The ONE Book

Oneness in Hundreds of Hues
Gleaming in Nations and Ages

Compiled and Edited by
Ronald Jorgensen & William Leon

Published 2019

ISBN 978-0-997719-30-7

Layout and design by Robin Sherman; updated 5.23.2020

For more information or to suggest expressions for future publications, please contact:
Bill Leon, Ph.D.
17027 37th Ave. NE
Lake Forest Park, WA 98155 USA
Phone: 206.914.6663
Email: billleon@geoeducation.org
Also see: www.theonebook.world to view or offer new expressions.

Note about the cover image
The cover image is of the Helix Nebula, a composite image taken with the Advanced Camera for Surveys aboard NASA/ESA Hubble Space Telescope and the Mosaic II Camera on the 4-meter telescope at Cerro Tololo Inter-American Observatory in Chile.

If we could have painted an appropriate image, it would have contained these elements:

1) the darkness of space implying mystery and the paradox of emptiness/invisibility where it is really full of dark matter, waves, and other realities that exist beyond our narrow spectrum of vision, yet which can be sensed in other ways;

2) lights of hope and wisdom scattered in what seem to be random ways that are somehow ordered;

3) the perception that some lights are brighter than others, but it may only be that they are closer (more familiar);

4) the knowledge that some of these lights are actually galaxies with millions of stars and planets and what we can perceive is only the faintest glimmer of their greatness or the gases emitted as they "die";

5) the sense of movement provided by the glowing stars and by the tinted gases between them which (like waves of consciousness) are ancient in origin but still expanding and evolving rapidly; and

6) the energy behind what we see that literally shines through them.

But we did not have to imagine and paint this. It really exists. And the expressions gathered here have many of these same qualities and more.

NASA and the European Space Agency describe it this way:
"The object is so large that both telescopes were needed to capture a complete view. The Helix is a planetary nebula, the glowing gaseous envelope expelled by a dying, sun-like star. The Helix resembles a simple doughnut as seen from Earth. But looks can be deceiving. New evidence suggests that the Helix consists of two gaseous disks nearly perpendicular to each other."

Cover photo credit: NASA, ESA, C.R. O'Dell (Vanderbilt University), and M. Meixner, P. McCullough, and G. Bacon (Space Telescope Science Institute)

This book is dedicated to

The Mother

of Sri Aurobindo Ashram

who inspired it and who guided and supported us in its birth and development.

Contents

Prologue

Oneness. How can such a simple word encompass such a profound and enigmatic phenomenon? Oneness is the essence of creativity, of consciousness, of enlightenment, of all that is. It is the essence of who and what we are, rather than who and what we appear to be. And yet the hills and valleys of the lives that we traverse on a daily basis seem to belie this basic truth. If this is who and what we really are, why is it so difficult to believe this? David Bohm, the eminent physicist, asked if everything in the cosmos is one, why do we appear to be separate? If we are One, is individuality a mirage? Is the mind? Are we truly interconnected – or entangled, as Bohm and other quantum physicists might say – or is Oneness just a fairy tale we tell ourselves to keep away the forces of darkness and death that threaten to overwhelm us? If we are One, what is the point of the chaos and conflict that describes so much of our collective existence? Is the Universe (or Multiverse, as I prefer to call it) a random collection of meaningless events or is there a great purpose – a Unity – at its core?

I have wrestled with these questions for many years. They nearly drove me to despair. But then, when I was 25 years old, I suffered three cardiac arrests which propelled me into three powerful near-death experiences that showed me that Oneness is indeed the ground of all being. That brief but timeless immersion in the extraordinary beauty, goodness, love, and intelligence that I encountered changed the course of my life. I became a psychologist and a professor and dedicated myself to the study of consciousness, a subject which I have been privileged to teach at the University of Washington for the past 20 years. This has allowed me to introduce hundreds of students to the mystery of Oneness and encourage them to ask their own questions and open themselves to their own direct experiences.

An ancient Zen koan asks us to consider what the Infinite does not know. The answer is "finitude," a condition that underlies our experience as humans. As I tell my students, we are non-physical beings having a physical experience. We become amnesiac when we undertake an adventure in physicality. We forget who we really are as we become immersed in, fascinated by, and hypnotized by the diversity and individuality of ourselves, each other, and all that surrounds us. Perhaps the forgetfulness itself is an important component of a Whole that is constantly evolving, expanding, integrating, learning from, and absorbing into itself the unique experiences that constitute Oneness. But, because we forget, we need to be reminded of the Unity that gives meaning and purpose to our seemingly separate lives.

We are reminded in so many ways. The literature of mysticism and transpersonal psychology, of meditation and spirituality, of this book itself, are replete with these reminders. Some call them samadhi, some nirvana, some enlightenment, some states of grace. They come to us and upon us in deeply personal and mysterious ways, from reveries, lucid dreams, and psychoactive drugs to near death events and everything in between. They can be prepared for through prayer or the rigorous study of meditation, but that does not mean that they can be ordered at will. Indeed, they more often arise spontaneously and unpredictably through prosaic activities such as gazing at a sunset, listening to music, or contemplating a work of art. One need not be a person of faith to experience Oneness for it is deeply embedded in secularity as well as spirituality. But no matter how they arise, experiences of Oneness transform us. They weave themselves deeply into the fabric of our lives and remind us that Oneness is always at play in the Multiverse.

Yet even after we are graced with these experiences we forget. And that is why this book is so important. Through the words and experiences of poets, scholars, scientists, mystics, artists, writers, yogis, monks, Taoists, Sufis, priests and nuns we are reminded that no matter where we drop in to the whole, we have always been there. This wisdom resonates. Something deep within stirs.

And stir us it must, for our collective amnesia has led the human species to create unprecedented challenges on an unprecedented scale that threaten the very existence of the biosphere. At the dawn of the nuclear age and in the wake of devastating global conflict, Albert Einstein warned us that "the world that we have made as a result of the level of thinking we have done thus far creates problems that we cannot solve at the same level at which we have created them. . . . We shall require a substantially new manner of thinking if humankind is to survive." Now more than ever we need to remember our interconnectedness, our entanglement, our Oneness if we are to evolve as a species and find real solutions to the problems we have created by embracing wholeheartedly the illusion of separateness. As the editors of this volume tell us, "the experience of oneness changes everything in a person's life and world." If we take the risk, individually and collectively, to remember who we really are we can leap from where we are to where we have never been before and go on from there.

Kathleen Noble, Ph.D.
Professor of Consciousness
University of Washington, Bothell

Preface

Like a warm heart beating a rhythm rhyming our lives, we know we are one — in ourselves, with others, with the Earth, and far more. It thrills. It comforts. It teaches. It confirms over and over like bedrock where we repeatedly return. **Oneness means everything affects everything as if all is one reality — which it is.**

You may already be aware an experience of oneness can bring sobs of joy, a startling shock of sensitivity, even moments of enlightenment. And then just how unpredictable it is, emerging in meditation or work or play, inhabiting a crisis or the rosiness of a sublime vacation, or discovered in a simple conversation or a struggle twined with great difficulty. You can find it in solitude, with a crowd of thousands, and in coupled intimacy. So it is no surprise an experience of oneness may appear deep within you and, too, all the way to the cosmos and beyond. No matter if it's in our discovery of subtleties in the structure of an atom, amazement flooding our moments with a flower or painting, or plumbless awe confronting a Hubble telescope image of the Sombrero Galaxy, don't we feel blessed in wonder, gratitude, and a rooted enthusiasm for our own lives?

Though oneness seems a rare experience, it is even more miraculous in its common disguises. For, being universal and universalizing, who or what does it not touch, though easily missed in the ruts of our familiar habitual view?

In these pages you will find proof and inspiration. Written by more than 500 amazing authors from over 100 nations on all continents over the entire length of recorded history with a considerable amount of it recent, The One Book miraculously reveals more than 600 facets of oneness in over 1,000 quotations, poems, proclamations, jokes, meditations, and exclamations. These are not just from professors in their windows or spiritual teachers in their robes, nor just from philosophers and novelists, but from people in over 130 settings such as folklore, music, farming, revolution, mysticism, and astronomy — from witnesses who include women, children, youth, poets, artists, politicians, scientists, athletes, truck drivers and horseback riders.

We avoid cliché-like expressions to offer ambushes of freshness and a depth of originality that can awaken a person to the seemingly invisible yet very palpable internetting of wonders in oneness we all share. For as a great poet wrote, "To feel love and oneness is to live."

You may be delighted or challenged by such facets of oneness as accuser–accused, animals, beauty, butchering, color, compassion, culture, discovery, divinity, falsehood, fish, geometry, golf, happiness, healing, ignorance, infinity, laughter–tears, liberty, loss, Martians, metallurgy, mischief, nature, need, occultism, oppression, pain, prayer, race, religions, science, service, silliness, sorrow–joy, sound, spirit, synergy, time, touch, transformation, and truth. Besides these forty-some facets of oneness, the several hundred found inside the book can take you wherever you dream or imagine going, with surprise after game-changing and happy surprise.

This is not a book designed for self-improvement. We like you the way you are. Yet it is easy to sense that you, like us, in reading these provocative passages from one-liners to essays to mystic visions, would be hard-pressed not to become a greater and more fascinating person, a naturally potent player in your own way for our Earth's and our peoples' happier future. Reading them has been doing that to us while compiling the work, and we're delighted for your possibilities, too. Whether you are an atheistic humanist or a pagan mystic, a Harlem Christian or a Hare Krishna, a political conservative or a community organizer, a hard-core sexual athlete or champion of chastity, a protector of the wilderness or a sophisticated city dweller, a peasant farmer, a heavy labor worker, or radical militant, in these pages you will find resonance, wholeness, and community where you might not expect it. Oneness knows no boundaries or any exclusivity. Simply turning these pages you are part of it in the fullness of welcome. We wish you delight!

Introduction

This book is about something people say just cannot be put into words — oneness. This mistaken belief was a motivation for making this book. We feel that oneness is in everything and everything is one. The evidence is all around us.

We have found over 1,000 examples from over 500 people who see this, who have expressed it eloquently and who can help you experience it tangibly. Our goal is to share these expressions of oneness with others who may feel jolted by the competition in much of life or by its fractional, contentious, and tense landscapes. We are confident they may sense, beneath noises of disconnection, the harmony that bears it all, which is usually missed in habitual glances.

The expressions touch over 600 facets of oneness from over 130 settings and surprise one like the opening of hidden doors into those realms. They come from ancient through modern times right into the present; and the authors hail from all the inhabited continents and a hundred nations — widely surpassing the representation in other international anthologies we have seen.

So this book is not just a read. It is an invitation to an experience. Because that experience changes everything in a person's life and world, we are thrilled to offer it.

Origin of the One Book

I [Ron] was living at the Sri Aurobindo Ashram, practicing Integral Yoga in South India and working for an organization named World Union. The leader of the Ashram was Mirra Alfassa, known as the Mother. Her role was central.

In a meeting with organizers of World Union, its leaders identified many plans they had for encouraging nations to come into closer relations. When asked for her opinion, the Mother said a book of expressions on oneness from cultures around the world would be useful, too.

Seeing the notes of that meeting around 12 years later, I asked the then chairman of World Union, M. P. Pandit, what happened to the book idea. He looked directly into me, and with a power of authority I cannot explain said, "You do it." I immediately sensed this imperative and started collecting expressions from sources I thought were far and wide.

After returning to the United States, Bill joined me in 1984, and my impression of far and wide was considerably magnified. Together — also with the help of many others — we have expanded and completed this work. It has grown into what I would call a genuine world eye.

Breadth of Expression

The book is unique in its devotion to a massive theme that has been articulated in so many ways by people all over the world and throughout the span of human history. Experience of and searching for oneness are themes that resound in every culture and in every inquiry into the nature of existence. Against the striking paucity of publications on oneness, this book has emerged to provide its massive, accessible collection of expressions on oneness like a first sunrise. It is a work to be enjoyed, used, and perhaps lived by not only the casual reader but also teachers, clergy, therapists, political figures, speech writers, journalists, scholars, and professionals in an abundance of disciplines.

Its pages bristle with startlingly fresh penetrations into the mystery and many-sided reality of oneness in facets such as beauty, love, power, life, peace, justice, joy, nation, world, and nature. Unexpectedly, it also has facets of absurdity, defeat, division, chaos, evil, falsehood and death — all moving out of their apparent imprisonment toward the truth of their liberation in the unveiling of oneness. Yet these seventeen facets represent only a few degrees of the sphere. We have identified hundreds more such as discovery, time, music, art, science, mind, feeling, body, East & West, bureaucracy, politics, health & disease, inner & outer, family, universe, wisdom . . . and oneness in itself.

And the variety is not limited to just these facets. The five hundred authors come from numerous settings like art, poetry, baseball, ecology, Sufism, social justice, philosophy, geography, revolution, architecture, music, feminism, Buddhism, economics, yoga, Native traditions, education, politics, Christianity, skepticism, nationalism, Hinduism, communism, Judaism, literature, mysticism, biology, drama, romanticism, transcendentalism, humanism, Theosophy, physics, history, anthropology, Taoism, psychology, Kwanzaa, and Zoroastrianism. These authors felt oneness and expressed it throughout every age and across every land and culture on Earth.

Structure of the Book

Though Ron began this collection while in India, legions of people have contributed expressions over the years. We found many in original texts from a wide variety of fields and traditions. When we found them in books of quotations, we went whenever possible to the original source and usually expanded the text. We did this to provide more of a context for the reader and to provide direction for further exploration. We also sought to verify the expressions and to correct any errors in them. Where this may not be complete, we welcome any additional edits or insights.

The expressions are grouped in twelve chapters that, in general, expand outward to encompass greater geographic breadths and larger groupings of people and other phenomena. But within each chapter you will find expressions in the realms of the individual, the universe, and the gamut in between. Too, we noticed a profusion of pairs and groupings of expressions that naturally fit together and we placed them in succession. Often they express similar experiences from different settings or cultures. Sometimes they seem contradictory. Generally there is a progression of greater depth and profundity as one reads through each chapter, inspiring more contemplation toward the end.

For each expression, we provide information we feel helps one understand its context. This is rare in books of quotations. Each expression has one or more identified facets of oneness (e.g., between lovers, with nature), its author (if known), the author's setting or area of endeavor (e.g., art, baseball, Christianity), the author's nationality, and the date of origin (we use BCE to designate Before the Common/Current Era which is numerically equivalent to dates commonly referred to as BC in the Gregorian calendar).

Authors often transcended their original field or were notable in many fields. It undoubtedly helped them see unity in a much greater arc. One of the richest examples was Leonardo Da Vinci who was first famous as a painter but was notably accomplished in a wide variety of other areas. When this has occurred, we list their original field of endeavor.

Numerous authors moved and fulfilled their greatness or destiny in countries they adopted later in life. Mother Theresa was born in Macedonia, grew up in Albania and founded her iconic order, the Missionaries of Charity, in India. Many also lived in nations which no longer exist with the same name or territory. For nation of origin we list current country names and put the older countries or nations in parentheses. Saint Augustine illustrates that with a designation of Algeria (Rome) because where he lived was then controlled by Rome. We also note the nations or tribes of indigenous people in parentheses.

When we could not determine the date of publication or when the author did not publish at all, his or her earthly exit is the date given. This provides a historical marker.

To help researchers, writers, and all curious readers find expressions of special interest, we created four indices (merged together) that allow the reader to look up expressions by author, setting, nation, and facet of oneness (e.g., in life, with others). Only the key words of the facets (e.g., life, others) are indexed, but other key words that are part of the expressions are also indexed. The fourth aspect of the index is in some ways the most interesting as it lays bare the stunning and mystical diversity of our vast life of oneness.

We feel this collection will grow in your world as you find and share new expressions, on our website, and perhaps in future published volumes. We would like your help in expanding it. You can send new expressions to us at billleon@geoeducation.org or to 17027 37th Avenue NE, Lake Forest Park, WA, 98155, USA or add them to our blog at **www.theonebook.world**. If you do, please provide as much documentary information as you can about the author, setting, nation, facet of oneness, and original source. Most important, though, send it even if you lack all of this information and we will work on it.

Descriptions of Oneness

You may feel or know what oneness is. But how can one describe it? Below are some attempts by us, each striving to be succinct and yet, of course, failing to cover the vastness — all that is.

- Oneness is the assurance of unity.
- Oneness is the absolute certainty of being part of an inextricable whole with some other "part(s)," "thing(s)" or "person (s)" that we generally conceive of as separate.
- Oneness is the deep and certain understanding that "the other" is a false perception and that, in reality, unity of being is an indisputable fact — even while a person may simultaneously perceive the self, others or objects as separate entities.
- Oneness means everything affects everything as if all is one substance — which it is.
- Oneness is a condition of existence where nothing can happen without affecting everything else.
- Oneness means there is no ultimate enemy.
- Oneness means you are never alone.
- Oneness means the center is everywhere.
- Oneness means all is special.
- Oneness means when all the contradictions are located on the whole globe of reality, they are simply varying expressions of the whole.
- Oneness means ultimately there are no secrets.
- Oneness means the worst, the most objectionable, the most disgusting person you can think of is also in your mirror.
- Oneness means if you are still in disagreement, you didn't finish the discussion.
- Oneness means your frown is the backside of your smile.
- Oneness makes the dilemma of Natural Evil a joke.
- Oneness means arrogance has no place to stand.
- Oneness means the devil is a part of the play.
- The realization of oneness would change all our pastimes and hobbies from trivial to beautiful.
- Oneness means that drunkenness — escaping from a harder reality — loses its pizzazz.
- With oneness, age is not a drag and infancy is not a limitation.
- Oneness means that competition (in friendships, businesses, games, politics, etc.) is a much more trivial game than we ever thought.
- Oneness means that the end of hate is the beginning of love.
- Oneness means that there is no one you can be indifferent to because there is no one you are disconnected from.
- Oneness means it is not just we who call the shots, the shots call us.
- Oneness means exclusivity is a dead end — like the false bottom in the magician's box.
- Oneness means habits give way to discoveries; limits to illimitability.
- Oneness means you have to struggle to be unhappy — and you still lose.

- Oneness means that the saying, "Work is play and play is work" is easy to understand.
- Oneness means to think inside the box and outside the box simultaneously.
- Oneness means that if it is either true or untrue, you have not fully investigated it yet.
- Oneness means you don't just have hope and faith — you know it is all right when you become fully aware.
- Oneness means this list of descriptions can never be complete.

That's enough by us! But it is important to remember what you read in the book are just expressions of oneness. As beautiful and masterful as some of them are, they cannot be oneness or the full experience of the author, but can only *invoke* it. They are in this way mantric. By reading them, we may be able to have our own experiences of oneness — perhaps akin to the ones of the authors. That's why we have selected these expressions — for their evoking power. We have selected these expressions because we feel that they will evoke feelings of oneness in some. That is their purpose here.

But in any case, each experience of oneness is unique. *What a beautiful paradox!* Even if we are all experiencing the same type of oneness (with God, with our team, with our lover, with our nation) it will be different for each us due to our individuality.

In describing what a "spiritual theorem" is, the Mother explained how spiritual experiences are unique but also more "real" and why they are important.

A theorem is the statement of a truth which has been arrived at through reasoning. The word is used quite concretely in mathematics and all the external sciences. From the philosophical point of view it is the same thing. In the present instance, the spiritual theorem of existence may be stated in this way: the Absolute in the relativities or Oneness in multiplicity. . . . And to really understand what it means, one feels that philosophy is always skirting the truth, like a tangent that draws closer and closer but never touches — that there is something that escapes. And this something is in truth everything.

To understand these things . . . there is only experience — to live this truth, not to feel it in the way the ordinary senses do but to realize within oneself the truth, the concrete existence of both states, simultaneously, existing together even while they are opposite conditions. All words can lead only to confusion; only experience gives the tangible reality of the thing: the simultaneous existence of the Absolute and the relativities, of Oneness and multiplicity, not as two states following each other and one resulting from the other, but as a state which can be perceived in two opposite ways depending on . . . the position one takes in relation to the Reality.

Words in themselves falsify the experience. To speak in words one must take not a step backwards but a step downwards, and the essential truth escapes. One must use them simply as a more or less accessible path to reach the thing itself which cannot be formulated. And from this point of view no formulation is better than any other; the best of all is the one that helps each one to remember, that is, the way in which the intervention of the Grace has crystallised in the thought.

Probably no two ways are identical, everyone must find his own. But one must not be mistaken, it is not "finding" by reasoning, it is "finding" by aspiration; it is not by study and analysis, but by the intensity of the aspiration and the sincerity of the inner opening.

When one is truly and exclusively turned to the spiritual Truth, whatever name may be given to it, when all the rest becomes secondary, when that alone is imperative and inevitable, then, one single moment of intense, absolute, total concentration is enough to receive the answer.

The experience comes first, in this case, and it is only later, as a consequence and a memory that the formulation becomes clear. In this way one is sure not to make a mistake. The formulation may be more or less exact, that is of no importance, so long as one doesn't make a dogma out of it.

It is good for you, that is all that is needed. If you want to impose it on others, whatever it may be, even if it is perfect in itself, it becomes false. . . .

(Silence)

The path must be shown and the doors opened but everyone must follow the path, pass through the doors and go towards his personal realisation.

The only help one can and should receive is that of the Grace which formulates itself in everyone according to his own need.

We stand in debt to what she has said. So all this book can do is offer the doors of its pages.

In reading the expressions gathered here, you may experience that these doors lead you outward to new vistas, to pleasing landscapes, to humorous epiphanies, but also to challenging climbs up steep ridges where mind wobbles on the knife edge of doubt and incredulity before finding a new plateau of peaceful repose. You may also find these doors open inward to deeper parts of yourself: parts not yet explored, perhaps feared, perhaps secretly sought and when found, discovered to be most familiar, to be your true home.

You may be surprised that these invitations are not just from saints and sages. We were delighted to find them from children, truck drivers, politicians, adventurers, artists, warriors, cooks, geographers, physicists, biologists, anthropologists, and the so-called ordinary people from the diversity of nations, cultures and eons.

You may find that to experience and express oneness requires no special talent, training, no high intellect. It may, in fact, be inborn or genetically hard-wired into our being in one or more of its physical, mental, vital, psychic or spiritual sheaths. You may become more aware of oneness in you and in more aspects of your life, finding your own doors. When you do, and if you choose to express your experience, we hope you will share them with us and your dear ones.

As we expand in new directions the walls recede. What separated us in conflicts with each other, the world at large, and with our own selves can show itself as our all, the all that is.

Use of the Book

Of course, how one approaches these expressions is left to you. Some of you may start on page one and keep going. Others may open it randomly. Still others may search by author, setting, nation, or facet. There are four indices integrated in the back you can consult to see which of these are in the book. Then you can search by those key words and find them.

Reading them aloud — especially the poetic works — evokes their mantric qualities. The sounds of the words bring forth the vibration of oneness infused in the text. Whatever your approach, we suggest that upon reading an expression, you pause and let it sink in. Active contemplation may be your way of exploration. If it is, have at it. But even so, take some time with each expression to just let it be; let it sing to you; let it settle into you; quiet the common human tendency to 'try to understand it.' If you can quiet yourself, you may find that it brings even more joy, understanding, and wisdom. Let it open a new door for you or one you have been through before. Use it to see in a new light what it shows you. Each is a glimpse of a part of all that is and can take you to the rest — not just to see it — but also to be it. Above all, enjoy the ride.

The primary purpose of this book is to provide mantric-like catalysts for people to have their own experiences of oneness after reading the expressions. Words are seeds. We take them into us through our ears, eyes, and fingers and sort them in our minds to keep the most useful and meaningful. We re-arrange them and the ideas they convey and re-use them internally and externally. When our words or those of others have special significance, we recognize it immediately. Some make you laugh. Some make you stop and think. Others make you stop thinking and just experience. The words in these expressions on oneness are seeds imbued with these qualities. They come from the flowers and fruits of personal experiences of oneness. When planted and nurtured, they will grow again in the reader.

Like all living things, these expressions are unique experiences of a hidden form. The biologist would call them phenotypes of common genotypes. The spiritualist would call them manifestations of the spirit within. They grew out of particular soils (nations) in particular climates (historical, cultural, and professional settings). Even though individual authors may share all of these, they will experience the world uniquely and will express their realizations differently. The permutations are endless.

As in biological evolution, ideas evolve and are expressed differently through the ages or in different settings. Yet we can take the seeds from a thousand-year-old tree and plant them in different ecological niches and — with proper care — they can grow and thrive. Likewise, we can take the ides and expressions of oneness of authors from different nations, cultures, settings, and times and plant them in our minds and hearts, and — with reflection — they can grow into our own unique experiences of oneness.

We have spent decades collecting the seeds you will find here. They are viable and waiting to be planted anew. Our purpose is not to gather examples of oneness or to compare them across authors, continents or centuries, or to encourage readers to marvel at their eloquence — though all that is evident. Our purpose is to catalyze the experience of oneness in those who gaze at these gems. No matter the writer's skill, you cannot truly know his or her experience. But you can have your own. These seeds are yours to plant, nurture, harvest and scatter. As more of us experience and act from a oneness consciousness, we will increase harmony and wholeness on all scales of existence.

With love for you to your unlimited best,
    Ron and Bill

> *Mind seeks for light, for knowledge, — for knowledge of the one truth basing all, an essential truth of self and things, but also of all truth of diversity of that oneness, all its detail, circumstance, manifold way of action, form, law of movement and happening, various manifestation and creation; for thinking mind the joy of existence is discovery and the penetration of the mystery of creation that comes with knowledge.*

    Sri Aurobindo *The Life Divine*

Origins

in diversity

Oneness is the soul of multitude.

Sri Aurobindo   Yoga   India   1950

in ease   in duality

Taking hold, one's astray in nothingness;
Letting go, the Origin's regained.

Kokai   Zen Buddhism   Japan   1420

in truth

All truths come from the same Source.

Sun Bear and Wabun   Native America   America (Chippewa)   1980

in dream

There is a dream dreaming us.

Kalahari Bushman Proverb   Mythology   Botswana   Traditional

in dream

The notion of this universe, its heavens, hells, and everything within it, as a great
dream dreamed by a single being in which all the dream characters are dreaming too,
has in India enchanted and shaped the entire civilization.

Joseph Campbell   Mythology   United States   1974

in dream

Schopenhauer in his poetically speculative essay "On an Apparent Intention in the Fate of the Individual" proposes an image of this whole vast universe, this marvelous multiplicity of phenomena conditioned by time and space, as "a vast dream, dreamed by a single being, in such a way that all the dream characters dream too; so that everything interlocks and harmonizes with everything else."

Arthur Schopenhauer   Metaphysics   Germany   1810

of creation   in diversity

From the Tao, the One is created;
From the One, Two;
From the Two, Three;
From the Three, Ten Thousand Things.

Lao Tzu   Taoism   China   500 BCE

unity in creation

The one is made up of all things, and all things issue from the one.

Heraclitus of Ephesus   Philosophy   Greece   475 BCE

with the Divine   in eternity

He is indivisible and the One, but seems to divide himself in forms and creatures and appears as all the separate existences. All things are eternally born from him, upborne in his eternity, taken eternally back into his oneness.

The Bhagavad Gita   Hinduism   India   600 BCE

in language

The word is the great-grandson of the original Source.

Ramana Maharshi   Hinduism   India   1931

poetry—spirit

The Eskimo word for to make poetry is the word to breathe; both are derivatives of anerca, the soul, that which is eternal: the breath of life. A poem is words infused with breath or spirit: "Let me breathe of it," says the poet-maker and then begins: "One has put his poem in order on the threshold of his tongue."

Edmund Carpenter   Poetry   Canada (Inuit)   1959

of the elements   in transformation

In China . . . the elements are five. . . . They are wood, fire, earth, metal, and water, usually understood as giving rise to each other in that order: wood producing fire by being consumed as fuel: fire producing earth by yielding ashes; earth producing metal by fostering the growth of metallic ores within its rocks; metal producing water by secreting or attracting dew when metal mirrors are exposed at night; and water then producing wood again by entering into the substances of plants.

Joseph Needham   Taoism   China   1956

itself

When we delve deeply into the meaning of unity, we will find that it is the source and centre of all true values.

N. Sri Ram   Theosophy   India   1973

in source

The tabernacle of unity hath been raised; regard ye not one another as strangers. Ye are the fruits of one tree and the leaves of one branch.

Bahá'u'lláh   Bahá'í   Iran (Persia)   1863

with work

No man is born into the world whose work
Is not born with him; there is always work,
And tools to work withal, for those who will;
And blessed are the horny hands of toil!

James Russell Lowell   Romanticism   United States   1848

in home

Home — the nursery of the infinite.

William Ellery Channing   Unitarianism   United States   1887

in balance   in God

The flowing out of God always demands a flowing back.

Jan Van Ruysbroeck   Mysticism   Belgium   1321

micro–macro

That very law which moulds a tear
And bids it trickle from its source, —
That law preserves the earth a sphere,
And guides the planets in their course.

Samuel Rogers   Romanticism   United Kingdom   1780

God–world

The world is but a ray emanating from the sun of His face.

Azar Kayvan   Zoroastrianism   Iran (Persia)   1570

God–creation

God says:

"I am the day unto myself, not formed by the sun, but rather,
forming the sun,
igniting it.

I am the understanding not understood, but rather,
allowing all understanding, illuminating it."

Hildegard of Bingen   Mysticism   Germany   1163

out of God

I do actually see that whatever is, is God. It is He who has become all these things!

Sri Ramakrishna   Hinduism   India   1900

in origin

There is no difference among classes of people. All the world is of divine origin.

Mahabharata   Hinduism   India   400 BCE

in God   micro–macro

Whither shall I go from Thy spirit? or whither shall I flee from Thy presence? If I ascend up into heaven, thou art there: if I make my bed in hell, behold, thou art there. If I take the wings of the morning, and dwell in the uttermost parts of the sea; Even there shall Thy hand lead me, and Thy right hand shall hold me. If I say, Surely the darkness shall cover me; even the night shall be light about me. Yea, the darkness hideth not from thee; but the night shineth as the day: the darkness and the light are both alike to thee.

Torah   Judaism   Israel   970 BCE

in origin   spirit–matter

If, as Hawking and many other scientists say, the Big Bang explosion resulted in life as we know it today, then the seeds of all things, ourselves included, were present at the birth of creation, and every scrap of matter and energy and blood and bones and thought present in the cosmos today could be traced back to the origins of the universe from one small subatomic particle of light. That makes us each sparks of the same light. It also makes each of us a hologram of the entire event. The energies that fragmented and separated and multiplied as the young universe expanded and cooled continue to operate in the beating of our hearts and the movements of our bodies, as well as in the alignment and behavior of the stars. We and they — all things and everything are a connected whole. That is the meaning of "We are one." The evolution of the universe, then, is continuing not only around us but within us. Our thoughts, our dreams, and our awareness are part of that universe, the physical and the spiritual inextricably bound together.

Shirley MacLaine   Mysticism   United States   1989

in natural law

The scientist's religious feeling takes the form of a rapturous amazement at the harmony of natural law, which reveals an intelligence of such superiority that, compared with it, all the systematic thinking and acting of human beings is an utterly insignificant reflection.

Albert Einstein   Physics   Germany   1956

in consciousness

Everything begins in consciousness; everything exists because of consciousness and everything advances with the evolution of consciousness.

Howard John Zitko   Education   United States   1947

in diversity

In unity there is the infinite interfusion of diversities but in each diversity we find the total potentiality of unity.

Chang Chung-yuan   Taoism   China   1963

form–formlessness

[Mentally created deities] should be regarded as the two-faced unity which appears as form and is, in essence, the formless Void.

Alexandra David-Neel   Buddhism   France   Traditional

of the soul   in infinity

In her beginningless infinity
Through her soul's reaches unconfined she gazed;
She saw the undying fountains of her life,
She knew herself eternal without birth.

Sri Aurobindo   Yoga   India   1950

of time

Our destiny exercises its influence over us even when, as yet, we have not learned its nature: it is our future that lays down the law of our today.

Friedrich Nietzsche   Existentialism   Germany   1878

in time

There lies a somnolent lake
Under a noiseless sky,
Where never the mornings break
Nor the evenings die.

Trumbull Stickney   Poetry   United States   1890

in time

As the sun,
Ere it is risen, sometimes paints its image
In the atmosphere, so often do the spirits
Of great events stride on before the events,
And in to-day already walks to-morrow.

Friedrich Schiller   Drama   Germany   1799

actual—potential

Within a tree there is a tree which does not yet exist.
Now its twigs tremble in the wind.

Within a blue sky there is a blue sky which does not yet exist.
Now a bird cuts across its horizon.

Within a body there is a body which does not yet exist.
Now its sanctuary accumulates fresh blood.

Within a city there is a city which does not yet exist.
Now its plazas sway before me.

  Kora Rumiko   Poetry   Japan   1960

in silence

Why, know you not soul speaks to soul?
I say the use of words shall pass —
Words are but fragments of the glass,
But silence is the perfect whole.

  Joaquin Miller   Poetry   United States   1860

in itself

For one throb of the artery,
While on that old grey stone I sat
Under the old wind-broken tree,
I knew that One is animate,
Mankind inanimate phantasy.

  William Butler Yeats   Poetry   Ireland   1921

micro—macro

A creature whose sphere of vision is a speck, whose experience is a second, sees the pencil of Raphael moving over the canvas of the Transfiguration. It sees the pencil moving over its own speck, during its own second of existence, in one particular direction, and it concludes that the formula expressing that direction is the secret of the whole.

Goldwin Smith   History   United Kingdom   1840

in God

Oh, where is the sea? the fishes cried,
As they swam its crystal clearness through.

Minot Judson Savage   Theism   United States   1860

in spirit

As the water and its bubbles are one — for the bubble has its birth in water, floats on water, and is ultimately resolved into water — so the Jivâtman [individual spirit] and the Paramâtman [spirit] are in essence one and the same. . . .
   What is the nature of the union of the Jivâtman and the Paramâtman? It is like the union of the hour and the minute hands at twelve o'clock.

Sri Ramakrishna   Hinduism   India   1900

in God

It is of more worth to God, his being brought forth spiritually in the individual virgin or good soul, than that he was born of Mary bodily. But this involves the notion of our being the only Son whom the Father has eternally begotten. When the Father begat all creatures he was begatting me; I flowed out with all creatures while remaining within in the Father.

Meister Eckhart   Mysticism   Germany   1300

in time   with fish   in evolution

After history, I thought of other subjects we did at school; geography, zoology. . . . They say that the human embryo goes through various stages. First, it's a fish then apparently an amphibian, and after that it gradually grows into something like an ape. What do you make of that?! So fish, and even frogs, were given some chance of jumping around and showing off their paces in my body. Only I can see that our teacher didn't get around to telling me that these are not just abstract stages that my organism went through while it was an imbecile embryo gradually forming in my mother's womb. In those golden days I was twin and partner, as it were, to some quite specific living carp which had perhaps swum in the river Amazon eighteen million years ago. And all other fish, every one of them, found a home in my contemporaries.

   For now I was firmly convinced that none of us will ever disappear and, in the words of the song, "will never and nowhere go under." We shall simply move to other, and perhaps even more comfortable quarters.

Abram Terts (Andrei Donatovich Sinyavsky)   Existentialism   Russia   1950

God—creation

How wonderful
is the wisdom
in the God-head's heart.

It is the heart that sees
the primordial eternity
of every creature.

When God gazes upon the countenance
of humankind,
the face that he formed,
he contemplates his work
in its totality,
its totality in this human form.

How wonderful is this breath then,
this breath that awakened humankind.

Hildegard of Bingen   Mysticism   Germany   1163

in light   creationism–physics

The tendency of modern physics is to resolve the whole material universe into waves and nothing but waves; these are waves of two kinds; bottled up waves which we call matter and unbottled waves which we call radiation or light. If annihilation of matter occurs, the process is merely that of unbottling imprisoned wave energy and letting it fall to travel through space. These concepts reduce the whole universe to a world of light, potential and existent, so that the whole story of creation can be told with perfect accuracy and completeness in the six words, "God said, "Let there be light!"

Sir James Jeans   Physics   United Kingdom   1930

from the godhead

His name is hidden from his children in his name, "Amen"... Thy beauties seize and carry away all hearts; the love of thee maketh the arms to drop, thy beautiful deeds make the hands to tremble, all hearts melt at the sight of thee, O Form, ONE, creator of all things, O One, Only, maker of things which are. Men came forth from his eyes, the gods sprang into being at the utterance of his mouth.

Unknown   Egyptian Religion   Egypt   1240 BCE

through emptiness

Subtlety is infinitely small. All things originate from ultimate smallness and later achieve completion, begin from nothingness and then grow. Therefore constantly void of desire and empty, one may discern the mystery of the origin of things.

Wang Pi   Taoism   China   249

being–doing

Subatomic interactions, therefore, are interactions of energy with energy. At the subatomic level there is no longer a clear distinction between what is and what happens, between the actor and the action. At the sub-atomic level the dancer and the dance are one.

Gary Zukav   Physics   United States   1979

inner—outer

The understanding of Tao is an inner experience in which distinction between subject and object vanishes.

Chang Chung-yuan   Taoism   China   1963

in duality   above—below

The image of an axial ladder let down through an opening in midsky, as though from the golden sun-door of noon to the navel of the earth, is a universal mythological motif, the mythic prototype, in fact, of the stairway of the temple tower. At the summit, the place of the union (or identity) of heaven and earth, eternity and time, where the two are one and the One becomes two, Quetzalcoatl sits in the naked state symbolic of unconditioned being. His posture is that of a child listening, but also talking, to its parents. Between them, receiving their words, he is at the coming together of their powers — each of the two, meanwhile, representing but one half of the dual appearance, in the place "where duality begins," of that ultimate "One" which is finally neither one nor many but unmeasured. Reuniting their powers in himself (as their son), he thus actually transcends them as an image of that which, anteceding them, is both twoness and oneness, beyond imaging, beyond thought, beyond the categories even of "being," "nonbeing," and "beyond." And he is in this sense verily a paradox, an incarnation of the Inconceivable, as he descends the ladder of manifestation to this earth, voluntarily assuming, in descending, the limitations inevitably imposed upon life by the conditions of time and space. These are represented in the tokens of his powers, which in the regions above are all about him as potential, and which in the course of his descent are taken on as the masks represented in the ritual gear of his cult and expounded in his myth.

Joseph Campbell   Mythology   United States   1974

through individualization   good–evil

Instead of being conscious of your external form and of everything in your being which makes of you a separate individuality, if you were conscious of the vital forces which move everywhere or of the inconscient that is at the base of all, you would have the feeling of a mass moving with all kinds of contradictory movements but which could not be separated from each other; you would not have the feeling of being an individual at all: you would have the feeling of something like a vibration in the midst of the whole. Well, the original Will was to form individual beings capable of becoming conscious once again of their divine origin. Because of the process of individualization one must feel separate if one is to be an individual. The moment you are separated, you are cut off from the original consciousness, at least apparently, and you fall into the inconscient. For the only thing which is the Life of life is the Origin, if you cut yourself off from that, consciousness naturally is changed into unconsciousness. And then it is due to this very unconsciousness that you are no longer aware of the truth of your being. . . . It is a process. You cannot argue whether it is inevitable or evitable; the fact is it is like that. This process of formation and creation is the reason why purity no longer manifests in its essence and in its purity but through the deformation of unconsciousness and ignorance. . . .

That is why there is all this ugliness, there is death; that is why there is illness; that is why there is wickedness; that is why there is suffering. There is no remedy, there is only one way for all these things. All this is there in different domains and with different vibrations, but the cause of all is the same. It is inconscience produced because of the necessity of individual formation. . . .

And so, the remedy? Since such is the cause, the only way of putting everything right is to become conscious once again. And to do this is very simple, very simple.

Suppose that there are in the universe two opposing and contradictory forces, as some religions have preached: there was good and evil, and there always will be good and evil, there will be a conflict, a battle, a struggle. The one that is stronger, whether it be the good or the evil, will win; if there is more of the good, the good will win and if there is more of the evil, the evil will win; but the two will always exist. If it were like that, it would be hopeless; one wouldn't have to say that it is either difficult or easy, it would be impossible. One would not be able to get out of it. But actually that is not so.

Actually there is but one Origin and this origin is the perfection of Truth, for that is the only thing which truly exists; and by exteriorizing, projecting, scattering itself, it brings forth what we see, and a crowd of tiny heads, very gentle, very brilliant, in search of something they have not yet seized but which they can seize, because what they are in search of is within them. That is a certainty. It may take more or less time, but it is sure to come. The remedy is at the very core of the evil. Voilà.

The Mother   Yoga   France   1953

spirit in creations

I have felt
A presence that disturbs me with the joy
Of elevated thoughts; a sense sublime
Of something far more deeply interfused,
Whose dwelling is the light of setting suns,
And the round ocean and the living air,
And the blue sky, and in the mind of man;
A motion and a spirit, that impels
All thinking things, all objects of all thought,
And rolls through all things. . . .

    William Wordsworth   Mysticism   United Kingdom   1798

in the spirit

Across the covert air the spirit breathes,
A body of the cosmic beauty and joy
Unseen, unguessed by the blind suffering world,
Climbing from Nature's deep surrendered heart
It blooms forever at the feet of God,
Fed by life's sacrificial mysteries.
Here too its bud is born in human breasts;
Then by a touch, a presence or a voice
The world is turned into a temple ground
And all discloses the unknown Beloved.

    Sri Aurobindo   Yoga   India   1950

in time   in self

One realm we have never conquered: the pure present. One great mystery of time is
terra incognita to us: the instant. The most superb mystery we have hardly recognized:
the immediate, instant self. The quick of all time is the instant. The quick of all the
universe, of all creation, is the incarnate, carnal self. Poetry gave us the clue: free verse:
Whitman. Now we know.

    D.H. Lawrence   Literature   United Kingdom   1919

in balance

Pushing any truth out very far, you are met by a counter-truth.

Henry Ward Beecher   Abolitionism   United States   1867

spirit–matter

There is no spirit which is not matter-enveloped: there is no matter which is not spirit-ensouled. The highest separated Self has its film of matter, and though such a Self is called "a spirit" because the consciousness-aspect is so predominant, nonetheless is it true that it has its vibrating sheath of matter, and that from this sheath all impulses come forth, which affect all other denser material sheaths in succession.

Annie Besant   Theosophy   United Kingdom   1915

human–God

When the Osiris of a man has entered into heaven as a living soul, he is regarded as one of those who "have eaten of the eye of Horus"; he walks among the living ones, he becomes "God, the son of God" and all the gods of heaven become his brethren.

Unknown   Egyptian Religion   Egypt   1240 BCE

heaven and Earth

Men had but one pair of primitive ancestors; they sprang from the vast heaven that exists above us, and from the earth which lies beneath us. They were called Rangi and Papa . . . they still both clave together. Because of this . . . there was darkness. . . .
   The offspring of Rangi and Papa became restless within their cramped quarters and debated whether they should kill their parents or send them apart. Tu-of-the-angry-face cried, "Let us slay them." But Tane, father of the forests and creatures of the forests argued, "It is better to rend them apart, and let heaven stand far above us, and the earth lie under our feet." . . .
   Afterwards clear light increased upon the earth and all the beings who had been hidden between Papa and Rangi multiplied. Ever since then Papa and Rangi have dwelled apart, but her loving sighs still rise up to him as mist and his tears fall as dew drops.

Roslyn Poignant   Mythology   Australia   Traditional

of opposites   God–devil   saints–sinners   creationism–evolution

"I believe the divine Spirit. . . the elan vital . . . brought about the organic evolution through the action of Darwinian Selection." If we follow this to its natural conclusion we must acknowledge that the creative force behind it all animates and directs the sinners as well as the saints and so must be symbiotic union of both God and the Devil in a further religious reduction to monotheism.

Alister Hardy   Biology   United Kingdom   1968

God–man

His head struck the sides of the cart. His body could be seen at every lurch. A man was being crushed to dust. Wretches! They were forgetting that this man contained God!

Yes, this man is God; this man is the God who crushes your conscience to dust, if you have one; who burns your heart, if it has not already melted in the fires of your infamy. The one the country has martyred is God himself as righteousness, as the universal idea of spontaneous generosity. Beat him, wound him, bruise him. You people are too vile for him to return blow for blow and wound for wound. I feel this God within me, I have this God within me: this God within me has compassion for you, more compassion than horror or scorn.

José Marti   Revolution   Cuba   1870

in evolution

From center to circumference, from the imperceptible vesicle to the uttermost conceivable bounds of the Kosmos, those glorious thinkers, the Occultists, trace cycle merging into cycle, containing and contained in an endless series. The embryo evolving in its pre-natal sphere, the individual in his family, the family in the state, the state in mankind, the Earth in our system, that system in its central universe, the universe in the Kosmos, and the Kosmos in the ONE CAUSE. . . .

Helena Petrovna Blavatsky   Theosophy   Russia   1888

in origin

[The] Buddha Supreme is a personification of the Dharmakaya, "Law Body" of the universe, which though screened from us by the obscuring and projecting powers of maya is nevertheless the ground, substance, support, and reality of all being and of all things. The proper way to think of it is — paradoxical — not to think of it; for all thought is conditioned by maya, that is to say by concepts, categories, and the laws of grammar, whereas the reference of the term Dharmakaya is beyond categories, even beyond those of "being" and "nonbeing"; indeed, beyond the category "beyond." Hence the terms I have just used, namely "ground," "substance," "support," and "reality," do not describe it. One might think or speak of it (which, however, is no "it") as a "void" in the sense of "without characteristics," or as nirvana, "blown out" in the sense approximately of deus absconditus. Positively conceived, however, it is termed the Dharmakaya.

Joseph Campbell   Mythology   United States   1974

itself

Thus the principle of Unity pervades the Four Seas; the permeation of it fills up all Heaven and Earth. In compactness it is as pure as unpolished jade; in a state of diffusion it is as turbid as muddy water. Yet turbid as it is, it becomes gradually clear; from emptiness it becomes full; it ripples placidly like a deep abyss; it drifts along like floating clouds; to all appearance non-existing; it yet exists; to all appearance lost, it is still preserved. Multifarious as are created things, they all pass through its portal, the origin of all emerges from its gate. Its movements are invisible, its transformations like those of Spirit; its actions leave no vestiges; ever behind, and yet before all.

Huai-Nan-Tsze   Taoism   China   1938

in sound

Aum [Sometimes spelled "Om."] [The Hindus regard Aum as the creative sound which builds up the worlds. When the mystic has become capable of hearing all together the sounds and voices of all beings and things that exist and move, he then perceives the one and only Aum.]

Alexandra David-Neel   Buddhism   France   Traditional

the necessity of oneness

Man as he is is not sufficient to himself, nor separate, nor is he the Eternal and the All; therefore by himself he cannot be the explanation of the cosmos of which his mind, life and body are so evidently an infinitesimal detail. The visible cosmos too, he finds, is not sufficient to itself, nor does it explain itself even by its unseen material forces; for there is too much that he finds both in the world and in himself which is beyond them and of which they seem only to be a face, an epidermis or even a mask. Neither his intellect, nor his intuitions, nor his feeling can do without a One or a Oneness to whom or to which these world forces and himself may stand in some relation which supports them and gives them their significance. He feels that there must be an Infinite which holds these finites, is in, behind and about all this visible cosmos, bases the harmony and interrelation and essential oneness of multitudinous things. His thought needs an Absolute on which these innumerable and finite relativities depend for their existence, an ultimate Truth of things, a creating Power or Force or a Being who originates and upholds all these innumerable beings in the universe. Let him call it what he will, he must arrive at a Supreme, a Divine, a Cause, an Infinite and Eternal, a Permanent, a Perfection to which all tends and aspires, or an All to which everything perpetually and invisibly amounts and without which they could not be.

Sri Aurobindo   Yoga   India   1940

in contradictions

there is no birth,
nor is there death;
there is no beginning,
nor is there any ending;
nothing is identical with itself,
nor is there any diversification;
nothing comes into existence,
nor does anything go out of existence.

Nágárjuna   Buddhism   India   250

in diversity

A Spirit who is no one and innumerable,
The one mystic infinite Person of his world
Multiplies his myriad personality,
On all his bodies seals his divinity's stamp
And sits in each, immortal and unique.

Sri Aurobindo   Yoga   India   1950

Creations

humanity–literature

Camerado, this is no book,
Who touches this touches a man. . . .

Walt Whitman   Mysticism   United States   1855

through time

Lend me the stone strength of the past and I will lend to you
The wings of the future, for I have them.

Robinson Jeffers   Poetry   United States   1923

life–beauty–justice

Living well and beautifully and justly are all one thing.

Socrates   Philosophy   Greece   450 BCE

micro–macro

Once the inter-relation of all created things is even dimly sensed, one cannot be small.
The mantle of magnitude is over the most humble part of the whole.

Betty White   Dance   United States   1942

of events

If the nose of Cleopatra had been shorter, the whole face of the earth would have been
changed.

Blaise Pascal   Mathematics   France   1670

through time   in education

A teacher affects eternity; he can never tell where his influence stops.

Henry Adams   History   United States   1907

science–politics

The language of science is universal, and perhaps scientists have been the most international of all professions in their outlook. . . . Every time you scientists make a major invention, we politicians have to invent a new institution to cope with it — and almost invariably, these days, it must be an international institution.

John F. Kennedy   Politics   United States   1950

spirit–matter

We Africans have never devised a metaphysical system which divided matter from Spirit, therefore we have never had a dislike for the so-called "gross appetites."

Unknown   Metaphysics   Nigeria (Yoruba)   Traditional

in balance

Wisdom rises upon the ruins of folly.

Thomas Fuller   Christianity   United Kingdom   1630

through gossip   through thought   good–evil

See what gossip does. It begins with evil thought, and that in itself is a crime. For in every one and in everything there is good; in everyone and in everything there is evil. Either of these we can strengthen by thinking of it. . . .

J. Krishnamurti   Theosophy   India   1909

thought—action

When a thought of good or evil import is begotten in our brain, it draws to it impulses of like nature as irresistibly as the magnet attracts iron filings.

Helena Petrovna Blavatsky   Theosophy   Russia   1877

in work   with the godhead

That's why I was not afraid; I knew that if the work was mine it would die with me. But I knew it was his work, that it will live and bring much good.

Mother Theresa   Christianity   Macedonia, Albania   1976

creator—creation

Creation
is allowed
in intimate love,
to speak
to the Creator
as if to a lover.

Creation
is allowed
to ask
for a pasture,
a homeland.

Out of the Creator's fullness,
this request is granted to creation.

Hildegard of Bingen   Mysticism   Germany   1163

soul–creator–creation

I am restless. I am athirst for far-away things.
My soul goes out in a longing to touch the skirt of the dim distance.
O Great Beyond, O the keen call of thy flute!
I forget, I ever forget, that I have no wings to fly, that I am bound in this spot evermore.

I am eager and wakeful, I am a stranger in a strange land.
Thy breath comes to me whispering an impossible hope.
Thy tongue is known to my heart as its very own.
O Far-to-seek, O the keen call of thy flute!
I forget, I ever forget, that I know not the way, that I have not the winged horse.

I am listless, I am a wanderer in my heart.
In the sunny haze of the languid hours, what vast vision of thine takes shape in the blue of the sky!
O Farthest end, O the keen call of thy flute!
I forget, I ever forget, that the gates are shut everywhere in the house where I dwell alone!

Rabindranath Tagore   Poetry   India   1915

God–self in poetry

Glorious indeed is the world of God around us, but more glorious the world of God within us. There lies the Land of Song; there lies the poet's native land.

Henry Wadsworth Longfellow   Poetry   United States   1839

in work

Labour without joy is base. Labour without sorrow is base. Sorrow without labor is base. Joy without labour is base.

John Ruskin   Christianity   United Kingdom   1867

in unity

In the past, separateness was right. The great course of the divine life-stream was dividing itself into multiplicity; it was needed to build up the individual centres of consciousness. So long as a centre needs strengthening, separateness is on the side of progress. Souls at one period need to be selfish; they cannot do without selfishness in the early stages of growth. But now the law of progressing life for the more advanced is the outgrowing of separateness, and the seeking to realise unity. We are now on the path towards unity; we are approaching nearer and nearer to each other. We must now unite, in order to grow further. The purpose is the same, though the method has changed in the evolution through the ages. The public conscience is beginning to recognise that not in separateness but in unity, there lies the true growth of a nation. We are trying to substitute arbitration for war, co-operation for competition, protection of the weak for trampling them under foot, and all this, because the line of evolution now goes towards unity and not towards separateness. Separation is the mark of descent into matter, and unification is the mark of the ascent to Spirit. The world is on the upward trend, although thousands of souls may lag behind. The ideal now is for peace, co-operation, protection, brotherhood and helpfulness. The essence of sin now lies in separateness.

Annie Besant   Theosophy   United Kingdom   1899

in polarities   silence–speech

Ptahhotep: "What have you learned during your struggles to keep silent? Have you only learned the art of keeping silent?"
Haich: "No, Father, that was simply impossible. While I was struggling with silence, I simultaneously had to struggle with speech. To the same extent that I have mastered silence, I have also mastered speech. This is because silence means not talking, and talking means not keeping silent. I wasn't able to separate these two things. I've discovered that silence and speech are two different sides of the same unit, like the two sides of a coin.

Elisabeth Haich   Yoga   Hungary   1960

in complementarity

Equality is false; it's the devil's concept. Our concept is complementary. Complementary means you complete or make perfect that which is imperfect.

Maulana Karenga   Kwanzaa   United States   1973

in dance

Negress my hot uproar of Africa
My land of riddle and my fruit of reason
You are dance by the naked joy of your smile
By the offering of your breasts and your secret powers
You are dance by golden legends of bridal nights
By new times and ancestral rhythms
Negress multiply triumph of dreams and stars
Mistress obedient to the embrace of Koras
You are dance by dizziness
By the magic of loins beginning the world anew
You are dance
And around me the myths burn
Around me the wigs of learning
In great fires of joy in the sky of your steps
You are dance
And the false gods burn beneath your vertical flame
You are the face of the initiate
Sacrificing madness beside the guardian tree
You are the idea of the All and the voice of the Ancient.
Gravely launched to attack chimeras
You are the Word that explodes
In miraculous spray on the shores of oblivion.

David Mandessi Diop   Poetry   France, Senegal   1950

science–religion

Though religion may be that which determines the goal, it has, nevertheless, learned from science, in the broadest sense, what means will contribute to the attainment of the goals it has set up. But science can only be created by those who are thoroughly imbued with the aspiration toward truth and understanding. This source of feeling, however, springs from the sphere of religion. To this there also belongs the faith in the possibility that the regulations valid for the world of existence are rational, that is, comprehensible to reason. I cannot conceive of a genuine scientist without that profound faith. The situation may be expressed by an image: science without religion is lame, religion without science is blind.

Albert Einstein   Physics   Germany   1954

wisdom—peace

The heart of the wise man lies quiet like limpid water.

Unknown   Proverb   Cameroon   Traditional

in contradiction

Overcome anger by love, ill-will by good will; overcome the greedy with liberality, the liar with truth.

Gautama Buddha   Buddhism   Nepal, India (Kapilavastu)   483 BCE

through time

In this spiritual world there are no time divisions such as the past, present and future; for they have contracted themselves into a single moment of the present where life quivers in its true sense. . . . The past and the future are both rolled up in this present moment of illumination, and this present moment is not something standing still with all its contents, for it ceaselessly moves on.

D.T. Suzuki   Zen Buddhism   Japan   1968

of insignificant things   part—whole

Think naught a trifle, though it small appear;
Small sands the mountain, moments make the year;
And trifles life.

Edward Young   Poetry   United Kingdom   1765

miracles—nature

Miracles are not contrary to nature but only contrary to what we know about nature.

Saint Augustine   Christianity   Algeria (Rome)   430

in silence

Learn this of the waters: Loud splatters the streamlet, the ocean's depths are silent.

    Gautama Buddha   Buddhism   Nepal, India (Kapilavastu)   483 BCE

beauty—truth

Beauty is truth's smile
when she beholds her own face
in a perfect mirror.

    Rabindranath Tagore   Poetry   India   1928

in process

Arts and sciences are not cast in a mould, but are formed and perfected by degrees, by often handling and polishing, as bears leisurely lick their cubs into form.

    Michel de Montaigne   Existentialism   France   1580

in sculpture   in balance

The more the marble wastes,
The more the Statue grows.
    Michelangelo   Art   Italy   1564

art—godhead

Characteristically, African sculpture is hewn out of single pieces of wood. This is to enable the work to keep its integrity and also the wood to keep its grain. Besides, the form of the wood itself may determine the over-all expression in the work. In the carving of deities the god himself is supposed to intervene and impose the form he wishes to take. The result is the artist's unconscious expression of the god, manipulated, directed, and realized by the god himself through the wood.

    Kofi Awoonor   Poetry   Ghana   1975

natural potential in carving

As the carver holds the unworked ivory lightly in his hand, turning it this way and that, he whispers, "Who are you? Who hides there?" And then: "Ah, seal!" He rarely sets out to carve, say, a seal, but picks up the ivory, examines it to find its hidden form and, if that's not immediately apparent, carves aimlessly until he sees it, humming or chanting as he works. Then he brings it out: Seal, hidden, emerges. It was always there. He didn't create it: he released it; he helped it step forth.

Edmund Carpenter   Art   United States   1973

in innate form

Those who rely upon the arc, the line, compasses and the square to make correct forms injure the natural construction of things. Those who use cords to bind and glue to piece together interfere with the natural character of things. . . . There is an ultimate reality in things. . . . Things in their ultimate reality are curved without the help of arcs, straight without lines, round without compasses, and rectangular without right angles. . . . In this manner all things create themselves from their own inward reflection and none can tell how they come to do so.

Chuang Tzu   Taoism   China   286 BCE

in calligraphy   inner–outer

When one is going to hold the brush one must draw back his vision and reverse his hearing, discard all thoughts and concentrate on spiritual reality. When his mind is tranquil and his breath harmonious his brush-work will penetrate into subtlety. If his mind is not tranquil this writing will not be straight. If his breath is not harmonious the characters will fall short. . . . Tranquility means harmony in thoughtlessness.

Yu Shin-nan   Taoism   China   700

in balance   in painting

Where things grow and expand that is K'ai; Where things are gathered up, that is ho. When you expand (K'ai) you should think of gathering up (ho) and then there will be structure; when you gather up (ho) you should think of expanding (K'ai) and then you will have inexpressible effortlessness and an air of inexhaustible spirit. In using the brush and in laying out the composition, there is not a moment when you can depart from K'ai-ho.

Unknown   Taoism   China   Traditional

in architecture

The timeless way: It is a process which brings order out of nothing, but ourselves; it cannot be attained, but it will happen of its own accord, if we will only let it. . . .

There is one timeless way of building.
   It is thousands of years old, and the same today as it has always been.
   The great traditional buildings of the past, the villages and tents and temples in which man feels at home, have always been made by people who were very close to the center of this way. It is not possible to make great buildings, or great towns, beautiful places, places where you feel yourself, places where you feel alive, except by following this way. And, as you see, this way will lead anyone who looks for it to buildings which are themselves as ancient in their form, as the trees and hills, and as our faces are.

Christopher Alexander   Architecture   United States   1979

truth–error

Truth is always twins; for every truth is accompanied by its facsimile error — which is the application of that by literal-minded people.

Christopher Morley   Journalism   United States   1910

in wholeness

By plucking her petals, you do not gather the beauty of the flower.

Rabindranath Tagore   Poetry   India   1928

in silence

The flowering moments of the mind
Drop half their petals in our speech.

Oliver Wendell Holmes   Poetry   United States   1840

in qualities

What the imagination seizes as beauty must be true.

John Keats   Romanticism   United Kingdom   1817

in beauty   spirit—matter

Beauty needs no justification. If one creates something of real beauty, it is part of what should exist, not part of any personal achievement.

N. Sri Ram   Yoga   India   1973

in mythology   in heritage

It has actually been from the one great, variously inflected and developed literate world-heritage that all the philosophies, theologies, mysticisms, and sciences now in conflict in our lives derive. These are in origin one; one also in their heritage of symbols; different, however, in their histories, interpretations, applications, emphases, and local aims.

Joseph Campbell   Mythology   United States   1974

in process

Thou canst not travel on the Path before thou hast become that Path itself.

Unknown   Buddhism   India   Traditional

of time

As if you could kill time without injuring eternity.

Henry David Thoreau   Transcendentalism   United States   1862

eternity–time

I saw the starry Tree
Eternity
Put forth the blossom Time.

Robert Buchanan   Mysticism   United Kingdom   1860

time–eternity   surface–depths

Time is but the shadow of the world upon the background of Eternity.

Jerome K. Jerome   Christianity   United Kingdom   1900

in beauty   in death

What is lovely never dies,
But passes into other loveliness.

Thomas Bailey Aldrich   Poetry   United States   1860

afflictions–blessings

Afflictions are the best blessings in disguise.

Unknown   Proverb   Africa   Traditional

speech—action

There is a weird power in a spoken word. . . . And a word carries far — very far — deals destruction through time as the bullets go flying through space.

Joseph Conrad   Skepticism   Ukraine (Poland)   1900

in sound

OM [also written AUM] is interpreted as the seed sound, the energy sound, the shakti, all being. . . .

The A [in AUM] is announced with open throat; the U carries the sound-mass forward; and the M, then, somewhat nasalized, brings all to a close at the lips. So pronounced, the utterance will have filled the whole mouth with sound and so have contained (as they say) all the vowels. Moreover since consonants are regarded in this thinking as interruptions of vowel sounds, the seeds of all words will have been contained in this enunciation of AUM, and in these, the seed sounds of all things. Thus words, they say, are but fragments or particles of AUM, as all forms are particles of that one Form of forms that is beheld when the rippling surface of the mind is stilled in yoga.

Joseph Campbell   Mythology   United States   1974

in truth   beyond polarities

The Zen-school . . . refuses to recognize the opposition of concepts in classical Buddhism, that between Sansara, the "stream" of incessant being, and Nirvana, the running dry of the stream: in truth both are one. "The highest truth," it says in an early Zen text, "is not difficult, it only spurns choice;" that is, the rational urge to expound either "a" or "non-a" as the truth and not both at once. Hence the Absolute may not be apprehended through anything universal, instead it may be apprehended through the tangible and concrete, through something that we experience.

Martin Buber   Hasidism   Austria   1958

spirit–matter   in supramental perception

The sharp division which practical experience and long habit of mind have created between Spirit and Matter has no longer any fundamental reality. The world is a differentiated unity, a manifold oneness, not a constant attempt at compromise between eternal dissonances, not an everlasting struggle between irreconcilable opposites. An inalienable oneness generating infinite variety is its foundation and beginning; a constant reconciliation behind apparent division and struggle combining all possible disparities for vast ends in a secret Consciousness and Will which is ever one and master of all its own complex action, appears to be its real character in the middle; we must assume therefore that a fulfilment of the emerging Will and Consciousness and a triumphant harmony must be its conclusion. Substance is the form of itself on which it works, and of that substance if Matter is one end, Spirit is the other. The two are one: Spirit is the soul and reality of that which we sense as Matter; Matter is a form and body of that which we realise as Spirit.

Sri Aurobindo   Yoga   India   1940

in separation   in matter

The sense of Unity becomes real only when tested by differences, when it asserts itself in the midst of separation, when it is carried into every detail and particular ill in the world of obstructive matter.

N. Sri Ram   Theosophy   India   1973

of darkness and light   of sorrow and joy

I know all about darkness.
Therefore I believe light is coming.

Hideo Oguma   Poetry   Japan   1940

in color

In black there are all colors
   Where darkness always the light
      Iridescent the raven's wing in sunlight

Brooke Medicine Eagle   Native America   America (Sioux, Nez Perce)   1991

in harmony

The sun cannot rise in wrath.

Unknown   Proverb   Nigeria (Yoruba)   Traditional

in imagination

Imagination . . . is the liquid solution in which art develops the snapshots of reality.

Palinurus (Cyril Connolly)   Literature   United Kingdom   1944

thought–things   mental–physical

What is life, if not to pull the strings
Of thought that pull those grosser strings whereby
We pull our limbs to pull material things
Into such shapes as in our thoughts doth lie?

Samuel Butler   Humanism   United Kingdom   1860

in creation

They're not epics, but that doesn't matter a pin,
In creating, the only hard thing's to begin;
A grass-blade's no easier to make than an oak;
If you've once found the way, you've achieved the grand stroke.

James Russell Lowell   Literature   United States   1848

mysticism–politics   in process

Everything begins in mysticism and ends in politics.

Charles Péguy   Poetry   France   1890

through work

When men are rightly occupied, their amusement grows out of their work, as the colour-petals out of a fruitful flower.

John Ruskin   Socialism   United Kingdom   1871

in diversity

Below the Buddhic level diversity is more apparent than unity, but it is through living amidst that diversity that perception and realization of unity become possible.

G.S. Arundale   Theosophy   United Kingdom   1926

unity–multiplicity

The creation depends on and moves between the biune principle of unity and multiplicity; it is a manifoldness of idea and force and form which is the expression of an original unity, and it is an eternal oneness which is the foundation and reality of the multiple worlds and makes their play possible. Supermind therefore proceeds by a double faculty of comprehensive and apprehensive knowledge; proceeding from the essential oneness to the resultant multiplicity, it comprehends all things in itself as itself the One in its manifold aspects and it apprehends separately all things in itself as objects of its will and knowledge. While to its original self-awareness all things are one being, one consciousness, one will, one self-delight and the whole movement of things a movement one and indivisible, it proceeds in its action from the unity to the multiplicity and from multiplicity to unity, creating an ordered relation between them and an appearance but not a binding reality of division, a subtle unseparating division, or rather a demarcation and determination within the indivisible.

Sri Aurobindo   Yoga   India   1940

in contradictions   in the logic of the Infinite

An original and ultimate consciousness would be a consciousness of the Infinite and necessarily unitarian in its view of diversity, integral, all-accepting, all-embracing, all-discriminating because all-determining, an indivisible whole-vision. It would see the essence of things and regard all forms and movements as phenomenon and consequence of the essential Reality, motions and formations of its power of being. It is held by the reason that truth must be empty of any conflict of contradictions: if so, since the phenomenal universe is or seems to be the contrary of the essential Brahman it must be unreal; since individual being is the contrary of both transcendence and universality, it must be unreal. But what appear as contradictions to a reason based on the finite may not be contradictions to a vision or a larger reason based on the infinite. What our mind sees as contraries may be to the infinite consciousness not contraries but complementaries: essence and phenomenon of the essence are complementary to each other, not contradictory, — the phenomenon manifests the essence; the finite is a circumstance and not a contradiction of the infinite; the individual is a self-expression of the universal and the transcendent, — it is not a contradiction or something quite other than it, it is the universal concentrated and selective, it is one with the Transcendent in its essence of being and its essence of nature. In the view of this unitarian comprehensive seeing there is nothing contradictory in a formless Essence of being that carries a multitude of forms, or in a status of the Infinite supporting a kinesis of the Infinite, or in an infinite Oneness expressing itself in a multiplicity of beings and aspects and powers and movements, for they are beings and aspects and powers and movements of the One. . . . To understand truly the world-process of the Infinite and the Time-process of the Eternal, the consciousness must pass beyond this finite reason and the finite sense to a larger reason and spiritual sense in touch with the consciousness of the Infinite and responsive to the logic of the Infinite which is the very logic of being itself and arises inevitably from its self-operation of its own realities, a logic whose sequences are not the steps of thought but the steps of existence.

Sri Aurobindo   Yoga   India   1940

of poetry

The construction of poetry's stories should be clearly like that in a drama; they should be based on a single action, one that is a complete whole in itself, with a beginning, middle and end, so as to enable the work to produce its own proper pleasure with all the organic unity of a living creature.

Aristotle   Philosophy   Greece   350 BCE

in silence with worlds

Friends, I sang as a bird sings
at daybreak. In all agreement
with one single world.
But how could one live in a world
where things had a single name?

Then I made up words.
And words perched, warbling, on the head
of objects.

Reality, thus, came to have
as many heads as words.
And when I tried to express sadness and joy
words settled upon me, obedient
to my slightest lyrical gesture.

Now I must be mute.
I am sincere only when silent.

So, only when I am silent
do they settle upon me — words —
a flock of birds in a tree
at nightfall.

    Cassiano Ricardo   Poetry   Brazil   1915-1965

in time in seasons

The sprouting grass waiting for spring,
and the grass that begins to wither, were once the same
wild grass of the moor.
Sooner or later
they surely meet with autumn
and end in the season of weariness.

    Gió   Buddhism   Japan   1100

spirit–matter

The electron on which forms and worlds are built,
  Leaped into being, a particle of God.
A spark from the eternal Energy spilt,
  It is the Infinite's blind minute abode.

In that small flaming chariot Shiva rides.
  The One devised innumerably to be;
His oneness in invisible forms he hides,
  Time's tiny temples to eternity.

Atom and molecule in their unseen plan
  Buttress an edifice of strange onenesses,
Crystal and plant, insect and beast and man, —
  Man on whom the World-Unity shall seize,

Widening his soul-spark to an epiphany
Of the timeless vastness of Infinity.

  Sri Aurobindo   Yoga   India   1940

in spirit

There is no freedom, no fulfillment in quantity — or in money — but only in the giving and receiving of quality in a creative sharing in that infinite ocean of potentialities which is spirit.

  Dane Rudhyar   Astrology   France   1970

in work

Ye now are in an age in which if ye shirk even one tenth of what is ordained ye shall be ruined. After this will come a time when he who will do e'en one tenth of what is ordered now will be redeemed.

  Mohammed   Islam   Saudi Arabia   632

aspirations–children

Life's aspirations come
In the guise of children.

Rabindranath Tagore   Poetry   India   1928

rights–duties

The true source of rights is duty. If we all discharge our duties, rights will not be far to
seek. If leaving duties unperformed we run after rights, they will escape us like a will-
o'-the-wisp. The more we pursue them, the farther will they fly.

Mahatma Gandhi   Nationalism   India   1925

in purity

As long as I am this or that, or have this or that, I am not all things and I have not all
things. Become pure till you neither are nor have either this or that; then you are
omnipresent and, being neither this nor that, are all things.

Meister Eckhart   Mysticism   Germany   1300

person–elements–universe

Thus he spake, and once more into the cup in which he had previously mingled the
soul of the universe he poured the remains of the elements, and mingled them in much
the same manner; they were not, however, pure as before, but diluted to the second
and third degree. And having made it he divided the whole mixture into souls equal in
number to the stars, and assigned each soul to a star; and having placed them as in a
chariot, he showed them the nature of the universe, and declared to them the laws of
destiny, according to which their first birth would be one and the same for all — no one
should suffer a disadvantage at his hands. . . .

Plato   Platonism   Greece   360 BCE

unmanifest–manifest

The soul is a figure of the Unmanifest,
The mind labours to think the Unthinkable,
The life to call the Immortal into birth,
The body to enshrine the Illimitable.

Sri Aurobindo   Yoga   India   1950

form–formlessness

Form is emptiness, emptiness is form.

Unknown   Buddhism   India   1000

with creation

Teach me, like you, to drink creation whole
And, casting out myself, become a soul.

Richard Wilbur   Poetry   United States   1961

beauty–ugliness darkness–light

As life unfolds in the higher regions it is the law of nature that between beauty and
ugliness the pendulum of experience and understanding shall swing with increasing
violence, until the intimate knowledge of darkness awakens within us a perfect
appreciation of light.

G.S. Arundale   Theosophy   United Kingdom   1935

through time

The whole is a great circle, and every part influences every other part, while "past" and
"future" depend on the point at which you place yourself on the circle. This is what is
meant, I think, by the somewhat apocalyptic saying that "the future influences the
past." Anyhow, it is clear that it does as a matter of fact, even if it is not clear how.

Annie Besant   Theosophy   United Kingdom   1900

in golf

"A round of golf," he said in his Journal notes, "partakes of the journey, and the journey is one of the central myths and signs of Western Man. It is built into his thoughts and dreams, into his genetic code." . . .

So Shivas Irons would have us learn to enjoy what is while seeking our treasure of tomorrow. And — you might have guessed it — a round of golf is good for that, ". . . because if it is a journey, it is a round: it always leads back to the place you started from . . . golf is always a trip back to the first tee, the more you play the more you realize you are staying where you are." By playing golf, he said, "you re-enact that secret of the journey. You may even get to enjoy it.

   Michael Murphy   Yoga   United States   1972

in consciousness   in common sense   in experience

"Common Sense" is an eloquent testimony to the oneness of our indwelling lives; we see all things around us on the physical plane in the same way, because our apparently separate consciousnesses are all really part of the One Consciousness ensouling all forms. We all respond in the same general way, according to the stage of our evolution, because we share the same consciousness; and we are affected similarly by the same things because the action and reaction between them and ourselves is the interplay of the One Life in varied forms.

   Annie Besant   Theosophy   United Kingdom   1915

of time

Time pours out its measureless froth and
the near and the far still unopened
and midday comes and evening comes,
no midday there, no evening, eternal floods
that swim in the wind, the fog, the light, the world
and this tangle moves off into endlessness
like a gigantic shimmering silk cocoon. . . .

   Sándor Weöres   Poetry   Hungary   1940

through concentration

You've discovered that concentration cannot be a permanent condition, but only a transition between the projected world and being. When you concentrate your thoughts on something, you can't stop with just thinking, because concentration leads you back to yourself, and you become the very thing you're concentrating on. From thinking you progress through concentration into a state of being! Thinking ceases completely and the thinker becomes identical with what he is thinking. To think something means to project a thought outwardly by means of the intellect, as if by means of a mirror, hence to step out of oneself. Through concentration we draw the projection back again, and what is thought becomes identical with the thinker, with the person himself. The two factors are joined in a perfect unity. That which is created goes back into the creator!

   Elisabeth Haich   Yoga   Hungary   1960

inner—outer

To build a house in the world of man
And not to hear the noise of horse and carriage,
How can this be done? —
When the mind is detached, the place is quiet.
I gather chrysanthemums under the eastern hedgerow
And silently gaze at the southern mountains.
The mountain air is beautiful in the sunset,
And the birds flocking together return home.
In all these things there is a real meaning,
Yet when I want to express it, I become lost in no-words.

   T'ao Ch'ien   Taoism   China   427

person—things

He who possesses an understanding of reality can reach the subtlety of things in accordance with their natural spontaneity. His mind interfuses and his spirit becomes one with things. Silently he comes into accord with their action and non-action. When he reaches this invisible fountain, he can express it in all forms in which both appearances and essence move and vibrate. Hence, the forms are given the breath of life and move with their own rhythm.

   Weng Fang-kang   Taoism   China   1818

stability—movement   in multiplicity   in Shiva's dancing

Stability and movement, we must remember, are only our psychological representations of the Absolute, even as are oneness and multitude. The Absolute is beyond stability and movement as it is beyond unity and multiplicity. But it takes its eternal poise in the one and the stable and whirls round itself infinitely, inconceivably, securely in the moving and multitudinous. World-existence is the ecstatic dance of Shiva which multiplies the body of the God numberlessly to the view: it leaves that white existence precisely where and what it was, ever is and ever will be; its sole absolute object is the joy of the dancing.

Sri Aurobindo   Yoga   India   1940

in division

Why I like to divide things is because such division must be based upon the totality of things. The creation of one rests upon the all. Why I dislike to complete things is because completeness means containing everything. Therefore it is isolated and self-sufficient, rejecting the relation to other things.

Chuang Tzu   Taoism   China   286 BCE

power—wisdom

Until philosophers are kings, or the kings and princes of this world have the spirit and power of philosophy, and political greatness and wisdom meet in one, and those commoner natures who pursue either to the exclusion of the other are compelled to stand aside, cities will never have rest from their evils — nor the human race, as I believe, — and then only will this our State have a possibility of life and behold the light of day.

Plato   Platonism   Greece   387 BCE

of vision   through time

To the spiritual eagle eye of the seer and the prophet of every race, Ariadne's thread stretches beyond that "historic period" without break or flow, surely and steadily into the very night of time; and the Land which holds it is too mighty to drop it, or even let it break.

Helena Petrovna Blavatsky   Theosophy   Russia   1888

in multiplicity   the mathematics of oneness

We see that the Absolute, the Self, the Divine, the Spirit, the Being is One; the Transcendental is one, the Cosmic is one: but we see also that beings are many and each has a self, a spirit, a like yet different nature. And since the spirit and essence of things is one, we are obliged to admit that all these many must be that One, and it follows that the One is or has become many; but how can the limited or relative be the Absolute and how can man or beast or bird be the Divine Being? But in erecting this apparent contradiction the mind makes a double error. It is thinking in the terms of the mathematical finite unit which is sole in limitation, the one which is less than two and can become two only by division and fragmentation or by addition and multiplication; but this is an infinite Oneness, it is the essential and infinite Oneness which can contain the hundred and the thousand and the million and billion and trillion. Whatever astronomic or more than astronomic figures you heap and multiply, they cannot overpass or exceed that Oneness; for, in the language of the Upanishad, it moves not, yet is always far in front when you would pursue and seize it. It can be said of it that it would not be the infinite Oneness if it were not capable of an infinite multiplicity; but that does not mean that the One is plural or can be limited or described as the sum of the Many: on the contrary, it can be the infinite Many because it exceeds all limitation or description by multiplicity and exceeds at the same time all limitation by finite conceptual oneness. Pluralism is an error because, though there is the spiritual plurality, the many souls are dependent and interdependent existences; their sum also is not the One nor is it the cosmic totality; they depend on the One and exist by its Oneness: yet the plurality is not unreal, it is the One Soul that dwells as the individual in these many souls and they are eternal in the One and by the one Eternal. This is difficult for the mental reason which makes an opposition between the Infinite and the finite and associates finiteness with plurality and infinity with oneness; but in the logic of the Infinite there is no such opposition and the eternity of the Many in the One is a thing that is perfectly natural and possible.

Sri Aurobindo   Yoga   India   1940

in contradiction   in process

If simple unity could be adequately perceived by the sight or by any other sense, then . . . there would be nothing to attract towards being; but when there is some contradiction always present, and one is the reverse of one and involves the conception of plurality, then thought begins to be aroused within us, and the soul perplexed and wanting to arrive at a decision asks "What is absolute unity?" This is the way in which the study of the one has a power of drawing and converting the mind to the contemplation of true being.

Plato   Platonism   Greece   387 BCE

in contradiction   in education

To complement this movement of inner discovery, it would be good not to neglect the development of the mind. For the mental instrument can equally be a great help or a great hindrance. In its natural state the human mind is always limited in its vision, narrow in its understanding, rigid in its conceptions, and a constant effort is therefore needed to widen it, to make it more supple and profound. So it is very necessary to consider everything from as many points of view as possible. Towards this end, there is an exercise which gives great suppleness and elevation to the thought. It is as follows: a clearly formulated thesis is set; against it is opposed its antithesis, formulated with the same precision. Then by careful reflection the problem must be widened or transcended until a synthesis is found which unites the two contraries in a larger, higher and more comprehensive idea.

The Mother   Yoga   France   1950

micro–macro

A handful of sand is an anthology of the universe.

David McCord   Poetry   United States   1920

micro–macro

In the heaven of Indra, there is said to be a network of pearls so arranged that if you look at one you see all the others reflected in it. In the same way each object in the world is not merely itself but involves every other object and in fact is everything else.

Sir Charles Eliot   Huayan Buddhism   United Kingdom   1935

micro—macro

In every particle of dust, there are present Buddhas without number. On the point of a single hair a whole Buddha land may be seen.

Unknown   Buddhism (Huayan)   China   100 BCE

above—below in architecture

The whole cosmos is regarded as pervaded by a single life, in such a way that there is a harmony recognized between the upper and lower modes of Being and Becoming. The informing thought of the Sumerian world feeling is: "What is above is below"; and from this two directions of spiritual movement are projected: the Above comes downward, the Below mounts aloft. The spatial symbol of this world feeling is the stepped Sumerian temple-tower with its various cosmological names, such as, "Temple of the Seven Conveyers of the Commands of Heaven and Earth," "Temple of the Foundation of Heaven and Earth", etc., the stages of the tower corresponding to the different levels of doctrine of the ranges of the upper world. . . .

Accordingly, the earthly order corresponds to the heavenly. Every priest-king in his own domain (which is a miniature of the cosmos) is by the grace of his god a consummate image of the godhead. And this idea lives on even after the high symbolic period passes. Every throne is the image of a heavenly throne. The king's court reflects that of his god. As steps are mounted to a throne, so one mounts the stages to heaven. Moreover, the same thought can be recognized in the structure of any temple. The forecourt leads to the sanctuary, and the sanctuary to the inner shrine, where the image represents the seat of the supreme god. The spatial symbolism of such a temple-form corresponds to that of the ziggurat projected on a flat surface: the penetration ever deeper inward being equivalent to the ascent ever higher aloft.

Alfred Jeremias   Archeology   Germany   1929

in multiplicity

There is that unmanifest Unknowable; there is this manifest knowable, partly manifest to our ignorance, manifest entirely to the divine Knowledge which holds it in its own infinity. If it is true that neither our ignorance nor our utmost and widest mental knowledge can give us a hold of the Unknowable, still it is also true that, whether through our knowledge or through our ignorance, That variously manifests itself; for it cannot be manifesting something other than itself, since nothing else can exist: in this variety of manifestation there is that Oneness and through the diversity we can touch the Oneness. . . . We see that these apparently opposite terms of One and Many, Form and the Formless, Finite and Infinite, are not so much opposites as complements of each other; not alternating values of the Brahman which in its creation perpetually loses oneness to find itself in multiplicity and, unable to discover itself in multiplicity, loses it again to recover oneness, but double and concurrent values which explain each other; not hopelessly incompatible alternatives, but two faces of the one Reality which can lead us to it by our realisation of both together and not only by testing each separately, — even though such separate testing may be a legitimate or even an inevitable step or part of the process of knowledge. Knowledge is no doubt the knowledge of the One, the realisation of the Being; Ignorance is a self-oblivion of Being, the experience of separateness in the multiplicity and a dwelling or circling in the ill-understood maze of becomings: but this is cured by the soul in the Becoming growing into knowledge, into awareness of the Being which becomes in the multiplicity all these existences and can so become because their truth is already there in its timeless existence. The integral knowledge of Brahman is a consciousness in possession of both together, and the exclusive pursuit of either closes the vision to one side of the truth of the omnipresent Reality. The possession of the Being who is beyond all becomings, brings to us freedom from the bonds of attachment and ignorance in the cosmic existence and brings by that freedom a free possession of the Becoming and of the cosmic existence. The knowledge of the Becoming is a part of knowledge; it acts as an Ignorance only because we dwell imprisoned in it, avidyāyām antare, without possessing the Oneness of the Being, which is its base, its stuff, its spirit, its cause of manifestation and without which it could not be possible.

In fact, the Brahman is one not only in a featureless oneness beyond all relation, but in the very multiplicity of the cosmic existence. Aware of the works of the dividing mind but not itself limited by it, It finds its oneness as easily in the many, in relations, in becoming as in any withdrawal from the many, from relations, from becoming. Ourselves also, to possess even its oneness fully, must possess it — since it is there, since all is that — in the infinite self-variation of the cosmos. The infinity of the multiplicity finds itself explained and justified only when it is contained and possessed in the infinity of the One; but also the infinity of the One pours itself out and possesses itself in the infinity of the Many.

Sri Aurobindo   Yoga   India   1940

52

in vibration

All energy, all the forces of the universe, are movements which emanate from one point — their own center — and radiate in circular waves in all directions, manifesting themselves as vibrations or oscillations. These manifestations of force cease only when the forces that have gotten out of balance regain their primordial state of equilibrium, the divine unity. Hence when we speak of the "primordial state" we mean the state in which all material phenomena have ceased to exist. In its true essence, matter, too, is motion, and if this motion comes to stop, matter must necessarily cease to exist. As long as the three-dimensional material world exists, its mutable law is that of unrest, of movement. . . .

So, throughout the universe, countless varieties of vibrations are at work, ranging from the shortest to the longest wave length. Every form of creation, beginning with the celestial bodies and ranging all the way down to the tiniest monocellular creature — all the myriad manifestations of creation are the effects of various forms of these rays. We live in these various rays whether we know it or not; even more, these forms of energy have built and formed us human beings and are constantly at work in our body, our mind, and our entire being. The whole universe consists of these various vibrations. The source of these creative vibrations we call God.

Elisabeth Haich   Yoga   Germany   1960

spirit—matter

Since, then, we admit both the claim of the pure Spirit to manifest in us its absolute freedom and the claim of universal Matter to be the mould and condition of our manifestation, we have to find a truth that can entirely reconcile these antagonists and can give to both their due portion in Life and their due justification in Thought, amercing neither of its rights, denying in neither the sovereign truth from which even its errors, even the exclusiveness of its exaggerations draw so constant a strength. For wherever there is an extreme statement that makes such a powerful appeal to the human mind, we may be sure that we are standing in the presence of no mere error, superstition or hallucination, but of some sovereign fact disguised which demands our fealty and will avenge itself if denied or excluded. Herein lies the difficulty of a satisfying solution and the source of that lack of finality which pursues all mere compromises between Spirit and Matter. A compromise is a bargain, a transaction of interests between two conflicting powers; it is not a true reconciliation. True reconciliation proceeds always by a mutual comprehension leading to some sort of intimate oneness. It is therefore through the utmost possible unification of Spirit and Matter that we shall best arrive at their reconciling truth and so at some strongest foundation for a reconciling practice in the inner life of the individual and his outer existence.

Sri Aurobindo   Yoga   India   1940

spirit—matter

Hell split across its huge abrupt facade
As if a magic building were undone,
Night opened and vanished like a gulf of dream.
Into being's gap scooped out as empty Space
In which she had filled the place of absent God,
There poured a wide intimate and blissful Dawn;
Healed were all things that Time's torn heart had made
And sorrow could live no more in Nature's breast:
Division ceased to be, for God was there.
The soul lit the conscious body with its ray,
Matter and Spirit mingled and were one.

Sri Aurobindo   Yoga   India   1950

of opposites

Harmony would lose its attractiveness if it did not have a background of discord.

Unknown   Taoism   China   Traditional

success—failure   in work

One man may hit the mark, another blunder; but heed not these distinctions. Only from the alliance of the one, working with and through the other, are great things born.

Antoine de Saint-Exupéry   Literature   France   1948

in work   in butchering

Prince Wen Hui's cook was carving up an ox. Every touch of his hand, every heave of his shoulder, every step of his foot, every thrust of his knee, with the slicing and parting of the flesh, and the zinging of the knife — all was in perfect rhythm, just like the Dance of the Mulberry Grove or a part in the Ching Shou symphony.

Prince Wen Hui remarked, "How wonderfully you have mastered your art."

The cook laid down his knife and said, "What your servant really cares for is Tao, which goes beyond mere art. When I first began to cut up oxen, I saw nothing but oxen. After three years of practicing, I no longer saw the ox as a whole. I now work with my spirit, not with my eyes. My senses stop functioning and my spirit takes over. I follow the natural grain, letting the knife find its way through the many hidden openings, taking advantage of what is there, never touching a ligament or tendon, much less a main joint."

"A good cook changes his knife once a year because he cuts, while a mediocre cook has to change every month because he hacks. I've had this knife of mine for nineteen years and have cut up thousands of oxen with it, and yet the edge is as if it were fresh from the grindstone. There are spaces between the joints. The blade of the knife has no thickness. That which has no thickness has plenty of room to pass through these spaces. Therefore, after nineteen years, my blade is as sharp as ever. However, when I come to a difficulty, I size up the joint, look carefully, keep my eyes on what I am doing, and work slowly. Then with a very slight movement of the knife, I cut the whole ox wide open. It falls apart like a clod of earth crumbling to the ground. I stand there with the knife in my hand, looking about me with a feeling of accomplishment and delight. Then I wipe the knife clean and put it away."

"Well done!" said the Prince. "From the words of my cook, I have learned the secret of growth."

Guo Xiang   Xuanxue Taoism   China   312

in art

It needs a certain purity of spirit to an artist, of any sort. . . . This is the beginning of all art, visual or literary or musical: be pure in spirit. It isn't the same as goodness. It is much more difficult and nearer the divine. The divine isn't only good, it is all things.

One may see the divine in natural objects: I saw it today, in the frail, lovely little camellia flowers on long stems. . . . I saw them like a vision. So now, I could paint them.

. . . I believe one can only develop one's visionary awareness by close contact with the vision itself: that is, by knowing pictures, real vision-pictures, and by dwelling on them, and really, dwelling in them. It is a great delight to dwell in a picture. But it needs a purity of spirit, a sloughing of vulgar sensation and vulgar interest, and above all, vulgar contact, that few people know how to perform. . . . Art is a form of supremely delicate awareness and atonement — meaning at-oneness, the state of being at one with the object. Art is the great atonement in delight — for I can never look on art save as a form of delight.

D.H. Lawrence   Literature   United Kingdom   1929

in art

Poetry, painting, and calligraphy, for their highest achievements, are all derived from a common ground. From a thorough study of one of these arts one can be led to a deep understanding of the others, because they all share primordial roots and radiate into the depths of one another.

Chang Chung-yuan   Taoism   China   1963

in art   painting–poetry

Simonides calls painting silent poetry, and poetry, speaking painting.

Plutarch of Chaeronea   Moralism   Greece   120 BCE

with music

A mighty elemental force is music.
The more obscure is it, the greater is
The power it wields, the more is there
                    of magic
In every note. . . . Suffice it that it fills
My tearless eyes with tears. . . .
                    A mellow languor,
It courses through the veins of humankind
And is, unseen, dissolved like salt in water
In everything....

Yevgeni Vinokurov   Poetry   Russia   1966

with greatness

When the high heart we magnify,
And the clear vision celebrate,
And worship greatness passing by,
Ourselves are great.

John Drinkwater   Drama   United Kingdom   1919

with the will of the Divine

As soon as I have no longer any material responsibilities, all thoughts about these things flee far away from me, and I am solely and entirely occupied with Thee and Thy service. Then, in that perfect peace and serenity, I unite my will to Thine, and in that integral silence I listen to Thy truth and hear its expression. It is by becoming conscious of Thy Will and identifying ours with Thine that there is found the secret of true liberty and all-puissance, the secret of the regeneration of forces and the transfiguration of the being.

To be constantly and integrally at one with Thee is to have the assurance that we shall overcome every obstacle and triumph over all difficulties, both within and without.

O Lord, Lord, a boundless joy fills my heart, songs of gladness surge through my head in marvellous waves, and in the full confidence of Thy certain triumph I find a sovereign Peace and an invincible Power. Thou fillest my being, Thou animatest it, Thou settest in motion its hidden springs, Thou increasest tenfold its love; and I no longer know whether the universe is I or I the universe, whether Thou art in me or I in Thee; Thou alone art and all is Thou; and the streams of Thy infinite grace fill and overflow the world.

Sing O lands, sing O peoples, sing O men,
The Divine Harmony is there.

The Mother   Yoga   France   1914

with the Divine   in action

To be merged both in Thee and in Thy work . . . to be no longer a limited individuality . . . to become the infinitude of Thy forces manifesting through one point . . . to be freed from all shackles and all limitations . . . to rise above all restrictive thought . . . to act while remaining outside the action . . . to act with and for individuals while seeing only Oneness, the Oneness of Thy Love, Thy Knowledge, Thy Being . . . O my divine Master, eternal Teacher, Sole Reality, dispel all darkness in this aggregate Thou hast formed for Thy service, Thy manifestation in the world. Realise in it that supreme consciousness which will awaken the same consciousness everywhere.

Oh, no longer to see appearances which incessantly change; always to contemplate in everything and everywhere only Thy immutable Oneness!

O Lord, all my being cries to Thee in an irresistible call; wilt Thou not grant that I may become Thyself in my integral consciousness, since in truth I am Thou and Thou art I?

The Mother   Yoga   France   1914

of opposites   in truth

Even as the dairy-maid, pulling and slacking
The two ends of the churning string by turns,
Churns out the golden butter from the milk,
E'en so the sage, working alternately
At both the two inevitable sides
Of every question, finds the perfect Truth.

Amrita Chandra Suri   Jainism   India   1933

of truth   beyond confinement

What kind of truth is it which has these mountains as its boundary and is a lie beyond them?

Michel de Montaigne   Existentialism   France   1580

in truth

Truth, whose center is everywhere and its circumference nowhere, whose existence we cannot disimagine; the soundness and health of things, against which no blow can be struck, but it recoils on the striker.

Ralph Waldo Emerson   Transcendentalism   United States   1882

action–inaction

He who in action can see inaction and can see action still continuing in cessation from works, is the man of true reason and discernment among men; he is in Yoga and a many-sided universal worker (for the good of the world, for God in the world).

Unknown   Yoga   India   600 BCE

in surrender   during difficulties

When physical conditions are a little difficult and some discomfort follows, if one knows how to surrender completely before Thy will, caring little for life or death, health or illness, the integral being enters immediately into harmony with Thy law of love and life, and all physical indisposition ceases, giving place to calm well-being, deep and peaceful.

I have noticed that when one enters into an activity that necessitates great physical endurance, what tires one most is anticipating beforehand all the difficulties to which one will be exposed. It is much wiser to see at every moment only the difficulty of the present instant; in this way the effort becomes much easier for it is always proportionate to the amount of strength, the resistance at one's disposal. The body is a marvellous tool, it is our mind that does not know how to use it and, instead of fostering its suppleness, its plasticity, it brings a certain fixity into it which comes from pre-conceived ideas and unfavourable suggestions.

But the supreme science, O Lord, is to unite with Thee, to trust in Thee, to live in Thee, to be Thyself; and then nothing is any longer impossible to a man who manifests Thy omnipotence.

Lord, my aspiration rises to Thee like a silent canticle, a mute adoration, and Thy divine Love illumines my heart.

O divine Master, I bow to Thee!

The Mother   Yoga   France   1914

self–God

When man seeks God outside himself, he can often be "thinking" about God, he can be "praying" to God, he can be "loving" God with his whole being, but all this doesn't mean he has become identical with God. For man can never find God by seeking outside himself!

   The creator in man is man's own self whose last manifestation, farthest from his own center, is the little "I", his personal "I-consciousness." The personal "I" within him is the image of God mirrored by matter — in the body. Thus when man seeks to return to God, and re-establish his identity with him he must follow the same path with his consciousness: he must draw his consciousness more and more from his own little personal "I" — deeper and deeper into himself — turning to his own true self, to his creator, until he consciously recognizes himself in Him. But this doesn't mean that the creature — the person — recognizes itself in this condition. As an imaginary being, it has no true existence and cannot really achieve self-knowledge. On the contrary, the creator recognizes himself in the created, in the person. This is the only possibility for overcoming the state of separation and bringing back the consciousness into the state of unity; the individual stops thinking about himself and instead becomes himself, recognizes himself. In this condition, the recognizer, the recognized, and the recognition are one and the same. The self — the creator — recognizes its self in itself!

   Man can only experience God in this way. This is resurrection! In this state he recognizes that his own self has created him and is constantly creating him, hence that his own self is his creator. He likewise realizes that the one and only self is the creator of the entire universe! As a result of this divine self-recognition he simultaneously experiences the creative cosmic all-consciousness. At the same time as he achieves self-recognition, he achieves recognition of everything, omniscience!

   Elisabeth Haich   Yoga   Hungary   1960

in virtue

Virtue is the adherence in action to the nature of things, and the nature of things makes it prevalent. It consists in a perpetual substitution of being for seeming, and with sublime propriety God is described as saying, I AM.

   Ralph Waldo Emerson   Transcendentalism   United States   1841

identity and difference   unity and multiplicity   in the logic of the Infinite

The Identical to our notions is the Immutable; it is ever the same through eternity, for if it is or becomes subject to mutation or if it admits of differences, it ceases to be identical; but what we see everywhere is an infinitely variable fundamental oneness which seems the very principle of Nature. The basic Force is one, but it manifests from itself innumerable forces; the basic substance is one, but it develops many different substances and millions of unlike objects; mind is one but differentiates itself into many mental states, mind-formations, thoughts, perceptions differing from each other and entering into harmony or into conflict; life is one, but the forms of life are unlike and innumerable; humanity is one in nature, but there are different race types and every individual man is himself and in some way unlike others; Nature insists on tracing lines of difference on the leaves of one tree; she drives differentiation so far that it has been found that the lines on one man's thumb are different from the lines of every other man's thumb so that he can be identified by that differentiation alone, — yet fundamentally all men are alike and there is no essential difference. Oneness or sameness is everywhere, differentiation is everywhere; the indwelling Reality has built the universe on the principle of the development of one seed into a million different fashions. But this again is the logic of the Infinite; because the essence of the Reality is immutably the same, it can assume securely these innumerable differences of form and character and movement, for even if they were multiplied a trillionfold, that would not affect the underlying immutability of the eternal Identical. Because the Self and Spirit in things and beings is one everywhere, therefore Nature can afford this luxury of infinite differentiation: if there were not this secure basis which brings it about that nothing changes yet all changes, all her workings and creations would in this play collapse into disintegration and chaos; there would be nothing to hold her disparate movements and creations together. The immutability of the Identical does not consist in a monotone of changeless sameness incapable of variation; it consists in an unchangeableness of being which is capable of endless formation of being, but which no differentiation can destroy or impair or minimise. The Self becomes insect and bird and beast and man, but it is always the same Self through these mutations because it is the One who manifests himself infinitely in endless diversity. Our surface reason is prone to conclude that the diversity may be unreal, an appearance only, but if we look a little deeper we shall see that a real diversity brings out the real Unity, shows it as it were in its utmost capacity, reveals all that it can be and is in itself, delivers from its whiteness of hue the many tones of colour that are fused together there; Oneness finds itself infinitely in what seems to us to be a falling away from its oneness, but is really an inexhaustible diverse display of unity. This is the miracle, the Maya of the universe, yet perfectly logical, natural and a matter of course to the self-vision and self-experience of the Infinite.

Sri Aurobindo   Yoga   India   1940

of contradictions   human striving–divine will

With the same accuracy, one can say that all is divine or that nothing is divine. Everything depends upon the angle from which one looks at the problem.

Likewise, it can be said that the divine is a perpetual becoming and yet also, that it is immutable for all eternity.

To deny or affirm God's existence is equally true, but each is only partially true. It is by rising above both affirmation and negation that one may draw nearer the truth.

It can further be said that whatever happens in the world is the result of divine will, but also that this will has to be expressed and manifested in a world that contradicts or deforms it; these are two attitudes having, respectively, the practical effect of either submitting with peace and joy to whatever happens or, on the contrary, ceaselessly fighting for the triumph of what should be. To live the truth one must know how to rise above both attitudes and combine them.

The Mother   Yoga   France   1954

Self

of self

Talk as much philosophy as you please, worship as many gods as you like, observe all ceremonies, sing devoted praises to any number of divine beings — liberation never comes, even at the end of a hundred aeons, without the realization of Oneness of Self.

Shankara   Ontology   India   800

as the means of knowledge   the supramental perception

. . . man is separated in his mind, his life, his body from the universal and therefore, even as he does not know himself, is equally and even more incapable of knowing his fellow-creatures. He forms by inferences, theories, observations and a certain imperfect capacity of sympathy a rough mental construction about them; but this is not knowledge. Knowledge can only come by conscious identity, for that is the only true knowledge, — existence aware of itself. We know what we are so far as we are consciously aware of ourself, the rest is hidden; so also we can come really to know that with which we become one in our consciousness, but only so far as we can become one with it. If the means of knowledge are indirect and imperfect, the knowledge attained will also be indirect and imperfect. It will enable us to work out with a certain precarious clumsiness but still perfectly enough from our mental standpoint certain limited practical aims, necessities, conveniences, a certain imperfect and insecure harmony of our relations with that which we know; but only by a conscious unity with it can we arrive at a perfect relation. Therefore we must arrive at a conscious unity with our fellow-beings and not merely at the sympathy created by love or the understanding created by mental knowledge, which will always be the knowledge of their superficial existence and therefore imperfect in itself and subject to denial and frustration by the uprush of the unknown and unmastered from the subconscient or the subliminal in them and us. But this conscious oneness can only be established by entering into that in which we are one with them, the universal; and the fullness of the universal exists consciently only in that which is superconscient to us, in the Supermind: for here in our normal being the greater part of it is subconscient and therefore in this normal poise of mind, life and body it cannot be possessed. The lower conscious nature is bound down to ego in all its activities, chained triply to the stake of differentiated individuality. The Supermind alone commands unity in diversity.

Sri Aurobindo   Yoga   India   1940

in self

If those who lead you say to you: "See, the Kingdom is in heaven," then the birds of heaven will precede you. If they say to you: "It is in the sea," then the fish will precede you. But the Kingdom is within you and it is without you. If you will know yourselves, then you will be known and you will know that you are the sons of the Living Father. But if you do not know yourselves, then you are in poverty and you are poverty.

Jesus Christ   Christianity   Palestine (Judea)   33

of knowledge

No man can reveal to you aught but that which already lies half asleep in the dawning of your knowledge.

Kahlil Gibran   Mysticism   Lebanon   1923

in contrast   in balance

He who sleeps in continual noise is wakened by silence.

William Dean Howells   Realism   United States   1860

by oneself

Neither by words nor by the patriarch;
Neither by colors nor by sound was I enlightened.
But, at midnight, when I blew out the candle and went to bed,
Suddenly, within myself, I reached the dawn.

Unknown   Zen Buddhism   China   Unknown

through the psychic being

It is the psychic personality in us that flowers as the saint, the sage, the seer; when it reaches its full strength, it turns the being towards the Knowledge of Self and the Divine, towards the supreme Truth, the supreme Good, the supreme Beauty, Love and Bliss, the divine heights and largenesses, and opens us to the touch of spiritual sympathy, universality, oneness. . . .

But it might seem then that by bringing this psychic entity, this true soul in us, into the front and giving it there the lead and rule we shall gain all the fulfilment of our natural being that we can seek for and open also the gates of the kingdom of the Spirit. . . . By itself the psychic being at a certain stage might be content to create a formation of truth, good and beauty and make that its station; at a farther stage it might become passively subject to the world self, a mirror of the universal existence, consciousness, power, delight, but not their full participant or possessor. Although more nearly and thrillingly united to the cosmic consciousness in knowledge, emotion and even appreciation through the senses, it might become purely recipient and passive, remote from mastery and action in the world; or, one with the static self behind the cosmos, but separate inwardly from the world-movement, losing its individuality in its Source, it might return to that Source and have neither the will nor the power any further for that which was its ultimate mission here, to lead the nature also towards its divine realisation. For the psychic being came into Nature from the Self, the Divine, and it can turn back from Nature to the silent Divine through the silence of the Self and a supreme spiritual immobility. Again, an eternal portion of the Divine, this part is by the law of the Infinite inseparable from its Divine Whole, this part is indeed itself that Whole, except in its frontal appearance, its frontal separative self-experience; it may awaken to that reality and plunge into it to the apparent extinction or at least the merging of the individual existence. A small nucleus here in the mass of our ignorant Nature, so that it is described in the Upanishad as no bigger than a man's thumb, it can by the spiritual influx enlarge itself and embrace the whole world with the heart and mind in an intimate communion or oneness. Or it may become aware of its eternal Companion and elect to live for ever in His presence, in an imperishable union and oneness as the eternal lover with the eternal Beloved, which of all spiritual experiences is the most intense in beauty and rapture. All these are great and splendid achievements of our spiritual self-finding, but they are not necessarily the last end and entire consummation; more is possible.

Sri Aurobindo   Yoga   India   1940

inner–outer   with the Divine

In moments when the inner lamps are lit
And the life's cherished guests are left outside,
Our spirit sits alone and speaks to its gulfs.
A wider consciousness opens then its doors;
Invading from spiritual silences
A ray of the timeless Glory stoops awhile
To commune with our seized illumined clay
And leaves its huge white stamp upon our lives.

Sri Aurobindo   Yoga   India   1950

person–Earth

I swear the earth shall surely be complete to him or her who
   shall be complete,
The earth remains jagged and broken only to him or her who
   remains jagged and broken.

Walt Whitman   Mysticism   United States   1855

with self

Irrigators guide water; fletchers straighten arrows; carpenters turn wood; wise people shape themselves.

Gautama Buddha   Buddhism   Nepal, India (Kapilavastu)   483 BCE

in opposition within one's self

The great thing about being your own worst enemy is that we're evenly matched.

Bob Thaves   Cartooning   United States   2013

with self

Though one should in battle conquer a thousand men a thousand times, he who conquers himself has the more glorious victory.

Gautama Buddha   Buddhism   Nepal, India (Kapilavastu)   483 BCE

in the heart

Call it any name, God, Self, the Heart or the Seat of Consciousness, it is all the same. The point to be grasped is this, that HEART means the very core of one's being, the Center, without which there is nothing whatever.

Ramana Maharshi   Hinduism   India   1931

in yoga   consciousness—source

The word "yoga" is from the Sanskrit verbal root yuj, meaning "to yoke, to join," to yoke one thing to another. What is to be joined through yoga is consciousness to its source, so that one lives in the knowledge of identity with that source and not merely with the limited ego of the daylight personality. Or to recast the idea in terms of lunar and solar light: what is to be joined is the reflected light of a sub-lunar, temporal consciousness to the timeless solar source of all light and all consciousness whatsoever.

Joseph Campbell   Mythology   United States   1974

in peace   despite desire

He attains peace, into whom all desires enter as waters into the sea (an ocean of wide being and consciousness) which is ever being filled, yet ever motionless — not he who (like troubled and muddy waters) is disturbed by every little inrush of desire.

The Bhagavad Gita   Hinduism   India   600 BCE

in meditation

True Meditation has no direction, goals, or method. All methods aim at achieving a certain state of mind. All states are limited, impermanent, and conditioned. Fascination with states leads only to bondage and dependency. True Meditation is abidance as primordial consciousness.

True Meditation appears in consciousness spontaneously when awareness is not fixated on objects of perception. When you first start to meditate, you notice that awareness is always focused on some object: on thoughts, bodily sensations, emotions, memories, sounds, etc. This is because the mind is conditioned to focus and contract upon objects. Then the mind compulsively interprets what it is aware of (the object) in a mechanical and distorted way. It begins to draw conclusions and make assumptions according to past conditioning.

In True Meditation all objects are left to their natural functioning. This means that no effort should be made to manipulate or suppress any object of awareness. In true meditation the emphasis is on being awareness: not on being aware of objects, but on resting as primordial awareness itself. Primordial awareness (consciousness) is the source in which all objects arise and subside. As you gently relax into awareness, into listening, the mind's compulsive contraction around objects will fade. Silence of being will come more clearly into consciousness as a welcoming to rest and abide. An attitude of open receptivity, free of any goal or anticipation, will facilitate the presence of silence and stillness to be revealed as your natural condition.

Silence and stillness are not states and therefore cannot be produced or created. Silence is the non-state in which all states arise and subside. Silence, stillness, and awareness are not states and can never be perceived in their totality as objects. Silence is itself the eternal witness without form or attributes. As you rest more profoundly as the witness, all objects take on their natural functionality, and awareness becomes free of the mind's compulsive contractions and identifications, and returns to its natural non-state of Presence.

The simple yet profound question, "Who am I?," can then reveal oneself to not be the endless tyranny of the ego – personality, but objectless Freedom of Being – Primordial Consciousness in which all states and all objects come and go as manifestations of the Eternal Unborn Self that YOU ARE.

Adyashanti   Buddhism   United States   2010

in awareness of the world

Man knows himself only to the extent that he knows the world; he becomes aware of himself only within the world, and aware of the world only within himself. Every object, well contemplated, opens up a new organ of perception within us.

Johann Wolfgang von Goethe   Literature   Germany   1823

in happiness   in work

Human happiness is the true odour of growth, the sweet exhalation of work.

David Grayson   Journalism   United States   1907

with self

This above all, to thine own self be true.
And it must follow, as the night the day
Thou canst not then be false to any man.

William Shakespeare   Drama   United Kingdom   1601

love

Of all the Qualifications, Love is the most important, for if it is strong enough in a man, it forces him to acquire all the rest, and all the rest without it would never be sufficient.

J. Krishnamurti   Theosophy   India   1909

in parts of oneself   inner–outer

Listen to a man's words and look at the pupil of his eye. How can a man conceal his character.

Mencius   Confucianism   China   289 BCE

in vision   in beauty

Never did eye see the sun unless it had first become sunlike, and never can the soul have vision of the First Beauty unless itself be beautiful.

Plotinus   Neo-Platonism   Italy   250

inner–outer

It is in the highest sense true that everyone perceives richness and beauty outside himself to the extent that he has both in his own heart.

Wilhelm von Humboldt   Philosophy   Germany   1835

knowledge–feeling   in harmony

The seat of knowledge is in the head; of wisdom, in the heart. We are sure to judge wrong if we do not feel right.

William Hazlitt   Humanism   United Kingdom   1823

laughter–tears   in balance

Laughter and tears are meant to turn the wheels of the same sensibility; one is wind-power and the other water-power, that is all.

Oliver Wendell Holmes   Poetry   United States   1858

loss–gain

When the heart weeps for what it has lost, the spirit laughs for what it has found.

Proverb   Sufism   Unknown   Traditional

in knowledge

Though a learned man may not possess a foot of land, the whole world is his country.

Unknown   Proverb   Romania   Traditional

inner—outer

What other liberty is there worth having, if we have not freedom and peace in our minds, if our inmost and most private man is but a sour and turbid pool?

Henry David Thoreau   Transcendentalism   United States   1862

in action   failure—success

The man who makes no mistakes does not usually make anything.

William Connor Magee   Christianity   Ireland   1868

person—humanity

One day a lion, looking down a well,
Saw what appeared to him a miracle,
Another lion's face that upward glared
As if the first to try his strength he dared.
Furious, the lion took a sudden leap
And o'er him closed the placid waters deep.
Thou who dost blame injustice in mankind,
'Tis but the image of thine own dark mind;
In them reflected all thy nature is
With all its angles and obliquities;
Around thyself thyself the noose hast thrown,
Like that mad beast precipitate and prone;
Face answereth to face, and heart to heart,
As in the well that lion's counterpart.
"Back to each other we reflections throw,"
So spoke Arabia's Prophet long ago;
And he who views men through self's murky glass
Proclaims himself no lion, but an ass.

Jalal ad-Din Rumi   Sufism   Tajikistan, Turkey (Persia)   1230

self–war

Instead of hating the people you think are warmakers, hate the appetites and the disorder in your own soul, which are the causes of war.

Thomas Merton   Christianity   United States   1962

inner peace–world peace

Without inner peace, it is impossible to have world peace.

H.H. the 14th Dalai Lama   Tibetan Buddhism   Tibet   1989

in freedom

All dogmatism has its roots in a self that wants to entrench itself and does not wish to be disturbed. When one is free within oneself one is really able to listen to others.

N. Sri Ram   Theosophy   India   1973

in diversity

If a man fasten his attention on a single aspect of truth and apply himself to that alone for a long time, the truth becomes distorted and not itself but falsehood.

Ralph Waldo Emerson   Transcendentalism   United States   1841

within

The world needs no sectarian church, whether of Buddha, Jesus, Mohammed, Swedenborg, Calvin, or any other. There being but ONE Truth, man requires but one church — the Temple of God within us, walled in by matter but penetrable by any one who can find the way.

Helena Petrovna Blavatsky   Theosophy   Russia   1877

God–soul

All religion, all life, all art, all expression come down to this: to the effort of the human soul to break through its barrier of loneliness, of intolerable loneliness, and make some contact with another seeking soul, or with what all souls seek, which is (by any name) God.

Don Marquis   Humor   United States   1934

in art

The artist was not a special kind of man, but every man a special kind of artist.

Ananda Coomaraswamy   Aesthetics   Sri Lanka   1900

in dance

Dance is the only art of which we ourselves are the stuff of which it is made.

Ted Shawn   Dance   United States   1955

in singing

And not only the mouth sings, but also the hands, feet, buttocks, sexual organs, the whole being is liquefied in sound, voice and rhythm.

Aimé Césaire   Nationalism   Martinique   1956

in balance

Listen, or thy tongue will keep thee deaf.

Unknown   Native America   America   Traditional

in balance

A curve for the shore,
A line for the lea,
A tint for the sky
Where the sunrise will be.
A stroke for a gull,
A sweep for the main;
The skill to do more—
With the will to refrain.

Ruth Mason Rice   Journalism   United States   1900

in time

Live every moment as though you were building a perfect temple.

N. Sri Ram   Theosophy   India   1973

as a point of concentration   of the universal

The fundamental error of the Mind is, then, this fall from self-knowledge by which the individual soul conceives of its individuality as a separate fact instead of as a form of Oneness and makes itself the centre of its own universe instead of knowing itself as one concentration of the universal.

Sri Aurobindo   Yoga   India   1940

in geography   in awareness

No matter where you go, there you are.

Earl Mac Rauch   Film   United States   1984

inner—outer

In the world there is naught so wondrous as the sun,
But the Sun of the soul sets not and has no yesterday.

Jalal ad-Din Rumi   Sufism   Tajikistan, Turkey (Persia)   1230

in character

Fools have their second childhood, but the Great
Still keep their first, and have no second state.

William Henry Davies   Poetry   United Kingdom   1890

in balance   through time

What is a great life but a thought of youth executed by mature age?

Alfred de Vigny   Drama   France   1863

through travel

I am a part of all that I have met.

Alfred Lord Tennyson   Romanticism   United Kingdom   1842

with food

To eat of something is to become identical with it; for what you eat is what you will
consist of, what you will be.

Elisabeth Haich   Yoga   Hungary   1960

micro—macro

The lion with all his hairs, taken together, is at the same time found within a single
hair.

Unknown   Buddhism   China   500 BCE

micro—macro   person—God

I am a single drop; how can it be
That God, the whole ocean, floweth into me?

   Angelus Silesius   Poetry   Poland   1657

micro—macro

In outward form thou art the microcosm
But in reality the macrocosm,
Seemingly the bough is the cause of the fruit,
But really the bough exists because of the fruit.

   Jalal ad-Din Rumi   Sufism   Tajikistan, Turkey (Persia)   1230

with humanity   through imagination

A man, to be greatly good, must imagine intensely and comprehensively; . . . the pains
and pleasures of his species must become his own.

   Percy Bysshe Shelley   Romanticism   United Kingdom   1812

in contentment

O soul! be content with a little
That thou may'st consider the sultan and the dervish as one.
Why goest thou before the king with entreaty?
When thou places avarice aside, thou art a king.

   Saadi   Islam   Iran (Persia)   1257

in action

No man's deeds are blotted out; each deed comes home. The doer finds the results of
his deeds awaiting him sooner or later.

   Gautama Buddha   Buddhism   Nepal, India (Kapilavastu)   483 BCE

In God

Those drunk with God, though they be thousands,
   yet are one;
Those drunk with lust, though it be a single one,
   he is a double.

   Shams-i-Tabrizi   Sufism   Iran (Persia)   1246

with knowledge

A man who knows a subject thoroughly, a man so soaked in it that he eats it, sleeps it and dreams it — this man can always teach with success, no matter how little he knows of technical pedagogy.

   H.L. Mencken   Criticism   United States   1922

knowledge–action

To understand is hard. Once one understands, action is easy.

   Sun Yat-sen   Nationalism   China   1910

in trivia

The turning points of lives are not the great moments. The real crises are often concealed in occurrences so trivial in appearance that they pass unobserved.

   William E. Woodward   History   United States   1928

in infinity

If the doors of perception were cleansed, everything would appear to man as it is, infinite.

   William Blake   Mysticism   United Kingdom   1827

of the soul

The soul can dream itself to be
Adrift upon an endless sea

Of day and night! The soul can seem
To be all things that it can dream!

Yet needs but look within to find
That which is steady in the wind!

That which the fire does not appal!
Which good and ill move not at all!

Which does not seek, or lack, or try!
And was not born, and cannot die!

James Stephens   Poetry   Ireland   1926

inner—outer   in symbols

The lotus . . . symbolizes both the sun as the heart of space and the heart as the sun of
the body, both moved by the same indwelling self, (atman). And accordingly, the lotus
open to the sun symbolizes the fully flowered knowledge of this mirrored truth, while
the lotuses in bud mark stages of approach to its realization.

Joseph Campbell   Mythology   United States   1974

in the self

In my birth all things were born, and I was the cause of my own self and all things . . .
and if I had not been, then God had not been either.

Meister Eckhart   Mysticism   Germany   1320

in person

All the great works and wonders that God has ever wrought . . . or even God Himself with all His goodness, can never make me blessed, but only in so far as they exist and are done and loved, known, tasted, and felt within me.

  Bijbel Archief   Theology   Germany   1497

near—far with God

When I found Him in my bosom,
Then I found Him everywhere,
In the bud and in the blossom,
In the earth and in the air;
And He spoke to me with clearness
From the silent stars that say
As ye find Him in His nearness,
Ye shall find Him far away.

  Walter Chalmers Smith   Poetry   United Kingdom (Scotland)   1840

in God

God is my center where I close him in;
My circumference when I melt in him.

  Angelus Silesius   Poetry   Poland   1657

inner—outer

God in me, God without! Beyond compare!
Being wholly here and wholly there!

  Angelus Silesius   Poetry   Poland   1657

in harmony

It is one of the attributes of God, one of the perfections which we contemplate in our idea of him, that there is no duality or opposition between his will and his vision, between the impulses of his nature and the events of his life. This is what we commonly designate as omnipotence and creation. Now, in the contemplation of beauty, our faculties of perception have the same perfection: it is indeed from the experience of beauty and happiness, from the occasional harmony between our nature and our environment, that we draw our conception of the divine life. There is, then, a real propriety in calling beauty a manifestation of God to the senses, since, in the region of sense, the perception of beauty exemplifies that adequacy and perfection which in general we objectify in an idea of God.

George Santayana   Philosophy   United States   1896

with God

O Lord, I, a beggar, ask of Thee more than a thousand kings may ask of Thee. Each one has something he needs to ask of Thee: I have come to ask Thee to give me Thyself.

Ansari of Heart   Sufism   Afghanistan   1088

of self and all

If one is not, then nothing is.

Plato   Platonism   Greece   387 BCE

in mind

One minute of sitting, one inch of Buddha,
Like lightning all thoughts come and pass.
Just once look into your mind-depths;
Nothing else has ever been.

Manzan   Zen Buddhism   Japan   1714

conscious–unconscious in art

In the moment of creation, when the artist is in the unconscious of conscious, he reflects the innocence of the uncarved block; when he is in the conscious of the unconscious he reflects the transparency of Heavenly radiance. Both aspects represent the state of no-thought, or nonbeing. . . . No matter whether the reflection is innocence or transparency, it is free from the conditions of subjectivity and objectivity. Yet it reveals them both.

Chang Chung-yuan   Taoism   China   1963

in parts of the body

As it is, there are many parts, yet one body. The eye cannot say to the hand, "I have no need of you" nor again the head to the feet, "I have no need of you." On the contrary, the parts of the body which seem to be weaker are indispensable. . . . God has so adjusted the body, giving greater honor to the inferior part, that there may be no discord in the body, but that the members may have the same care for one another. If a member suffers, all suffer together; if one member is honored, all rejoice together.

Saint Paul   Christianity   Turkey (Rome)   67

in parts of oneself

All the soarings of my mind begin in my blood.

Rainer Maria Rilke   Poetry   Germany   1921

body–soul

The human body is the best picture of the human soul.

Ludwig Wittgenstein   Philosophy   Germany   1953

soul–body

The soul is the voice of the body's interests.

George Santayana   Philosophy   United States   1905

soul–body   inner–outer   in sculpture

Before a Statue of Achilles

I gaze on thee as Phidias of old
Or Polyclitus gazed, when first he saw
These hard and shining limbs, without a flaw,
And cast his wonder in heroic mould.
Unhappy me who only may behold,
Nor make immutable and fix in awe
A fair immortal form no worm shall gnaw,
A tempered mind whose faith was never told!
The godlike mien, the lion's lock and eye,
The well-knit sinew, utter a brave heart
Better than many words that part by part
Spell in strange symbols what serene and whole
In nature lives, nor can in marble die.
The perfect body itself the soul.

George Santayana   Philosophy   United States   1888

in the body   inner–outer

Our life is but the soul made known by its fruits, the body. The whole duty of man may
be expressed in one line: Make to yourself a perfect body.

Henry David Thoreau   Transcendentalism   United States   1862

God–spirit

[Question]: God is infinite, the Jiva [individual soul] a finite being. How then can the
finite grasp the infinite?

[Answer]: It is like a doll of salt trying to fathom the depths of the ocean. In doing so
the salt doll is dissolved into the sea and lost. Similarly, the Jiva, in trying to measure
God, loses his individuality and becomes one with him.

Sri Ramakrishna   Hinduism   India   1900

with God

Duality exists as long as God is not identified within.

A pitcher holding water floats in the ocean and keeps its separate identity. Likewise, a being exists in duality as long as there is the ego of separateness: "I am this body, with this name, and this religion."

When the pitcher is broken, the water inside it disappears into the water of the ocean. There is no existence of the pitcher and separation of water — there remains only ocean. In the same way, when the ego that identifies with the body and makes a separateness is broken, the ego (ahamkara) dissolves into the Self (asmita, or beingness). Actually, the ego comes from the same source as the Self. The Self in the body is the existence of God within. As long as God is not identified within, we (the ego-self) will remain separate from the true Self (God).

Baba Hari Dass   Yoga   India   1986

in God

Whosoever has God in mind, singly and solely God, in all things, such a man carries God with him into all his works. He sees nothing but God, nothing seems good to him but God. He becomes one with God in every thought. Just as no multiplicity can dissipate God, so nothing can dissipate this man or make him multiple.

Meister Eckhart   Mysticism   Germany   1280

God–soul

I went from God to God, until they cried from me in me, "O thou I!"

Bayazid Bistami   Sufism   Iran (Persia)   874

in freedom   in life

He who is really free can wear any faith, or even stage or mode of living, and be his true self in it. He is free of all modes and forms, for he has found the Life in all things.

G.S. Arundale   Theosophy   United Kingdom   1935

in balance

He who is strong in faith, weak in understanding will generally place his confidence in good-for-nothing people and believe in the wrong object. He who is strong in understanding, weak in faith, leans towards dishonesty and is difficult to cure, like a disease caused by medicine. One in whom both are equal believes in the right object.

He who is strong in concentration, weak in energy, is overcome by idleness, since concentration partakes of the nature of idleness. He who is strong in energy, weak in concentration, is overcome by distractions, since energy partakes of the nature of distraction. Therefore they should be equal to one another, since from equality in both comes contemplation and ecstasy.

Saint Thomas Aquinas   Thomism   Italy   1274

self–history

I had the feeling that everything was being sloughed away; everything I aimed at or wished for or thought, the whole phantasmagoria of earthly existence, fell away or was stripped from me — an extremely painful process. Nevertheless something remained: it was as if I now carried along with me everything I had ever experienced or done, everything that had happened around me I might also say; it was with me and I was it. I consisted of all that, so to speak. I consisted of my own history, and I felt with great certainty: this is what I am. I am a bundle of what has been, and what has been accomplished.

This experience gave me a feeling of extreme poverty, but at the same time of great fullness. There was no longer anything I wanted or desired. I existed in an objective form; I was what I had been and lived. At first, the sense of annihilation predominated, of having been stripped and pillaged; but suddenly that became of no consequence. Everything seemed to be past; what remained was a fait accompli, without any reference back to what had been. There was no longer any regret that something had dropped away or been taken away. On the contrary; I had everything that I was, and that was everything.

Carl Jung   Psychology   Switzerland   1965

with humanity

Why are you unhappy?
Because 99.9 per cent
Of everything you think,
And of everything you do,
Is for yourself —
And there isn't one.

Wei Wu Wei (Terence Gray)   Taoism   United Kingdom   1963

in self   with God

The Disciple said to his Master: Sir, how may I come to the Supersensual Life so that I
may know God, and hear God speak?
The Master answered and said: Son, when thou canst throw thyself into THAT, where
no Creature dwelleth, though it be but for a Moment, then thou hearest what God
speaketh.
Disciple: Is that where no Creature dwelleth near at hand; or is it afar off?
Master: It is in thee. And if thou canst, my Son, for a while but cease from all thy
thinking and willing, then thou shalt hear the unspeakable Words of God.
Disciple: How can I hear Him speak, when I stand still from thinking and willing?
Master: When thou standest still from the thinking of self, and the willing of self; when
both thy intellect and will are quiet, and passive to the Impressions of the Eternal
Word and Spirit; and when thy Soul is winged up, and above that which is temporal,
the outward Senses, and the Imagination being locked up by holy Abstraction, then the
Eternal Hearing, Seeing, and Speaking will be revealed in thee; and so God heareth and
seeth through thee, being now the Organ of His Spirit; and so God speaketh in thee,
and whispereth to thy Spirit, and thy Spirit heareth His Voice.

Jacob Boehme   Theosophy   Germany   1622

in life

I do not cut my life up into days
but my day into lives, each day,
each hour, an entire life.

Juan Ramón Jiménez   Poetry   Spain   1957

with the soul

The soul is akin to the seas we ply.
Each swell resembles a midget ocean:
Dead if it's still; in the storm 'tis high,
And streams along with a sounding motion.

Einar Benediktsson   Poetry   Iceland   1900

with vice

There is no man who is not at some time indebted to his vices, as no plant that is not fed from manures.

Ralph Waldo Emerson   Transcendentalism   United States   1860

through evolution

Individuality is a conquest. And, as Sri Aurobindo says here [in the passage being studied], this first conquest is only a first stage, and once you have realized within you something like a personal independent and conscious being, then what you have to do is to break the form and go farther. For example, if you want to progress mentally, you must break all your mental forms, all your mental constructions to be able to make new ones. So, to begin with, a tremendous labour is required to individualize oneself, and afterwards one must demolish all that has been done in order to progress. . . . And if one observes very attentively, if creation had kept the memory of its origin, it would perhaps never have become a diverse multiplicity. There would have been at the center of each being the sense of perfect unity, and the diversity would — perhaps — never have been expressed.

   Through the loss of the memory of this unity began the possibility of becoming conscious of differences; and when one goes into the inconscient, at the other end, one falls back into a sort of unity that's unconscious of itself, in which the diversity is as unexpressed as it is in the origin.

   At both ends there is the same absence of diversity. In one case it is through a supreme consciousness of unity, in the other through a perfect unconsciousness of unity.

   The fixity of form is the means by which individuality can be formed.

The Mother   Yoga   France   1957

in balance

Whosoever is able to practice patience can be truly called a great and strong man, but he who is unable to endure abuse as happily as though he were drinking ambrosia, cannot be called one attained to knowledge of Dharma.

Gautama Buddha   Buddhism   Nepal, India (Kapilavastu)   483 BCE

in peace   with humanity

What man wants is peace in order that he may live. Defeating our neighbour doesn't give peace any more than curing cancer brings health. Man doesn't begin to live from triumphing over his enemy nor does he begin to acquire health through endless cures. The joy of life comes through peace, which is not static but dynamic. No man can really say that he knows what joy is until he has experienced peace. And without joy there is no life, even if you have a dozen cars, six butlers, a castle, a private chapel and a bomb-proof vault. Our diseases are our attachments, be they habits, ideologies, ideals, principles, possessions, phobias, gods, cults, religions, what you please. Good wages can be a disease just as much as bad wages. Leisure can be just as great a disease as work. Whatever we cling to, even if it be hope or faith, can be the disease which carries us off. Surrender is absolute: if you cling to even the tiniest crumb you nourish the germ which will devour you. As for clinging to God, God long ago abandoned us in order that we might realize the joy of attaining godhood through our own efforts. All this whimpering that is going on in the dark, this insistent, piteous plea for peace which will grow bigger as the pain and the misery increase, where is it to be found? Peace, do people imagine that it is something to be cornered, like corn or wheat? Is it something which can be pounced upon and devoured, as with wolves fighting over a carcass? I hear people talking about peace and their faces are clouded with anger or with hatred or with scorn and disdain, with pride and arrogance. There are people who want to fight to bring about peace — the most deluded souls of all. There will be no peace until murder is eliminated from the heart and mind. Murder is the apex of the broad pyramid whose base is the self. That which stands will have to fall. Everything which man has fought for will have to be relinquished before he can begin to live as man. Up till now he has been a sick beast and even his divinity stinks. He is master of many worlds and in his own he is a slave. What rules the world is the heart, not the brain. In every realm our conquests bring only death. We have turned our backs on the one realm wherein freedom lies. At Epidaurus, in the stillness, in the great peace that came over me, I heard the heart of the world beat. I know what the cure is: it is to give up, to relinquish, to surrender, so that our little hearts may beat in unison with the great heart of the world.

Henry Miller   Literature   United States   1941

in justice

Thus, in the soul of man there is a justice whose retributions are instant and entire. He who does a good deed is instantly ennobled. He who does a mean deed is by the action itself contracted. He who puts off impurity thereby puts on purity. If a man is at heart just, then in so far is he God; the safety of God, the immortality of God, the majesty of God do enter into that man with justice. If a man dissemble, deceive, he deceives himself, and goes out of acquaintance with his own being. Character is always known. Thefts never enrich; alms never impoverish; murder will speak out of stone walls. The least admixture of a lie — for example, the taint of vanity, any attempt to make a good impression, a favorable appearance — will instantly vitiate the effect. But speak the truth, and all things alive or brute are vouchers, and the very roots of the grass underground there do seem to stir and move to bear your witness. For all things proceed out of the same spirit, which is differently named love, justice, temperance, in its different applications, just as the ocean receives different names on the several shores it washes.

Ralph Waldo Emerson   Transcendentalism   United States   1838

in God   of self

The fourth aspect of religion is the idea of God. There will always be fights and discussions about it; one says, "The God of our family is one, the God of your family is another." . . . In the old times there was a dispute between the people who said that the God of Ben Israel was a special God; and so every community and every church made its God a special God. If there is a special God, it is not only a special God of a community but a God of every individual. For man has to make his own God before he realizes the real God. But that God which man makes within himself becomes in the end the door by which he enters the shrine of his innermost being, the real God, Who is in the heart of man. And then one begins to realize that God is not a God of a certain community or people, but that God is the God of the whole Being.

Hazrat Inayat Khan   Sufism   India   1927

in process

Non-po Tzu-Kuei asked Nu-yü: "You are of a high age and yet your complexion is like that of a child. How can that be done?" The latter answered: "I have achieved Tao." Then Nu-yü went on to explain: "There was Po Liang-I who had the talents of a genius, but lacked Tao to be a perfect man. . . . I tried to teach him so that he might become one. In three days he was able to free himself from the world. In another seven days he was free from all externalities. And in another nine days he was free from his own existence. Being free from his own existence," Nu-yü continued, "he had a vision of the rising sun. After that he was able to experience Oneness. After that there was no more distinction of past and present. Then he reached the state wherein there is neither living nor dying. Then he knew that the destruction of life did not mean death, and that birth did not mean life. He dealt with everything and accepted everything. All things proceed to destruction and all things proceed to construction. This is called tranquilization in confusion. Tranquilization in confusion means achievement through chaos."

Chuang Tzu   Taoism   China   286 BCE

with self

After nine years' study I can set my mind completely free, let my words come forth completely unbound as I speak. I do not know whether right and wrong, gain and loss, are mine or others. I am not aware that the old Master Shang Szu is my teacher and that Pai-kao is my friend. My self, both within and without, has been transformed. Everything about me is identified. My eye becomes my ear, my ear becomes my nose, my nose my mouth. My mind is highly integrated and my body dissolves. My bone and my flesh melt away. I cannot tell by what my body is supported or what my feet walk upon. I am blowing away, east and west, as a dry leaf torn from a tree. I cannot even make out whether the wind is riding on me or I am riding on the wind.

Lieh-tzu   Taoism   China   350 BCE

in time

At three
I didn't have a past

At five
my past was to yesterday

At seven
my past was to the age of warriors

At eleven
my past was to dinosaurs

At fourteen
my past was as the textbooks

At sixteen
I watched the infinity of the past with fear

At eighteen
I don't know what time is

Shuntaró Tanikawa   Poetry   Japan   1950

in self

The self — at one and the same time the self of all living creatures, and therefore my self — knows no bounds; so the entire universe is within me, and my self fills all the universe. Everything that is — I am! In everything I love, I love my self, for the only things we think we don't love are what we haven't yet come to recognize within ourselves.

   The self is life and the only reality, and whoever is initiated into the self — and in this way has come to know himself completely — loves everything and everyone equally, for he is one with them.

Elisabeth Haich   Yoga   Hungary   1960

in consciousness

Like waves beaten back from the shore, the human mind has always suffered humiliation at the frontiers of experience and thought. At the places of greatest stress, true and noble ideals have always fallen prisoner to unconscious fears, returning in disguise to haunt the mind with lies. . . . By interpreting and accepting its silent message we can learn to free the world and ourselves from the imperialism of the unconscious.

George Delf   Education   Unknown   1963

in love

But Savitri replied for man to Death:
"When I have loved for ever, I shall know.
Love in me knows the truth all changings mask.
I know that knowledge is a vast embrace:
I know that every being is myself,
In every heart is hidden the myriad One.
I know the calm Transcendent bears the world,
The veiled Inhabitant, the silent Lord:
I feel his secret act, his intimate fire;
I hear the murmur of the cosmic Voice.
I know my coming was a wave of God.
For all his suns were conscient in my birth,
And one who loves in us came veiled by death.
Then man was born among the monstrous stars
Dowered with a mind and heart to conquer thee."

Sri Aurobindo   Yoga   India   1950

with oneself in love

This was the commandment, "Thou shalt love thy neighbour as thyself," but when the commandment is rightly understood, it also says the converse, "Thou shalt love thyself in the right way."

Søren Kierkegaard   Existentialism   Denmark   1855

There are fascinating cases of children who can spontaneously remember details of a previous life. . . . One startling account of a child's memories of a past life came to the attention of the Dalai Lama, who sent a special representative to interview her and verify her account.

Her name was Kamaljit Kour, and she was the daughter of a schoolteacher in a Sikh family in the Punjab in India. One day, on a visit to a fair in a local village with her father, she suddenly asked him to take her to another village, some distance away. Her father was surprised and asked her why. "I have nothing here," she told him. "This is not my home. Please take me to that village. One of my school friends and I were riding on our bicycles when suddenly we were hit by a bus. My friend was killed instantly. I was injured in the head, ear, and nose. . . . As the doctors said I could not be cured, I asked my relatives to take me home." Her father was shocked, but when she insisted, he finally agreed to take her to the village, though he thought it was just a child's whim.

They went to the village together as promised, and she recognized it as they approached, pointing out the place where the bus had hit her, and asking to be put in a rickshaw, whereupon she gave directions to the driver. She stopped the rickshaw when they arrived at a cluster of houses where she claimed she had lived. The little girl and her bewildered father made their way to the house she said belonged to the former family, and her father, who still did not believe her, asked the neighbors whether there was family like the one Kamaljit Kour had described, who had lost their daughter. They confirmed the story, and told the girl's astonished father that Rishma, the daughter of the family, had been sixteen years old when she was killed; she had died in the car on the way home from hospital. . . .

When Rishma's grandfather and her uncles arrived, she recognized them and named them without mistake. She pointed out her own room, and showed her father each of the other rooms in the house. Then she asked for her schoolbooks, her two silver bangles and her two ribbons, and her new maroon suit. Her aunt explained that these were all things Rishma had owned. Then she led the way to her uncle's house, where she identified some more items. . . .

The family started to piece the story together. Kamaljit Kour was born 10 months after Rishma died. Although the little girl had not yet started school, she often pretended to read, and she could remember the names of all her school friends in Rishma's school photograph. Kamaljit Kour had also always asked for maroon-colored clothes. Her parents discovered that Rishma had been given a new maroon suit of which she was very proud, but she had never had time to wear it. The last thing Kamaljit Kour remembers of her former life was the lights of the car going out on the way home from the hospital; that must have been when she died.

Songyal Rinpoche   Tibetan Buddhism   Tibet   1992

in balance in simplicity

In the world, when people call anyone simple they generally mean a foolish, ignorant, credulous person. But real simplicity, so far from being foolish, is almost sublime. . . .

I should say that simplicity is an uprightness of soul which prevents self-consciousness. It is not the same as sincerity, which is a much humbler virtue. Many people are sincere who are not simple. They say nothing but what they believe to be true, and do not aim at appearing anything but what they are. But they are continually in fear of passing for something they are not, and so they are forever thinking about themselves, weighing their every word and thought, and dwelling upon themselves in apprehension of having done too much or too little. These people are sincere, but they are not simple. They are not at their ease with others, nor others with them. There is nothing easy, frank, unrestrained or natural about them. We feel that we would like less admirable people better, who were not so stiff!

One extreme as opposed to simplicity is to be absorbed in the world around and never turn a thought within, as is the blind condition of some who are carried away by what is pleasant and tangible. The other extreme is to be self-absorbed in everything, whether it be duty to God or other people, which makes a person wise in his own conceit — reserved, self-conscious, uneasy at the least thing which disturbs our inward self-complacency. Such false wisdom, in spite of its solemnity, is hardly less vain and foolish than the folly of those who plunge headlong into worldly pleasures. The first are impassioned by their outer surroundings, the others by what they believe themselves to be doing inwardly. . . .

Real simplicity lies in a happy medium, equally free from thoughtlessness and affection, in which the soul is not overwhelmed by external things so that it can look within, nor is it given up to the endless introspection that self-consciousness induces. The soul that looks where it is going, without losing time arguing over every step, or looking back perpetually, possesses true simplicity.

François Fénelon   Christianity   France   1715

inner–outer with oneself with God

What they [the early Quakers] did was to insist that religion is something that begins within the soul of man. They passed over, as Copernicus did, to a new centre . . . to ground religion for ever upon an inherent relation between God as living Spirit and the elemental spiritual nature of man. Religion, they believed, does not rise outside and flow in; it springs up inside and flows out.

Rufus Jones   Quakerism   United States   1927

in God

The Sufi has no individual will. His will is merged in the Will of God — his will becomes the very Will of God.

Jami   Sufism   Iran (Persia)   830

in polarities   manifest—unmanifest

As long as a creature seeks its complementary half outside itself, in the created, recognizable world, it will never find unity, simply because its complementary half isn't outside itself, manifested, separate from itself, but on the contrary, unseparated from itself, in its own unmanifested part, in its unconscious! No creature could exist if it did not have its other half in the unmanifested. Take yourself for example, little daughter. The opposite of everything you are and manifest in your conscious part is contained in your unconscious part which nevertheless belongs to you, and which you are just as much as you are your conscious, manifested part. You don't find your complimentary part outside yourself — in a man of flesh and blood, for example, but in the unconscious part of your true self. When you unite in your consciousness two halves of yourself, you've found your way back into the infinite all and nothing, you've become identical with God again!"

Elisabeth Haich   Yoga   Hungary   1960

with infinite   in person

Clouded and shrouded there doth sit
The Infinite
Embosomed in a man;
And thou art stranger to thy guest
And know'st not what thou dost invest. . . .

Then bear thyself, O man!
Up to the scale and compass of thy guest;
Soul of thy soul.
Be great as doth beseem
The ambassador who bears
The royal presence where he goes.

Ralph Waldo Emerson   Transcendentalism   United States   1882

in interbeing

I would like to present to you a form of Buddhism . . . called the Tiep Hien Order, the Order of "Interbeing."

The Tiep Hien Order was founded in Vietnam during the war. It derives from the Zen School of Lin Chi, and is the 42nd generation of this school. It is a form of engaged Buddhism, Buddhism in daily life, in society, and not just in a retreat center. . . .

Tiep means "to be in touch." The notion of engaged Buddhism already appears in the word tiep. First of all to be in touch with oneself. In modern society most of us don't want to be in touch with ourselves; we want to be in touch with other things like religion, sports, politics, a book — we want to forget ourselves. Anytime we have leisure, we want to invite something else to enter us, opening ourselves to the television and telling the television to colonize us. So first of all, "in touch" means in touch with oneself in order to find out the source of wisdom, understanding, and compassion in each of us. Being in touch with oneself is the meaning of meditation, to be aware of what is going on in your body, in your feelings, in your mind. . . .

The second part of the meaning of tiep is "to continue," to make something long-lasting. It means that the career of understanding and compassion started by the Buddhas and Bodhisattvas should be continued. This is possible only if we get in touch with our true self, which is like digging deep into the soil until we reach a hidden source of fresh water, and then the well is filled. When we are in touch with our true mind, the source of understanding and compassion will spring out. This is the basis of everything. Being in touch with our true mind is necessary for the continuation of the career started by the Buddhas and Bodhisattvas.

Hien means, "the present time." We have to be in the present time, because only the present is real, only in the present moment can we be alive. . . . Hien also means "to make real, to manifest, realization." Love and understanding are not only concepts and words. They must be real things, realized, in oneself and in society.

. . . we have translated Tiep Hien as interbeing. In the Avatamsaka Sutra it is a compound term which means "mutual" and "to be." . . . I am, therefore, you are. You are, therefore I am. That is the meaning of the word "interbeing." We inter-are.

Thich Nhat Hanh   Buddhism   Vietnam   1987

in androgyny

Male and female represent the two sides of the great radical dualism. But in fact they are perpetually passing into one another. Fluid hardens to solid, solid rushes to fluid. There is no wholly masculine man, no purely feminine woman.

Margaret Fuller   Feminism   United States   1845

in parts of oneself

Use what language you will, you can never say anything but what you are.

Ralph Waldo Emerson   Transcendentalism   United States   1861

with oneself

In oneself lies the whole world and if you know how to look and learn, then the door is there and the key is in your hand. Nobody on earth can give you either the key or the door to open, except yourself.

J. Krishnamurti   Theosophy   India   1972

in identity   in contemplation

In the Satipatthana Sutta, the basic manual on meditation from the time of the Buddha, it is recorded, "The practitioner will have to contemplate body in the body, feelings in the feelings, mind in the mind, objects of mind in objects of mind." The words are clear. The repetition, "body in the body," is not just to underline the importance of it. Contemplating body in the body means that you do not stand outside of something to contemplate it. You must be one with it, with no distinction between the contemplator and the contemplated. Contemplating body in the body means that you should not look on your body as the object of your contemplation. You have to be one with it. The message is clear. Non-duality is the key word for Buddhist meditation.

Thich Nhat Hanh   Buddhism   Vietnam   1987

in change   person—world

The individual is not apart from the world; he is its centre; when a change or transformation takes place in him, the circumference changes too, along with its relationship to him.

N. Sri Ram   Theosophy   India   1973

with one's nature

Better is one's own law of works, though in itself faulty, than an alien law well wrought out. One does not incur sin when one acts in agreement with the law of one's own nature.

The Bhagavad Gita   Hinduism   India   600 BCE

individuation to achieve oneness

The collectivity is a mass, a field of formation; the individual is the diviner of truth, the form-maker, the creator. In the crowd the individual loses his inner direction and becomes a cell of the mass body moved by the collective will or idea or the mass impulse. He has to stand apart, affirm his separate reality in the whole, his own mind emerging from the common mentality, his own life distinguishing itself in the common life uniformity, even as his body has developed something unique and recognisable in the common physicality. He has, even, in the end to retire into himself in order to find himself, and it is only when he has found himself that he can become spiritually one with all . . . .

Sri Aurobindo   Yoga   India   1940

with realization

Realization is nothing to be gained afresh; it is already there. All that is necessary is to get rid of the thought "I have not realized."

Ramana Maharshi   Hinduism   India   1931

in the soul

Though GOD is everywhere present, yet He is only present to thee in the deepest and most centered part of thy soul. The natural senses cannot possess God or unite thee to Him; nay, thy inward faculties of understanding, will and memory can only reach after God, but cannot be the place of his habitation in thee. But there is a root or depth of thee from whence all these faculties come forth, as lines from a center or as branches from the body of the tree. This depth is called the center, the fund or bottom of the soul. This depth is the unity, the eternity — I had almost said the infinity — of the soul; for it is so infinite that nothing can satisfy it or give it rest but the infinity of God.

William Law   Mysticism   United Kingdom   1710

in balance

The growth of wisdom may be gauged exactly by the diminution of ill-temper.

Friedrich Nietzsche   Existentialism   Germany   1880

in good and evil

Rabbi Shmelke and his brother once petitioned their teacher, the Preacher of Mezeritz, to explain to them the words of the Mishnah: "A man must bless God for the evil in the same way that he blesses Him for the good which befalls."

The Preacher replied: "Go to the House of Study, and you will find then a man smoking. He is Rabbi Zusya, and he will explain this to you."

When Rabbi Shmelke and his brother questioned Rabbi Zusya, he laughed and said: "I am surprised that the Rabbi sent you to me. You must go elsewhere and make your inquiry from one who has suffered tribulations in his lifetime. As for me, I have never experienced anything but good all my days."

But Rabbi Shmelke and his brother knew full well that from his earliest hour to the present he had endured the most grievous sorrows. Thereupon they understood the meaning of the words of the Mishnah, and the reason their Rabbi had sent them to Rabbi Zusya.

Unknown   Judaism   Israel   Unknown

wisdom—oneself

May I recognize whatever visions appear, as the reflections of my own consciousness.
May I know them to be of the nature of apparitions in the Intermediate State.
May I not fear the troops of my own thought forms, the Peaceful Deities and the Wrathful.

Padmasambhava   Tibetan Buddhism   Pakistan (India)   804

in criminality

The study of crime begins with the knowledge of oneself.

Henry Miller   Literature   United States   1920

person—humanity

We have to carry on the struggle against evil that is in mankind, not by judging others but by judging ourselves. Struggle with oneself and voracity towards oneself are the means by which we influence others.

Albert Schweitzer   Philosophy   France   1900

humility—vanity   of opposites

My humility! Thou art the very essence of my vanity.

Hazrat Inayat Khan   Sufism   India   1927

saint—sinner   in balance

Many of the insights of the saint stem from his experience as a sinner.

Eric Hoffer   Philosophy   United States   1954

in truth

A lie will easily get you out of a scrape, and yet strangely and beautifully, rapture possesses you when you have taken the scrape and left out the lie.

Charles Edward Montague   Journalism   United Kingdom   1922

inner–outer

The uttered part of a man's life . . . bears to the unuttered, unconscious part a small unknown proportion. He himself never knows it, much less do others.

Thomas Carlyle   Philosophy   United Kingdom   1820

in mind

Mind is a tissue woven of light and shade
Where right and wrong have sewn their mingled parts;
Or Mind is Nature's marriage of convenance
Between truth and falsehood, between joy and pain:
This struggling pair no court can separate.
Each thought is a gold coin with bright alloy
And error and truth are its obverse and reverse:
This is the imperial mintage of the brain
And of this kind is all its currency.

Sri Aurobindo   Yoga   India   1950

in healing   body–self

Writing of the cures at the classical Greek sanctuaries of healing, C. Keneyi remarks that "the patient himself was offered an opportunity to bring about the cure whose elements he bore within himself."

C. Kerényi   Greek Mythology   Hungary   1941

in difficulties

Though we sometimes speak of a primrose path, we all know that a bad life is just as difficult, just as full of obstacles and hardships, as a good one. The only choice is in the kind of life one would care to spend one's efforts on.

John Erskine   Christianity   United States   1943

in actions

One man cannot do right in one department of life whilst he is occupied in doing wrong in any other department. Life is one indivisible whole.

Mahatma Gandhi   Nationalism   India   1927

of sincerity

Sincerity is impossible, unless it pervade the whole being, and the pretence of it saps the very foundation of character.

James Russell Lowell   Literature   United States   1871

joy—sorrow

Your joy is your sorrow unmasked.

Kahlil Gibran   Mysticism   Lebanon   1923

in experience

The differences present in mind and matter eclipse the unity, only till the unity becomes a fact of one's own experience.

N. Sri Ram   Theosophy   India   1973

with life   inner—outer

He who would write heroic poems should make his whole life a heroic poem.

Thomas Carlyle   Philosophy   United Kingdom   1820

in commitment

There is nothing so easy but that it becomes difficult when you do it with reluctance.

Terence   Drama   Italy   163 BCE

criminality—divinity

No man can be an effective criminal unless he has a strong development of some divine quality. His badness is the result of unbalance — such as a great will-power and courage, or great intelligence — without love for his fellow-beings.

Annie Besant and C.W. Leadbeater   Theosophy   United Kingdom   1947

self—fortune

When, O spiritual one, thou hast become thy own fortune,
Then, being thyself thy fortune, thou wilt never lose it.
How, O fortunate one, canst thou ever lose thyself,
When thy real self is thy treasure and thy kingdom?

Jalal ad-Din Rumi   Sufism   Tajikistan, Turkey (Persia)   1230

itself

Unity has also the meaning of integrity, peace, and action that is choiceless, not arising out of the perplexities of dilemma and contradictions.

N. Sri Ram   Theosophy   India   1973

in insecurity

Security is mostly a superstition. It does not exist in nature, nor do the children of men as a whole experience it. Avoiding danger is no safer in the long run than outright exposure. Life is either a daring adventure or nothing.

Helen Keller   Social Activism   United States   1957

through acceptance   through denial

Do you wish to free yourself of mental and emotional knots and become one with the Tao?
If so, there are two paths available to you.
The first is the path with the acceptance.
Affirm everyone and everything.
Freely extend your goodwill and virtue in every direction, regardless of circumstances.
Embrace all things as part of the Harmonious Oneness, and you will begin to perceive it.
The second path is that of denial.
Recognize that everything you see and think is falsehood, and illusion, a veil over the truth.
Peel all the veils away, and you will arrive at the Oneness.
Though the paths are entirely different, they will deliver you to the same place:
Spontaneous awareness of the great Oneness.
Once you arrive there, remember: it isn't necessary to struggle to maintain unity with it.
All you have to do is participate in it.

Lao Tzu   Taoism   China   500 BCE

in contrast

Defects are the mirrors of the attributes of Beauty,
The base is the mirror of the High and Glorious One,
Because one contrary shows forth its contrary,
As honey's sweetness is shown by vinegar's sourness,
Who so recognizes and confesses his own defects
Is hastening in the way that leads to perfection!

Jalal ad-Din Rumi   Sufism   Tajikistan, Turkey (Persia)   1230

young–old

For as I like a young man in whom there is something of the old, so I like an old man in whom there is something of the young; and he who follows this maxim, in body will possibly be an old man, but he will never be an old man in mind.

Marcus Tullius Cicero   Philosophy   Italy   43 BCE

three aspects of the Self

These three are aspects of the one Existence. The first is based upon that self-knowledge which, in our human realization of the Divine, the Upanishad describes as the Self in us becoming all existences; the second on that which is described as seeing all existences in the Self; the third on that which is described as seeing the Self in all existences. The Self becoming all existences is the basis of our oneness with all; the Self containing all existences is the basis of our oneness in difference; the Self inhabiting all is the basis of our individuality in the universal.

Sri Aurobindo   Yoga   India   1940

in self

Anybody who knows the self completely and perfectly can manifest all the characteristics that exist in the universe, because all these characteristics are the various aspects of the one and only being that is, the one and only self.

Elisabeth Haich   Yoga   Hungary   1960

in balance   with opposites

When the perfect union of all energies in the four aspects of wholeness is attained, there arises a static state subject to no more change. In Chinese alchemy this state is called the "Diamond Body," corresponding to the corpus incorruptible of medieval alchemy, which is identical with the corpus glorificationis of Christian tradition, the incorruptible body of resurrection. This mandala shows, then, the union of all opposites, and is embedded between yang and yin, heaven and earth; the state of everlasting balance and immutable duration.

Carl Jung   Psychology   Switzerland   1930

the ego—others—the Divine

Man's freedom is relative and he cannot be held solely responsible for the imperfection of his nature. Ignorance and inconscience of Nature have arisen, not independently, but in the one Being; the imperfection of her workings cannot be entirely foreign to some will of the Immanence. It may be conceded that forces set in motion are allowed to work themselves out according to the law of their movement; but what divine Omniscience and Omnipotence has allowed to arise and act in Its omnipresence, Its all-existence, we must consider It to have originated and decreed, since without the fiat of the Being they could not have been, could not remain in existence. . . .

And first we must realise that the existence of ignorance, error, limitation, suffering, division and discord in the world need not by itself, as we too hastily imagine, be a denial or a disproof of the divine being, consciousness, power, knowledge, will, delight in the universe. They can be that if we have to take them by themselves separately, but need not be so taken if we get a clear vision of their place and significance in a complete view of the universal workings. A part broken off from the whole may be imperfect, ugly, incomprehensible; but when we see it in the whole, it recovers its place in the harmony, it has a meaning and a use. The Divine Reality is infinite in its being; in this infinite being, we find limited being everywhere, — that is the apparent fact from which our existence here seems to start and to which our own narrow ego and its ego-centric activities bear constant witness. But, in reality, when we come to an integral self-knowledge, we find that we are not limited, for we also are infinite. Our ego is only a face of the universal being and has no separate existence; our apparent separative individuality is only a surface movement and behind it our real individuality stretches out to unity with all things and upward to oneness with the transcendent Divine Infinity. Thus our ego, which seems to be a limitation of existence, is really a power of infinity; the boundless multiplicity of beings in the world is a result and signal evidence, not of limitation or finiteness, but of that illimitable Infinity. Apparent division can never erect itself into a real separateness; there is supporting and overriding it an indivisible unity which division itself cannot divide. This fundamental world-fact of ego and apparent division and their separative workings in the world existence is no denial of the Divine Nature of unity and indivisible being; they are the surface results of an infinite multiplicity which is a power of the infinite Oneness.

Sri Aurobindo   Yoga   India   1940

in peace

A woman's bathing in the stream.
Bemused, the sun upon her beams,
And on her shoulders gently lays
The fingers of its golden rays.

The willows cast their shadows far
To touch the woman's face and arms.
The reeds look on in silence bound,
Nor do the pebbles make a sound.

There is no evil anywhere,
No death, no sorrow, no despair,
No storms, no winter anymore,
No prison bars, no need, no war.

The world's at rest. Peace reigns supreme.
A woman's bathing in the stream.

Kaisyn Kuliev   Poetry   Russia   1940

in love

You have been told also that life is darkness, and in your weariness you echo what was said by the weary.
And I say that life is indeed darkness save when there is urge,
And all urge is blind save when there is knowledge,
And all knowledge is vain save when there is work,
And all work is empty save when there is love;
And when you work with love you bind yourself to yourself, and to one another, and to God.

Kahlil Gibran   Mysticism   Lebanon   1923

knowledge–love

The eternal, unbroken, natural state of abiding in the Self is Jnana (knowledge). To abide in the Self you must love the Self. Since God is verily the Self, love of the Self is love of God; and that is Bhakti (devotion to God). Jnana and Bhakti are thus one and the same.

Ramana Maharshi   Hinduism   India   1931

with the present

"You've begun to believe in a future eternal life?"

"No, not in a future eternal life, but in eternal life here. There are moments, you reach moments, and time suddenly stands still, and it will become eternal.". . .

"That'll scarcely be possible in our time .... In the Apocalypse the angel swears that there will be no more time."

"I know. That's very true; distinct and exact. When all mankind attains happiness then there will be no more time, for there'll be no need of it, a very true thought."

Fyodor Dostoyevsky   Literature   Russia   1872

life–death

O I see now that life cannot exhibit all to me, as the day cannot,
I see that I am to wait for what will be exhibited by death.

Walt Whitman   Mysticism   United States   1855

wisdom–love

The tongue of a wise man lieth behind his heart.

Ali Ibn Abi Talib   Islam   Saudi Arabia   661

in balance

He who is not happy with nothing will not be happy with everything; he who does not cherish the little things will not be thoughtful of the great things; he with whom sufficient is not enough is without virtue, for the physical body of man lives only from day to day; if you supply it with what it actually needs, you will still have time to meditate, while if you seek to supply it with all it wants, the task is without end.

Gautama Buddha   Buddhism   Nepal, India (Kapilavastu)   483 BCE

common–precious in piousness

I heard that in ancient times
A stone used, in the hands of the pious, to become silver;
Thou thinkest not that this speech is unreasonable,
When thou becomest content, silver and stone are alike to thee.

Saadi   Islam   Iran (Persia)   1257

with Being in enlightenment

The word enlightenment conjures up the idea of some super-human accomplishment, and the ego likes to keep it that way, but it is simply your natural state of felt oneness with Being. It is a state of connectedness with something immeasurable and indestructible, something, that almost paradoxically, is essentially you and yet is much greater than you. It is finding your true nature beyond name and form. The inability to feel this connectedness gives rise to the illusion of separation, from yourself and from the world around you. You then perceive yourself, consciously or unconsciously, as an isolated fragment. Fear arises, and conflict within and without becomes the norm. . . .

Being is the eternal, ever-present One Life beyond the myriad forms of life that are subject to birth and death. However, Being is not only beyond but also deep within every form as its innermost invisible and indestructible essence. This means that it is accessible to you now as your own deepest self, your true nature. But don't seek to grasp it with your mind. Don't try to understand it. You can know it only when the mind is still. When you are present, when your attention is full and intensely in the Now, Being can be felt, but it can never be understood mentally. To regain awareness of Being and to abide in that state of "feeling-realization" is enlightenment.

Eckhart Tolle   Spirituality   Germany   1997

with one's soul

Playing Catch with My Soul or If Rumi Played Baseball

To my child, "Catch!" you said,
The ball placed in my hand.

Later throws were longer, harder, tossed high.
I leapt for every one.

Some hit me in the head.
Needed that!

Some went down the hill into the woods;
I went searching
For years.

Sometimes I forgot about the ball;
Too busy working, worrying, wailing . . .

Then! From nowhere: "Catch!" you shouted.
Whirling, diving (in my suit on the sidewalk)
I caught the ball,
Joyous in tattered wool.

This time, I said, "Let's play!"
You responded as the ball;
Inside we crawled
And bounced as one.

Who's the thrower?
Who's the catcher?
Who's the ball?

To not know is bliss.
There is only the game.

William Leon   Yoga   United States   2012

in ecstasy   in dance

In the beauty of bodies wrought from rapture's lines,
Shapes of entrancing sweetness spilling bliss,
Feet glimmering upon the sunstone courts of mind,
Heaven's cupbearers bore round the Eternal's wine.
A tangle of bright bodies, of moved souls
Tracing the close and intertwined delight,
The harmonious tread of lives for ever joined
In the passionate oneness of a mystic joy
As if sunbeams made living and divine,
The golden-bosomed Apsara goddesses,
In groves flooded from an argent disk of bliss
That floated through a luminous sapphire dream,
In a cloud of raiment lit with golden limbs
And gleaming footfalls treading faery swards,
Virgin motions of bacchant innocences
Who know their riot for a dance of God,
Whirled linked in moonlit revels of the heart.

Sri Aurobindo   Yoga   India   1950

of the soul with the Divine   in the supramental perception

   The divine soul will be aware of all variation of being, consciousness, will and delight as the outflowing, the extension, the diffusion of that self-concentrated Unity developing itself, not into difference and division, but into another, an extended form of infinite oneness. It will itself always be concentrated in oneness in the essence of its being, always manifested in variation in the extension of its being. All that takes form in itself will be the manifested potentialities of the One, the Word or Name vibrating out of the nameless Silence, the Form realising the formless essence, the active Will or Power proceeding out of the tranquil Force, the ray of self-cognition gleaming out from the sun of timeless self-awareness, the wave of becoming rising up into shape of self-conscious existence out of the eternally self-conscious Being, the joy and love welling for ever out of the eternal still Delight. It will be the Absolute biune in its self-unfolding, and each relativity in it will be absolute to itself because aware of itself as the Absolute manifested but without that ignorance which excludes other relativities as alien to its being or less complete than itself.

Sri Aurobindo   Yoga   India   1940

with eternity   in change   in death

When death comes and whispers to me,
"Thy days are ended,"
let me say to him, "I have lived in love
and not in mere time."
He will ask, "Will thy songs remain?"
I shall say, "I know not, but this I know
that often when I sang I found my eternity."

"Let me light my lamp,"
says the star,
"and never debate
if it will help to remove the darkness."

Before the end of my journey
may I reach within myself
the one which is the all,
leaving the outer shell
to float away with the drifting multitude
upon the current of chance and change.

Rabindranath Tagore   Poetry   India   1926

in faith

Only the person who has faith in himself is able to be faithful to others.

Erich Fromm   Psychology   Germany   1947

with others   through liberation

The true solution can intervene only when by our spiritual growth we can become one self with all beings, know them as part of our self, deal with them as if they were our other selves; for then the division is healed, the law of separate self-affirmation leading by itself to affirmation against or at the expense of others is enlarged and liberated by adding to it the law of our self-affirmation for others and our self-finding in their self-finding and self-realisation. It has been made a rule of religious ethics to act in a spirit of universal compassion, to love one's neighbour as oneself, to do to others as one would have them do to us, to feel the joy and grief of others as one's own; but no man living in his ego is able truly and perfectly to do these things, he can only accept them as a demand of his mind, an aspiration of his heart, an effort of his will to live by a high standard and modify by a sincere endeavour his crude ego-nature. It is when others are known and felt intimately as oneself that this ideal can become a natural and spontaneous rule of our living and be realised in practice as in principle. But even oneness with others is not enough by itself, if it is a oneness with their ignorance; for then the law of ignorance will work and error of action and wrong action will survive even if diminished in degree and mellowed in incidence and character. Our oneness with others must be fundamental, not a oneness with their minds, hearts, vital selves, egos, — even though these come to be included in our universalised consciousness, — but a oneness in the soul and spirit, and that can only come by our liberation into soul-awareness and self-knowledge.

Sri Aurobindo   Yoga   India   1940

with the godhead

Here in this chamber of flame and light they met;
They looked upon each other, knew themselves,
The secret deity and its human part,
The calm immortal and the struggling soul.
Then with a magic transformation's speed
They rushed into each other and grew one.

Sri Aurobindo   Yoga   India   1950

Relations

with comrades

All for one; one for all.

Alexander Dumas   Literature   France   1840

in empathy

We help others, not by interfering with their lives nor by imposing our ideas on them, but always by acting in a spirit of sympathy and self-identification with them in their troubles and joys.

N. Sri Ram   Theosophy   India   1973

in thought   with others

The body travels more easily than the mind, and until we have limbered up our imagination we continue to think as though we had stayed home. We have not really budged a step until we take up residence in someone else's point of view.

John Erskine   Christianity   United States   1943

in thought

There's something so beautiful in coming to one's very own inmost thoughts in another. In one way it's one of the greatest pleasures one has.

Olive Schreiner   Feminism   South Africa   1880

in truth

When there is Brotherhood in truth, one's sole desire is that all that is best, purest, and most wonderful in another should come to flower.

N. Sri Ram   Yoga   India   1973

In silliness

I am part of the whole
The flag on your pole
I am the wheels of your car
The points on your star
The crust of your roll

I'm the blade of your skate
The latch on your gate
I'm the quilt on your bed
The hair on your head
The feet on your foot patrol

Deep in your heart
Be glad I'm a part
A part of the whole

I am part of the whole (don't ever doubt me)
Part of the whole (you'd be useless without me)
And keep in your heart
Be glad I'm a part
A part of the whole

I'm part of the whole
The beans in your casserole
The oars of your boat
The horns of your goat
The notes on your scroll

I'm the leaves of your tree
The wings of your bee
The hands of your clock
The heel of your sock
Your heart and your soul

Deep in your heart
Be glad I'm a part
A part of the whole

Unknown   Television   United States   1994

in diversity

The more different I am from others, the more I need to be supplemented by them in the Work.

N. Sri Ram   Theosophy   India   1973

quietude–joy

Lately I became aware of the meaning of Quietude.
Day after day I stayed away from the multitude.
I cleaned my cottage and prepared it for the visit of a monk
Who came to me from the distant mountains.
He descended from the cloud-hidden peaks
To see me in my thatched house.
Sitting in the grass we shared the resin of the pine.
Burning incense we read the sutras of Tao.
When the day was over we lighted our lamp.
The temple bells announced the beginning of the evening.
Suddenly I realized that Quietude is indeed Joy,
And I felt that my life has abundant leisure.

Wang Wei   Taoism   China   761

in danger

Great perils have this beauty, that they bring to light the fraternity of strangers.

Victor Hugo   Romanticism   France   1862

in humanity

In all the world there is no such thing as a stranger.

Kurozumi Munetada   Kurozumikyō   Japan   1846

in greeting

How are I? (common Jamaican greeting)

Furthermore, "I and I" is used instead of "We", and is used in this way to emphasize the equality between all people, in the recognition that the Holy Spirit within us all makes us essentially one and the same.

Unknown   Rastafari   Jamaica   1830

in greeting

Namaste (Sanskrit greeting)

The gesture Namaste represents the belief that there is a Divine spark within each of us that is located in the heart chakra. The gesture is an acknowledgment of the soul in one by the soul in another. "Nama" means bow, "as" means I, and "te" means you. Therefore, Namaste literally means "bow me you" or "I bow to you."

"The spirit in me respects the spirit in you," "the divinity in me bows to the divinity in you," and others are modern interpretations, extrapolated from the Sanskrit root of Namaste.

Unknown   Hinduism   India   Traditional

in greeting

Vanakam (Tamil greeting: I bow to Thee; in you surrender)

Unknown   Hinduism   India   Traditional

in greeting

Gruss Gott (Bavarian greeting: I greet God in you)

Unknown   Christianity   Germany   Traditional

person—others

An isolated individual does not exist. He who is sad, saddens others.

Antoine de Saint-Exupéry   Literature   France   1942

through kindness

Right from the moment of our birth, we are under the care and kindness of our parents. And then later on in our life, when we are oppressed by sickness and become old, we are again dependent, on the kindness of others. And since at the beginning and end of our lives, we are so dependent on others' kindness, how can it be in the middle we neglect kindness towards others?

H.H. the 14th Dalai Lama   Tibetan Buddhism   Tibet   1989

in giving

Those who give to us teach us to give.

Unknown   Proverb   Africa   Traditional

in giving

All that is not given is lost.

Unknown   Folklore   India   Traditional

in family

Every family should have as its motto, "My fear is for you." (Hofu ni Kwenu). If everyone accepts, "My fear is for you," when something happens, you will not think about yourself first, but about the other one.

Maulana Karenga   Kwanzaa   United States   1960

in delight   God–strangers

A little boy wanted to meet God. He knew it was a long trip to where God lived, so he packed his suitcase with a bag of potato chips and a six-pack of root beer and started his journey.

When he had gone about three blocks, he met an old woman. She was sitting in the park, just staring at some pigeons. The boy sat down next to her and opened his suitcase. He was about to take a drink from his root beer when he noticed that the old woman looked hungry, so he offered her some chips. She gratefully accepted it and smiled at him.

Her smile was so pretty that the boy wanted to see it again, so he offered her a root beer. Again, she smiled at him. The boy was delighted! They sat there all afternoon eating and smiling, but they never said a word.

As twilight approached, the boy realized how tired he was and he got up to leave; but before he had gone more than a few steps, he turned around, ran back to the old woman, and gave her a hug. She gave him her biggest smile ever.

When the boy opened the door to his own house a short time later, his mother was surprised by the look of joy on his face. She asked him, "What did you do today that made you so happy?"

He replied, "I had lunch with God." But before his mother could respond, he added, "You know what? She's got the most beautiful smile I've ever seen!"

Meanwhile, the old woman, also radiant with joy, returned to her home. Her son was stunned by the look of peace on her face and he asked, "Mom, what did you do today that made you so happy?"

She replied "I ate potato chips in the park with God." However, before his son responded, she added, "You know, he's much younger than I expected."

Unknown   Unknown   Unknown   Unknown

in sharing wisdom

A candle lights others and consumes itself.

Unknown   Proverb   United Kingdom   1855

in opposites   in balance

Opposites that meet certainly influence each other in ways that are sometimes catastrophic. I know too, by experience, that opposites must follow each other because they need each other to maintain a proper balance. Consequently there cannot be a giver who does not receive. There cannot be a receiver who does not give. When we don't have these opposites paired, it voids the action because it lacks completion.

Malidoma Patrice Somé   Shamanism   Burkina Faso   1993

in light and dark

I govern the light of the skies,
I govern the trees, grasses, and all
   other earthly greenings.

I order the wild creatures,
I order all creeping and crawling things
   over and under the earth.

Who would dare find fault with my
   methods?

In doing good,
the illumination of a good conscience
is like the light of the earthly sun.

If they do not see me in that light,
how can they see me in the dark of
   their hearts?

Hildegard of Bingen   Mysticism   Germany   1163

in kindness   in silence

The kindness I have longest remembered has been of this sort — the sort unsaid; so far behind the speaker's lips that almost it already lay in the heart.

Henry David Thoreau   Transcendentalism   United States   1843

of lovers

She closed her arms about his breast and head
As if to keep him on her bosom worn
For ever through the journeying of the years.
So for a while they stood entwined, their kiss
And passion-tranced embrace a meeting-point
In their commingling spirits one for ever,
Two-souled, two-bodied for the joy of Time.

Sri Aurobindo   Yoga   India   1950

in society

The practice of the Great Way, the illustrious men of the Three Dynasties — these I shall never know in person. And yet they inspire my ambition! When the Great Way was practiced, the world was shared by all alike. The worthy and able were promoted to office and men practiced good faith and lived in affection. Therefore they did not regard as parents only their own parents, or as sons only their own sons. The aged found a fitting close to their lives, the robust their proper employment; the young were provided an upbringing, and the widow and widower, the orphan and the sick, with proper care. Men had their tasks and women their hearths. They hated to see goods lying about in waste, yet they did not hoard them for themselves; they disliked the thought that their energies were not fully used, yet they used them not for private ends. Therefore all evil plotting was prevented and thieves and rebels did not arise, so that the people could leave their outer gates unbolted. This was the age of Grand Commonality.

Confucius   Confucianism   China   500 BCE

person–person   with the godhead

I do not agree with the big way of doing things. To us what matters is an individual. To get to love the person we must come in close contact with him. If we must wait till we get the numbers, then we will be lost in the numbers. And we will never be able to show that love and respect for the person. I believe in person to person; every person is Christ for me, and since there is only one Jesus, that person is only one person in the world for me at that moment.

Mother Theresa   Christianity   Macedonia, Albania   1976

with strangers   in danger

I told Tweed and Pumpy about the time when I was hitching over the mountains and I got a lift with a truckie in an interstate hauler. He told me about a friend of his who was killed coming down the mountains from the central west somewhere. The truckie told me this bloke had been his best friend. He said you just keep an eye out straight ahead young feller, and I'll show you where he got it.

It was at the crest of the mountain that his friend's major load brakes had failed. If that happens a driver only has one chance at a low gear to hold him going down. His friend had missed getting into upper gear, he was just going too fast. So he just headed down that mountain with a full load, out of gear and with only light cabin brakes that had no chance of even slowing him down.

The truckie told me about half a mile down the hill his friend would have been doing about sixty. He said with a full load you pick up speed pretty quick young feller. Have a look what's round this next bend.

Just around that bend was one of those safety ramps, dug into the mountain. Just an increasing upward slope off the road to the left. Any truckie in trouble pulls off onto the safety ramp and the slope will slow and stop him. It's like a waterhole in the outback or a plank of wood when you're drowning.

See that, the truckie said, them things have saved a lot of bloke's lives. Greatest idea any roadbuilder ever had. Well, he made it round this bend. He knew if he did he'd be right. Driving a full load up a safety ramp about sixty sure buggers a truck, but when she stops you're alive aren't you. Well, he pulled her round here and right in front of him was that ramp. You know what was in the middle of that ramp? A bloody little family having a picnic.

No bullshit. Smack in the middle, with a station wagon parked at the side, a bloke and his wife and two little girls on a rug eating bloody sandwiches.

He had about a hundred yards to decide whether to kill them or himself. He pulled away and kept going down the mountain and made three more bends in the road before he went off the edge. I saw him in the hospital a few days later, all hooked up to bloody gadgets and bottles. He told me that story in the afternoon and he died that night. He had two little girls of his own.

We just sat quietly for a while. Tweed sat hunched over, pulling at his beard. You could feel the cold coming out of the ground now. The fire died a bit and the dark came in slowly. Tweed . . . said you know what, I'll bet my life one of those parents looked up from a Vegemite sandwich and said look how fast that fool in the truck's going, they're a menace on the roads.

Christopher Lee   Labor   Australia   1975

in giving

There are those who give little of the much which they have — and they give it for recognition and their hidden desire makes their gifts unwholesome.

And there are those who have little and give it all.

These are the believers in life and the bounty of life, and their coffer is never empty.

There are those who give with joy, and that joy is their reward.

And there are those who give with pain, and that pain is their baptism.

And there are those who give and know not pain in giving, nor do they seek joy, nor give with mindfulness of virtue;

They give as in yonder valley the myrtle breathes its fragrance into space.

Through the hands of such as these God speaks, and from behind their eyes He smiles upon the earth.

Kahlil Gibran   Mysticism   Lebanon   1923

of humanity

The souls of emperors and cobblers are cast in the same mold. . . . The same reason that makes us wrangle with a neighbour causes a war betwixt princes.

Michel de Montaigne   Skepticism   France   1580

in process

For a long time we hated one another. Then we ignored one another. Then we began talking about one another. Then we began talking with one another. Then we began praying for one another. And now we are beginning to pray with one another. And when that is a fact, no one can safely erect barriers around where the relationship may go from here.

Robert McAfee Brown   Christianity   United States   1965

with enemies

Love your enemies and pray for those who persecute you so that you may be sons of your Father who is in heaven.

Jesus Christ   Christianity   Palestine (Judea)   33

in forgiveness

I would like to share with you two simple truths: there is nothing that cannot be forgiven, and there is no one undeserving of forgiveness. When you can see and understand that we are all bound to one another — by birth, by circumstance, or simply by our shared humanity — then you will know this to be true. I have often said that in South Africa there would have been no future without forgiveness. Our rage and our quest for revenge would have been our destruction. This is as true for us individually as it is for us globally.

Desmond Tutu   Christianity   South Africa   2014

victim—criminal

The robbed that smiles steals something from the thief...

William Shakespeare   Drama   United Kingdom   1603

with others

I desire not that fruit which is sought by causing pain to others!

Gautama Buddha   Buddhism   Nepal, India (Kapilavastu)   483 BCE

accuser—accused

He who accuses too many accuses himself.

Unknown   Proverb   Africa   Traditional

oppressed—oppressor

You can't hold a man down without staying down with him.

Booker T. Washington   Education   United States   1880

in conflict

A brand burns him who stirs it up

Unknown   Xhosa Proverb   South Africa (Xhosa)   Traditional

in cooperation

Who overcomes by force hath overcome but half his foe.

John Milton   Poetry   United Kingdom   1667

with humanity

It has always been a mystery to me how men can feel themselves honoured by the humiliation of their fellow beings.

Mahatma Gandhi   Nationalism   India   1927

in pain

Give nobody's heart pain so long as thou canst avoid it, for one sigh may set a whole world into a flame.

Saadi   Islam   Iran (Persia)   1258

beyond prejudice   through consciousness

We need to become conscious of every factor of prejudice in ourselves, every hardness in our natures, before we can live inwardly in contact with all beings and things.

N. Sri Ram   Theosophy   India   1973

With the oppressed   with all

[To a Common Prostitute]
Not till the sun excludes you do I exclude you . . . .

Walt Whitman   Mysticism   United States   1855

in hate   of races

Hear me, white brothers,
Black brothers, hear me:

I have seen the hand
Holding the blowtorch
To the dark, anguish-twisted body;
I have seen the hand
Giving the high-sign
To fire on the white pickets;
And it was the same hand,
Brothers, listen to me,
it was the same hand.

Hear me, black brothers,
White brothers, hear me:

I have heard the words
They set like barbed-wire fences
To divide you,
I have heard the words —
Dirty nigger, poor white trash —
And the same voice spoke them;
Brothers, listen well to me,
The same voice spoke them.

Robert E. Hayden   Poetry   United States   1941

in love

In love that seeks nothing for itself there can be no shadow of separateness.

N. Sri Ram   Theosophy   India   1973

in joy   in intimacy

Pathos is the sense of distance.

Antoine de Saint-Exupéry   Literature   France   1942

in strife

In the Aztec, Mayan, and general Middle American view, love, in the sense of Empedocles, plays no cosmic role whatsoever. On the contrary, as in Heraclitus, it is rather strife that holds opposites together: strife and strife alone supports and constitutes the world process.

Joseph Campbell   Mythology   United States   1974

with enemies

He that wrestles with us strengthens our nerves and sharpens our skill. Our antagonist is our helper.

Edmund Burke   Politics   Ireland   1761

in knowledge

If you do not understand a man you cannot crush him. And if you do understand him, very probably you will not.

G.K. Chesterton   Literature   United Kingdom   1910

in life

Honor life in all its forms; your own will be sustained.
Honor women; in honoring women you honor the gift of life and love.
Honor promises; by keeping your word you will be true.
Honor kindness; by sharing your gifts you will be kind.
Be peaceful; through peace all will find the Great Peace.
Be courageous; through courage all will grow in strength.
Be moderate in all things; watch listen and consider;
Your needs will be prudent.

Unknown   Native America   America (Chippewa)   Traditional _lover–infinity   micro–macro_

At times when my head
is cradled in the hot palms of your hands,
At times when my head
is laid in the scented sweetness of your lap,
I do not mind
nor call to mind
anything, anyone.
It is simply that my mind
is utterly, wholly won
to the belief that in Infinity
some planets whirl and swirl
as free of our laws of gravity
as of the grave cares of the World.

   Paruyr Sevak   Poetry   Armenia   1969

self–others

We can see through others only when we see through ourselves.

   Eric Hoffer   Philosophy   United States   1954

in person

There is one spectacle grander than the sea, that is the sky; there is one spectacle
grander than the sky, that is the interior of the soul.

   Victor Hugo   Romanticism   France   1862

good intention–power

A good intention clothes itself with sudden power.

   Ralph Waldo Emerson   Transcendentalism   United States   1860

in faith   in purity

He that is faithful in that which is least is faithful also in much; and he that is unjust in the least is unjust also in much.

Jesus Christ   Christianity   Palestine (Judea)   33

person–group

He who remains peaceful when his opponent is angered, preserves himself and others from great danger.

Gautama Buddha   Buddhism   Nepal, India (Kapilavastu)   483 BCE

of opposites

Many would be cowards if they had courage enough.

Thomas Fuller   History   United Kingdom   1630

of fear and love

. . . we live with fear. Fear that is hate,
fear that is ambition, competition, aggression,
fear that is loneliness, anger, bitterness, cruelty,
fear that is mistrust, envy, greed, vanity, . . . and yet
fear is only twisted love, love turned back
upon itself, devouring itself, hating itself,
love that was denied, love that was rejected. . . .

Manitonquat   Native America   America (Wampanoag)   1965

of all

Heart feels for heart, limb cries for answering limb;
All strives to enforce the unity all is.

Sri Aurobindo   Yoga   India   1950

between persons

Unperturbed and ever mindful, the perfect man never thinks of himself as being "better" or "worse" or the same as another — he finds no occasion to draw comparisons.

Gautama Buddha   Buddhism   Nepal, India (Kapilavastu)   483 BCE

through identification

[Question]: How do you know the character of a man by looking at his eyes?

[The Mother]: Not only by looking at his eyes. I know the character of a man through self-identification. And then outwardly, if you want, the eyes are like doors or windows: there are some which are open, so one enters within, goes very deep inside, and one may see everything that happens there. There are others which are partly open, partly closed; others still have a veil, a kind of curtain; and then there are others which are fastened, locked up, doors closed so well they cannot be opened. Indeed, this is already an indication, it gives an indication of the strength of the inner life, the sincerity and transparency of the being. And so, through these doors that are open I enter and identify myself with the person within. And I see what he sees, understand what he understands, think what he thinks, and I could do what he does (but usually I refrain from that!) and in this way I get to know what people are like. And it doesn't need much time; it goes very fast. It can even be done through a photograph, but not so well. A photograph captures only a moment, a minute of somebody; if there were many photographs. . . . But still, even with a photograph, by going a little deeper one can have a fairly clear idea. But all knowledge is knowledge by identification. That is, one must become that which one wants to know. One may surmise, imagine, deduce, one may reason, but one does not know.

The Mother   Yoga   France   1953

in identity

If we see things from the point of view of their differences, then even our inner organs are as far apart as the states of Ch'n and Yüeh. But if we see things from the point of view of their identity, then all things are one.

Chuang Tzu   Taoism   China   286 BCE

person—object

The next morning I am back in the temple garden. . . . I take my place again under the palm tree, concentrating on it.

When I begin this exercise, all kinds of extraneous thoughts disturbed me. I suddenly remembered what Menu told me the evening before — I noticed a bird in the fronds — then a gnat was humming about my ears. . . . But I chased away all foreign thoughts as they arose in me and concentrated only on the palm tree.

Now I am getting along better. Thoughts can no longer reach me and really disturb me. Previously I was still in the world of thoughts — among the thoughts. My thoughts were able to push me to and fro. But I did not let myself be pushed around. I stayed put just where I was, with the palm tree, gliding slowly and almost imperceptibly further and further into myself where thoughts could no longer follow and disturb me. Now and again a thought bobs up, creeping through my intellect like a tired traveller. From my secure position I observe this stray, straggling tired thought, but I don't bother it. . . . I think of the palm tree, . . . slowly, the palm tree fills my entire being.

Days go by, perhaps weeks too, I don't know. I don't know anything more that's going on in my outer world, as I am concentrating on the palm tree with all my attention. Then all of a sudden I have the odd feeling that I am no longer looking at the tree from the outside, but from the inside. To be sure I still perceive its outward form with my eyes, but I begin, to an ever-increasing extent, to see and experience the inner being, the animating creative principle of the palm, . . . to see it, to experience it, TO BE IT !

And finally there comes a moment in which I am suddenly conscious of the fact that the palm is no longer outside myself — no! — it never was outside — it was only false conception on my part — the palm tree is in me and I in it — I myself am the palm tree!

Elisabeth Haich   Yoga   Hungary   1960

in God

Answer the witness of God in every man, whether they are the heathen that do not profess Christ, or whether they are such as do profess Christ that have the form of godliness and be out of the power.

This is the word of the Lord God to you all and a charge to you all in the presence of the living God, be patterns, be examples in all countries, places, islands, nations, wherever you come; that your carriage and life may preach among all sorts of people, and to them; then you will come to walk cheerfully over the world, answering that of God in every one.

George Fox   Quakerism   United Kingdom   1672

in love   in service

Love is a being which lives in a realm larger than the realm of the individual, and speaks from a knowledge deeper than the knowledge of the individual. It dwells in truth between the creatures, that is, it dwells in God. Life covered and warranted by life, life growing forth into life, not until you realize this can you perceive the soul of the world. What is wanting in one man is supplied by another. If one man loves too little, another will love the more. Things help one another. But to help is to do spontaneously with concentrated will, my own part of doing. He who loves more does not preach of love to the other, but only loves; as it were, he does not trouble himself about the other. And so he who helps does not, as it were, trouble himself about the other, but does his own part with the intention of helping. This means: what is essentially happening between one being and another, happens not through their intercourse but through everyone's apparently unconnected and purposeless act. This is told in a parable: "If someone would sing and cannot lift up his voice, and another comes and begins to sing, then the first is enabled to join in the song. This is the secret of union." To help one another is not considered a task, but the self-evident reality on which the companionship of the Hasidism is based. To help is not a virtue, but a pulse of existence.

Martin Buber   Hasidism   Austria   1965

spiritual love

Spiritual love is a position of standing with one hand extended into the universe and one hand extended into the world, letting ourselves be a conduit for passing energy.

Christina Baldwin   Education   United States   1990

in marriage

"Marriage" always means a union of positive and negative. On earth, however, "marriage" means the vain attempt to achieve union with another being in the body. But the mystic union of the spirit takes place in the consciousness and brings complete, never-ending fulfillment; for the union with one's own complementary half means union with God. The circle is closed again!

Elisabeth Haich   Yoga   Hungary   1960

person—God   playing with God

The way my ideas think me
Is the way I unthink God.
As in the name of heaven I make hell
That is the way the Lord says me.

And all is adventure and danger
And I roll Him off cliffs and mountains
But fast as I am to push Him off
Fast am I to reach Him below.

And it may be then His turn to push me off,
I wait breathless for that terrible second:
And if He push me not, I turn around in anger:
"Oh, art thou the god I would have!"

Then He pushes me and I plunge down, down!
And when he comes to help me up
I put my arms around him saying, "Brother,
Brother". . . This is the way we are.

   Jose Garcia Villa   Poetry   The Philippines   1960

in love   with life

A life without love, without the presence of the beloved, is nothing but a mere magic-
lantern show. We draw out slide after slide, swiftly tiring of each, and pushing it back
to make haste for the next.

   Johann Wolfgang von Goethe   Literature   Germany   1830

in prayer

When you pray you rise to meet in the air those who are praying at that very hour, and
whom save in prayer you may not meet.

   Kahlil Gibran   Mysticism   Lebanon   1923

through love

For my part, I think the chief reason which prompted the invisible God to become visible in the flesh and to hold converse with men was to lead carnal men, who are only able to love carnally, to the beautiful love of his flesh, and afterwards, little by little, to spiritual love.

Saint Bernard   Christianity   France   1110

knowledge–action

"I am ashamed of my emptiness," said the Word to the Work.
"I know how poor I am when I see you," said the Work to the Word.

Rabindranath Tagore   Poetry   India   1900

work–love

Work is love made visible.

Kahlil Gibran   Mysticism   Lebanon   1923

God

Everyone that loves knows God, for God is love.

Saint John   Christianity   Palestine (Judea)   40

with the godhead

[Malcolm Muggeridge]: These leaders and these little children that you get off the street, they're not just destitute people, to be pitied, but marvelous people. Anyone who's well can pity a man who's sick. Anyone who has enough can pity someone who hasn't enough. But I think what you do is to make one see that these people are not just to be pitied; they are marvelous people. How do you do this?

[Mother Theresa]: That's just what a Hindu gentleman said: that they and we are doing social work, and the difference between them and us is that they were doing it for something and we were doing it to somebody. This is where the respect and the love and the devotion come in, that we give it and we do it to God, to Christ, and that's why we try to do it as beautifully as possible. Because it is a continual contact with Christ in his work, it is the same contact we have during Mass and in the Blessed Sacrament. There we have Jesus in the appearance of bread. But here in the slums, in the broken body, in the children, we see Christ and we touch him.

Mother Theresa   Christianity   Macedonia, Albania   1976

with God

While absorbed in his devotions, the Rabbi of Ladi was heard to say: "My Lord and God. I do not desire Thy Paradise; I do not desire the bliss of the After World; I desire only Thee Thyself."

Shneour Zalman   Judaism   Poland   1812

with God

A man knocks at his friend's door. The friend asks, "Who is there?" He answers "I." The friend sends him away. For a full year the grief of separation burns within him, then he comes and knocks again. To his friend's question, "Who is it?" he replies, "Thou." At once the room is opened to him, wherein is no space for two "I's," that of God (of the "friend") and that of the man.

Jalal ad-Din Rumi   Sufism   Tajikistan, Turkey (Persia)   1230

love–God

When you love you should not say, "God is in my heart," but rather, "I am in the heart of God."

Kahlil Gibran   Mysticism   Lebanon   1923

in the godhead

I arise to-day
Through the strength of heaven:
Light of sun,
Radiance of moon,
Splendor of fire,
Speed of lightning,
Swiftness of wind,
Depth of sea,
Stability of earth,
Firmness of Rock. . . .

Christ with me, Christ before me, Christ behind me.
Christ in me, Christ beneath me, Christ above me,
Christ on my right, Christ on my left,
Christ when I lie down, Christ when I sit down,
   Christ when I arise.
Christ in the heart of every man who thinks of me,
Christ in the mouth of every one who speaks of me,
Christ in every eye that sees me,
Christ in every ear that hears me.

I arise to-day
Through a mighty strength, the invocation of the Trinity,
Through belief in the threeness,
Through confession of the oneness
Of the Creator of Creation.

Saint Patrick   Christianity   Ireland   493

micro—macro   in nature

Reflected
in a dragonfly's eye —
mountains

Kobayashi Issa   Zen Buddhism   Japan   1827

of humanity

Great men are rarely isolated mountain-peaks; they are the summits of ranges.

T.W. Higginson   Unitarianism   United States   1911

spirit—technology

Technology can and is supposed to be attentive to what liberates the person toward taking care of the higher level of existence. But, to me, the role of technology must be to attend to the lower part of human existence, since a thing devoid of the spiritual cannot help reach out to the spirit. The spirit liberates the person to work with the things of the soul. Because this reaching out to the spiritual is not happening, the Machine has overthrown the spirit and, as it sits in its place, is being worshipped as spiritual. . . . Anyone who worships his own creation, something of his own making, is someone in a state of confusion.

Malidoma Patrice Somé   Shamanism   Burkina Faso   1993

in principle   in education

There is no teaching until the pupil is brought into the same state of principle in which you are; a transfusion takes place; he is you and you are he; then is a teaching, and by no unfriendly chance or bad company can he ever quite lose the benefit.

Ralph Waldo Emerson   Transcendentalism   United States   1841

science–religion

Neither in its impetus nor its achievements can science go to its limits without becoming tinged with mysticism and charged with faith.

Pierre Teilhard de Chardin   Christianity   France   1955

in light

Light is the first of painters. There is no object so foul that intense light will not make it beautiful.

Ralph Waldo Emerson   Transcendentalism   United States   1849

in light   in God

The light . . . is the Word of Life, the Word of Peace, the Word of Reconciliation, which makes of twain one new man and if ye do abide there, there is no division but unity in the life. . . . Therefore in the Light wait where the unity is, where the peace is, where the oneness with the Father and Son is, where there is no Rent or Division.

George Fox   Quakerism   United Kingdom   1656

inner–outer   with time

We are connected with our own age if we recognize ourselves in relation to outside events; and we have grasped its spirit when we influence the future.

Hans Hofmann   Art   Germany   1900

with language

I am happy to be bound to my mother tongue, bound as perhaps few are, bound as Adam was to Eve because there was no other woman, bound because it has been an impossibility for me to learn any other language, and thus an impossibility to act proud and haughty about my heritage; but I am also happy to be bound to a mother tongue which has a wealth of inner originality when it expands the souls and resounds sensually in one's ear with its sweet ring; a mother tongue which does not groan when it is involved with a difficult thought; and therefore there may be someone who believes it is unable to express the thought, for it alleviates the difficulty by articulating it; a mother tongue which does not pant and sound strained when confronted with the ineffable, but works with it in jest and in earnest until it is what is near, or does not seek deep down what lies close at hand, because in its happy relationship to the object it moves freely like a supernatural creature, and, like a child, brings forth the happy remark without really being conscious of it; . . . a language which understands jest as well as seriousness: a mother tongue which keeps its children captive with a chain, "easy to bear . . . yes, but hard to break!"

Søren Kierkegaard   Existentialism   Denmark   1845

in language   in translation

The awkwardness of presenting translations from American Indian poetry in the year 1971 is that it has become fashionable today to deny the possibility of crossing the boundaries that separate people of different races and cultures: to insist instead that black is the concern of black, red of red, and white of white. Yet the idea of translation has always been that such boundary crossing is not only possible but desirable. By its very nature, translation asserts or at least implies a concept of psychic and biological unity, weird as such an assertion may seem in a time of growing dis-integration. Each poem, being made present and translated, flies in the face of divisive ideology. The question for the translator is not whether but how far we can translate one another. Like the poet who is his brother, he attempts to restore what has been torn apart. Any arrogance on his part would not only lead to paternalism or "colonialism" (LeRoi Jones' term for it from a few years back), it would deny the very order of translation. Only if he allows himself to be directed by the other will a common way emerge, true to both positions.

Jerome Rothenberg   Literature   United States   1971

in supra-ethical action

In other words, ethics is a stage in evolution. That which is common to all stages is the urge of Sachchidananda towards self-expression. This urge is at first non-ethical, then infra-ethical in the animal, then in the intelligent animal even anti-ethical for it permits us to approve hurt done to others which we disapprove when done to ourselves. In this respect man even now is only half-ethical. And just as all below us is infra-ethical, so there may be that above us whither we shall eventually arrive, which is supra-ethical, has no need of ethics. The ethical impulse and attitude, so all-important to humanity, is a means by which it struggles out of the lower harmony and universality based upon inconscience and broken up by Life into individual discords towards a higher harmony and universality based upon conscient oneness with all existences. Arriving at that goal, this means will no longer be necessary or even possible, since the qualities and oppositions on which it depends will naturally dissolve and disappear in the final reconciliation.

Sri Aurobindo   Yoga   India   1940

connectivity

Mr. God,
   I think it is amazing the way everything fits together in the world. Look at heat in our houses, the moon, the sun and rain so farmers' plants will grow.
   How do you do it? Mirrors?
                    Judy [age 11]

Judy   Childhood   United States   1987

in connectivity

God has arranged all things in the world in consideration of everything else.

Hildegard of Bingen   Mysticism   Germany   1163

in space

Every exit is an entry somewhere else.

Tom Stoppard   Drama   United Kingdom   1967

micro—macro

A tree that can fill the span of a man's arms
Grows from a downy tip;
A terrace vine storeys high
Rises from hodfuls of earth;
A journey of a thousand miles
Starts from beneath one's feet.

Lao Tzu   Taoism   China   500 BCE

in relations

I do not think that the measure of a civilization is how tall its buildings of concrete are, but rather how well its people have learned to relate to their environment and fellow man.

Sun Bear and Wabun   Native America   America (Chippewa)   1980

nothing—everything

Ptahhotep: Pointing to the smooth, white surface of stone, he asks, "What do you see on this white surface?"
Haich: "Nothing," I reply.
Ptahhotep: "And what could you draw on it?"
Haich: "Everything."
Ptahhotep: "Now," says Ptahhotep, "this Nothing therefore contains Everything. In this condition both together form a perfect unity. Within this unity something can only become recognizable if it becomes separate and distinct from unity.

Elisabeth Haich   Yoga   Hungary   1960

in medicine   in music   in balance

Medicine, to produce health, has to examine disease, and music, to create harmony, must investigate discord.

Plutarch of Chaeronea   Moralism   Greece   120 BCE

146

in harmony

Sing and dance together and be joyous, but let each one of you be alone,
Even as the strings of a lute are alone though they quiver with the same music.

   Kahlil Gibran   Mysticism   Lebanon   1923

in opposites

Danger and delight grow on one stalk.

   Unknown   Proverb   United Kingdom   Traditional

in multiplicity

Plurality which is not reduced to unity is confusion; unity which does not depend on plurality is tyranny.

   Blaise Pascal   Mathematics   France   1662

in diversity

There never was in the world two opinions alike, no more than two hairs or two grains; the most universal quality is diversity.

   Michel de Montaigne   Skepticism   France   1580

in truth

There is but one Truth, and so the wise find nothing to debate.

   Gautama Buddha   Buddhism   Nepal, India (Kapilavastu)   483 BCE

of friends

Treat gossip about your friend as though it referred to you.

   Unknown   Proverb   Ethiopia   Traditional

in death

Death is a thing of grandeur. It brings instantly into being a whole new network of relations between you and the ideas, the desires, the habits of the man now dead. It is a rearrangement of the world.

Antoine de Saint-Exupéry   Literature   France   1942

in death and life

One cannot live with the dead;
Either we die with them,
Or we make them live again.
Or we forget them.

Louis Martin-Chauffier   Literature   France   1910

person–world

You influence the world even by your private thoughts and the feelings you nurse in the sanctum of your heart, your judgements on others, your aims and aspirations. There is nothing so private that it does not touch others directly or indirectly.

N. Sri Ram   Theosophy   India   1973

person–other

I don't ask for your pity, but just your understanding — not even that — no. Just for your recognition of me in you, and the enemy, time, in us all.

Tennessee Williams   Drama   United States   1959

with others

None of you is a believer so long as he does not prefer for his brother what he prefers for himself.

Mohammed   Islam   Saudi Arabia   662

between persons

My eye
is the lens

My Wink,
the shutter

I have a tiny darkroom
surrounded by hair,

and that's why
I don't carry a camera

Do you know, I've many pictures
of you inside me?

Ibaragi Noriko   Zen Buddhism   Japan   1955

through friendship

The friends of my friends are my friends.

Unknown   Proverb   France   Traditional

of friends

Her lips' remark was: "Oh, you kid!"
Her soul spoke thus (I know it did):
"O King of realms of endless joy,
My own, my golden grocer's boy."

Joyce Kilmer   Poetry   United States   1914

of distant friends

Nothing makes the earth seem so spacious as to have friends at a distance; they wake
the latitudes and longitudes.

Henry David Thoreau   Transcendentalism   United States   1843

of friends

But when two people are at one in their inmost hearts,
They shatter even the strength of iron or of bronze.
And when two people understand each other in their inmost hearts,
Their words are sweet and strong, like the fragrance of orchids.

Unknown   Taoism   China   1200 BCE

in family   in community

We are one people and must strive to act as one. As a people, our realities, life chances and possibilities are rooted in the quality of our relations with each other. Unity, thus, must begin on the basic level of family and extend outward in expanding concentric circles of our national community. For the state of the family is in a real sense a valid indication of the state of the national community. The lessons of who we are, our position and possibilities in life and the nature and need of building and maintaining quality and effective relations with each other are taught at an early age and in the context of the family.

Maulana Karenga   Kwanzaa   United States   1977

brother—God

You see your brother: you see your God.

Jesus Christ   Christianity   Palestine (Judea)   33

humanity—God

If a man say, I love God, and hateth his brother, he is a liar: for he that loveth not his brother whom he hath seen, how can he love God whom he hath not seen?

Saint John   Christianity   Palestine (Judea)   50

between generations

The son disgraces himself when he blames his father.

Unknown   Proverb   Africa   Traditional

between generations   in children

Children are life after death. We can't live after death any other way except through children and great works. Children make our works and everything else worthwhile.

Maulana Karenga   Kwanzaa   United States   1960

parent–child

You carry me within yourself,
My son,
and I'm scared,
I tremble for you.

Beneath the sun, into the fleece of corn
I've cast you,
I — your wandering,
your death.

The squirrel nibbles the cone with which it will hit you,
now rattles a volley on the typewriter —
and you're translated,
my son,
a little inaccurately,
as is the case with poetry.

Gloriously you cry
and condemn me
for life
to an anxious bliss.

Miroslav Florian   Poetry   Czech Republic   1950

family—other

The bond that links your true family is not one of blood, but of respect and joy in each other's life. Rarely do members of one family grow up under the same roof.

Richard Bach   Literature   United States   1977

through contemplation   with a stranger

The Buddha had a special way to help us understand the object of our perception. He said that in order to understand, you have to be one with what you want to understand. This is practice-able. About fifteen years ago, I used to help a committee for orphans, victims of war in Vietnam. From Vietnam, they sent out applications, one sheet of paper with a small picture of a child in the corner, telling the name, the age, and the conditions of the orphan. We were supposed to translate it from Vietnamese into French, English, Dutch, or German in order to seek a sponsor. . . .

Each day I helped translate about 30 applications into French. The way I did it was to look at the picture of the child. I did not read the application. I just took the time to look at the picture of the child. Usually after only 30 to 40 seconds, I became one with the child. I don't know how or why, but it's always like that. Then I would pick up the pen and translate the works from the application onto another sheet. Afterwards I realized that it was not me who had translated the application; it was the child and me, who had become one.

Thich Nhat Hanh   Buddhism   Vietnam   1987

in silence

There's no vocabulary
For love within a family, love that's lived in
But not looked at, love within the light of which
All else is seen, the love within which
All other love finds speech.
This love is silent.

T.S. Eliot   Literature   United Kingdom   1958

through women   through education

If you educate a man, you have educated a man; but if you educate a woman, you educate a family.

Unknown   Education   United States   Traditional

man—woman

Now it came to pass that man lacked
a help-mate that was his equal.

God created this help-mate in the form
of a woman — a mirror image of all that
was latent in the male sex.

In this way, man and woman are so
intimately related that one is the
work of the other.

Man can not be called man without woman.
Neither can woman be named woman without
man.

Hildegard of Bingen   Mysticism   Germany   1163

woman—man

Woman without man is like a field without seed.

Unknown   Proverb   Ethiopia   Traditional

in friendship   in homosexuality

If Emma's bosom heav'd a pensive sigh,
The tear stood trembling in Elfrida's eye;
If pleasure gladden'd her Elfrida's heart,
Still faithful Emma shar'd the larger part.

Unknown   Poetry   United States   1777

in sex

. . . the sex act, the act of love, can be one of the deepest means through which bliss can be attained.

Tantra is not teaching sexuality. It is simply saying that sex can be a source of bliss. And once you know that bliss, you can go further because you are grounded in reality. One is not to remain with sex forever, but you can use sex as a jumping point. That is what tantra means: you can use sex as a jumping point. And once you have known the ecstasy of sex, you can understand what mystics have been talking about — a greater orgasm, a cosmic orgasm.

... in human life, the sex act is the only act in which you come to feel a nonduality, in which you come to feel a deep oneness, in which the past disappears and the future disappears and only the present moment — the only real moment remains. So all those mystics who have really known oneness with existence itself, they have always used sexual terms and symbols for their experience to express it. There is no other symbology, there is no other symbology which comes near to it.

Sex is just the beginning, not the end. But if you miss the beginning, you will miss the end also, and you cannot escape the beginning to reach the end.

Bhagwan Shree Rajneesh   Philosophy   India   1974

in love

Sympathy constitutes friendship; but in love there is a sort of antipathy, or opposing passion. Each strives to be the other, and both together make up one whole.

Samuel Taylor Coleridge   Romanticism   United Kingdom   1830

in emotion

No one is so accursed by fate,
No one so utterly desolate,
But some heart, though unknown,
Responds unto his own.

Henry Wadsworth Longfellow   Poetry   United States   1842

of love apart

As lines, so loves oblique, may well
Themselves in every angle greet;
But ours, so truly parallel,
Though infinite, can never meet.

   Andrew Marvell   Poetry   United Kingdom   1678

in love

Love is the part, and love is the whole;
Love is the robe, and love is the pall;
Ruler of heart and brain and soul,
Love is the lord and the slave of all!

   George MacDonald   Romanticism   United Kingdom   1840

by love

There is no remedy for love but to love more.

   Henry David Thoreau   Transcendentalism   United States   1839

in love

In this great up-climbing, it is far better to suffer from love rather than to reject it, and
to harden your hearts against all ties and claims of affection. Suffer for love, even
though the suffering be bitter. Love, even though the love be an avenue of pain. The
pain shall pass away, but the love shall continue to grow, and in the unity of the Self
you shall finally discover that love is the great attracting force which makes all things
one.

   Annie Besant   Theosophy   United Kingdom   1908

in love

. . . Who shall set a shore to love?
When hath it ever swerved from death, or when
Hath it not burned away all barriers,
Even dearest ties of mother and of son,
Even of brothers?

Stephen Phillips   Drama   United Kingdom   1899

in love

When one loves somebody, everything is clear — where to go, what to do — it all takes
care of itself and one doesn't have to ask anybody about anything.

Maxim Gorky   Social Realism   Russia   1913

love–grace

Grace happens in the dimension of love. For love everything is always eternally
present. So if you are in love, grace can happen. But love is surrendering; love means
now the other has become more important than yourself. The other has become the
center; you are just the periphery. By and by you disappear completely, and the other
remains. In the right moment, grace is received.

So do not think of a master as one who can give you grace. Think of becoming a
helpless disciple — totally surrendered, in love. The master will come to you. When the
disciple is ready, the master always comes. It is not a question of physical presence;
when you are ready, from an unknown dimension of love, grace happens.

Bhagwan Shree Rajneesh   Philosophy   India   1974

in touch

Marriage a la Mode
Our souls sit close and silently within,
And their own web from their own entrails spin;
And when eyes meet far off, our sense is such,
That, spider like, we feel that tenderest touch.

John Dryden   Poetry   United Kingdom   1673

of lovers

As one too great for him he worships her;
He adores her as his regent of desire,
He yields to her as the mover of his will,
He burns the incense of his nights and days
Offering his life, a splendour of sacrifice.
A rapt solicitor for her love and grace,
His bliss in her to him is his whole world:
He grows through her in all his being's powers;
He reads by her God's hidden aim in things.

    Sri Aurobindo   Yoga   India   1950

in love

How vast a memory has Love!

    Alexander Pope   Poetry   United Kingdom   1707

in love

Do you remember that towering kiss? . . .
From that day forward —
  I don't know the date —
For me you became both light and breath.

    Unknown   Poetry   Russia   1900

in love

Others because you did not keep
That deep-sworn vow have been friends of mine;
Yet always when I look death in the face,
When I clamber to the heights of sleep,
Or when I grow excited with wine,
Suddenly I meet your face.

    William Butler Yeats   Poetry   Ireland   1919

with lover with the world   through time

Wheels whirred beneath me; and above,
where the star-tangling roof-tops flowed,
the moon rode with me as I rode
through shortening streets to meet my love.

This is not just what years recall:
forty years gone and more are less
than one breath-moment's happiness;
time has no part in it at all.

Drifts of our streaming life expand
into the neither now nor then
of movement become the world — as when
this hand goes out to touch her hand.

Robert D. FitzGerald   Poetry   Australia   1975

of lovers

In a wide moment of two souls that meet
She felt her being flow into him as in waves
A river pours into a mighty sea.
As when a soul is merging into God
To live in Him for ever and know His joy,
Her consciousness grew aware of him alone
And all her separate self was lost in his.
As a starry heaven encircles happy earth,
He shut her into himself in a circle of bliss
And shut the world into himself and her.
A boundless isolation made them one;
He was aware of her enveloping him
And let her penetrate his very soul
As is a world by the world's spirit filled,
As the mortal wakes into Eternity,
As the finite opens to the Infinite.
Thus were they in each other lost awhile,
Then drawing back from their long ecstasy's trance
Came into a new self and a new world.
Each now was a part of the other's unity,
The world was but their twin self-finding's scene
Or their own wedded being's vaster frame.
On the high glowing cupola of the day
Fate tied a knot with morning's halo threads
While by the ministry of an auspice-hour
Heart-bound before the sun, their marriage fire,
The wedding of the eternal Lord and Spouse
Took place again on earth in human forms:
In a new act of the drama of the world
The united Two began a greater age.
In the silence and murmur of that emerald world
And the mutter of the priest-wind's sacred verse,
Amid the choral whispering of the leaves
Love's twain had joined together and grew one.
The natural miracle was wrought once more:
In the immutable ideal world
One human moment was eternal made.

Sri Aurobindo   Yoga   India   1950

of the Divine   of the godhead

Along a road of pure interior light,
Alone between tremendous Presences,
Under the watching eye of nameless Gods,
His soul passed on, a single conscious power,
Towards the end which ever begins again.
Approaching through a stillness dumb and calm
To the source of all things human and divine.
There he beheld in their mighty union's poise
The figure of the deathless Two-in-One,
A single being in two bodies clasped,
A diarchy of two united souls,
Seated absorbed in deep creative joy;
Their trance of bliss sustained the mobile world.

Sri Aurobindo   Yoga   India   1950

Community

good—evil   with the wicked

Oftentimes have I heard you speak of one who commits a wrong as though he were not one of you, but a stranger unto you and an intruder upon your world.
But I say that even as the holy and the righteous cannot rise beyond the highest which is in each one of you,
So the wicked and the weak cannot fall lower than the lowest which is in you also.
And as a single leaf turns not yellow but with the silent knowledge of the whole tree,
So the wrong-doer cannot do wrong without the hidden will of you all.

Kahlil Gibran   Mysticism   Lebanon   1923

in crime

Commit a crime, and the earth is made of glass.
There is no such thing as concealment.

Ralph Waldo Emerson   Transcendentalism   United States   1841

love—God

Beloved, let us love one another; for love is of God, and he who loves is born of God and knows God. He who does not love does not know God; for God is love.

Saint John   Christianity   Palestine (Judea)   50

in God   with stupid people

And if even you see one who is extremely stupid, beware of insult to him or condemnation, for the insult would include God himself, who so created him.

Ivan Pososkov   Economics   Russia   1718

in God in life

Between the Kaaba and the wine-house no difference I see,
Whate'er the spot my eye surveys, there equally is He.

Hafez   Sufism   Iran (Persia)   1340

among the faithful

The faithful are one soul.

Jalal ad-Din Rumi   Sufism   Tajikistan, Turkey (Persia)   1230

leader–followers

Crazy Horse . . . [known to his own people as] Our Strange Man seemed to mean just that to many of his followers . . . and to many descendants of his enemies. . . . Even those sent out from the Missouri River forts felt it, men who had never seen Crazy Horse rally the warriors fleeing from a hard, uneven fight, or stand off a Snake charge alone, never watched him walk in silence through his village in peacetime, every face more alive for his passing.

Mari Sandoz   Native America   United States   1942

with humanity

Do not do to your neighbour what you yourself would not like; that is the whole of the law, and all the rest is but commentaries.

Unknown   Judaism   Israel   500

in collectivity

Dost thou not see that when ants assemble together
They bring trouble and torment to fighting lions?

Saadi   Islam   Iran (Persia)   1257

of collective strength

When spider webs unite, they can tie up a lion.

Unknown   Proverb   Ethiopia   Traditional

Africa–church in spirit

Black music, in all its forms, represents the highest artistic achievement of the race. It is the memory of Africa that we hear in the churning energy of the gospels. The memory of the Motherland that lingers behind the Christian references to Moses, Jesus and Daniel. The Black Holy Ghost roaring into some shack of a church, in the South, seizing the congregation with an ancient energy and power. The Black church, therefore, represents and embodies the transplanted African memory.

Larry Neal   Drama   United States   1972

in love

"Teacher, which is the Great Commandment in the law?" And he said to him "You shall love the Lord your God with all your heart, and with all your soul, and with all your mind. . . . And a second is like it, you shall love your neighbour as yourself."

Saint Matthew   Christianity   Israel (Galilee)   60

in religion

[by a child in Terezin concentration camp]

I am a Jew and will be a Jew forever.
Even if I should die from hunger,
never will I submit.
I will always fight for my people,
on my honor.
I will never be ashamed of them,
I give my word.

I am proud of my people,
how dignified they are.
Even though I am suppressed,
I will always come back to life.

Franta Bass   Childhood   Poland   1944

in unity

The Mishumaa Saba (the seven candles) represent the Nguzo Saba (The Seven Principles) which stand at the heart of the Kawaida value system. . . .

  The First Principle is Umoja (unity) which is a commitment to the principle and practice of togetherness and collective action on crucial levels, i.e., building and maintaining unity in the family, community, nation and race. This is the first and foundational principle because without unity our possibilities as a people are few and fragile if existent at all. The essentiality of unity cannot seriously be questioned. What is more often debated is the method by which this unity is achieved.

  Maulana Karenga   Kwanzaa   United States   1977

in work

The Third Principle is Ujima (collective Work and Responsibility) which is a commitment to active and informed togetherness on matters of common interest. It is also recognition and respect of the fact that without collective work and struggle, progress is impossible and liberation unthinkable.

  Moreover, the principle of Ujima supports the fundamental assumption that Black is not just an identity, but also a destiny and duty, i.e., a responsibility. In other words, our collective identity in the long run is a collective future.

  Thus, there is a need for us as self-conscious and committed people to share our future with our own minds and hands and share its hardships and benefits together.

  Ujima, as principle and practice, also means that we accept the fact that we are collectively responsible for our failures and setbacks as well as our victories and achievements.

  Maulana Karenga   Kwanzaa   United States   1977

ruler–ruled

Let any person who steals food or clothing, silver or gold, be examined whether he stole through need or poverty, and if it be found so, let not that thief be punished but let him who holds the office of steward be punished by removal from his position, since he has not taken care to provide for the needs of him who stole nor made a record of the needy, and let that thief be given the necessary clothing, food, land, and a house.

  Unknown   Government   Peru   1594

in collectivity

To be unified is to have the collective strength to confront and solve problems which are collective in nature. In fact, history has proved that a people united and conscious of their strengths and weaknesses cannot be defeated. But a people divided are doomed to a slow or quick destruction. Unity then is a vital principle and practice and without an active commitment to it, nothing else is really possible for us as a people and we are doomed to build houses we don't live in, live in cities structured around interests and aims other than our own, and fight wars for our oppressor in the name of freedom we don't even enjoy.

Maulana Karenga   Kwanzaa   United States   1977

with enemies

The murdered is not unaccountable for his own murder,
And the robbed is not blameless in being robbed.
The righteous is not innocent of the deeds of the wicked,
And the white-handed is not clean in the doings of the felon.
Yea, the guilty is oftentimes the victim of the injured,
And still more often the condemned is the burden bearer for the guiltless and unblamed.
You cannot separate the just from the unjust and the good from the wicked;
For they stand together before the face of the sun even as the black thread and the white are woven together.
And when the black thread breaks, the weaver shall look into the whole cloth, and he shall examine the loom also.

Kahlil Gibran   Mysticism   Lebanon   1923

with life

There was a sunrise falling like red blood. . . .
And men and women creeping through the red
Of the marvelous city, could not quite deny
All day the life that startled them: they said
Beautiful things, and wept, and wondered why.

Dorothy E. Reid   Poetry   United States   1770

in cities

Oh, blank confusion! true epitome
Of what the mighty City is herself,
To thousands upon thousands of her sons,
Living amid the same perpetual whirl
Of trivial objects, melted and reduced
To one identity.

William Wordsworth   Romanticism   United Kingdom   1850

in love

I once asked the Bishop of Geneva what one must do to attain perfection. "You must love God with all your heart," he answered, "and your neighbor as yourself."

"I did not ask wherein perfection lies, "I rejoined, "but how to attain it." "Charity," he said again, "that is both the means and the end, the only way by which we can reach that perfection which is, after all, but Charity itself. . . . Just as the soul is the life of the body, so charity is the life of the soul."

"I know all that," I said. "But I want to know how one is to love God with all one's heart and one's neighbor as oneself."

But again he answered, "We must love God with all our hearts, and our neighbor as ourselves."

"I am no further than I was," I replied, "Tell me how to acquire such love."

"The best way, the shortest and easiest way of loving God with all one's heart is to love him wholly and heartily!"

He would give me no other answer. At last, however, the Bishop said, "There are many besides you who want me to tell them the methods and systems and secret ways of becoming perfect, and I can only tell them that the sole secret is a hearty love of God, and the only way to attain that love is by loving. You learn to speak by speaking, to study by studying, to run by running, to work by working; and just so you learn to love God and man by loving. All those who think to learn in any other way deceive themselves. If you want to love God, go on loving Him more and more. Begin as a mere apprentice, and the very power of love will lead you on to become a master in the art. Those who have made most progress will continually press on, never believing themselves to have reached their end; for charity should go on increasing until we draw our last breath.

Jean-Pierre Camus   Christianity   France   1639

In conflict   in relationships

Perceive all conflict as patterns of energy seeking harmonious balance as elements in a whole.

Spiritual practice is really about weaving a network of good relationships.

Right relationship means right relationship with the elements, the land, the sacred directions. . . . The seed of pure mind is within all people. It is always there. It is not made impure. Our actions may be impure and set up a stream of reactions, but always we can come again to the seed of pure mind and right relationship. . . . It is time now for people to choose. The first step is to see the power of your own consciousness. . . . The common kernel is care for all beings, good relationship, cycles of reciprocity, generosity, giving of oneself, being an empty bowl so you can know what is.

Dhyani Ywahoo   Native America   America (Etowah Cherokee)

with women

Women who set a low value on themselves make life hard for all women.

Nellie McClung   Women's Suffrage Movement   Canada   1915

in the godhead   with outcasts

"For I was hungry and you gave me food, I was thirsty and you gave me drink, I was a stranger and you welcomed me. I was naked and you clothed me, I was sick and you visited me, I was in prison and you came to me." Then the righteous will answer him, "Lord, when did we see thee hungry and feed thee, or thirsty and give you drink? And when did we see you a stranger and welcome you, or naked and clothe you? And when did we see you sick or in prison and visit thee?" And the King will answer them, "Truly, I say to you, as you did it to one of the least of these my brethren, you did it to me."

Jesus Christ   Christianity   Palestine (Judea)   33

in service

The way of unity is love manifested as service.

N. Sri Ram   Theosophy   India   1973

in nature

The ox never thanks the pasture.

Unknown   Proverb   Haiti   Traditional

through love

To preserve the variety of personality within a common spirit of unity, no way matches the way of personal love.

Unknown   Intentional Community   United States   1970

in slander   in humility

Those who speak ill of me are really my good friends. When, being slandered, I cherish neither enmity nor preference, There grows within me the power of love and humility which is of the Unborn.

Yung-chia Ta-shih   Zen Buddhism   China   713

in balance

Sympathy moves from all to one, creativity moves from one to all. Without sympathy there is no ground of potentiality to support creativity. Without creativity there is no means of actuality to reveal sympathy. Sympathy and creativity move together hand in hand.

Chang Chung-yuan   Taoism   China   1963

of humanity

Nor knowest thou what argument
Thy life to thy neighbor's creed has lent.
All are needed by each one;
Nothing is fair or good alone.

Ralph Waldo Emerson   Transcendentalism   United States   1882

in collectivity

Pentecost was the call to spiritual unity among gospel believers. When the spirit descended on the disciples of Jerusalem, the same thing happened in Philadelphia, Alexandria, and at all other places where true believers dwelt. It was literally true that "there was but one heart and soul among the multitude of the believers."

Urantia Foundation   Urantia   United States   1955

through community

We owe a cornfield respect, not because of itself, but because it is food for mankind. In the same way, we owe our respect to a collectivity, of whatever kind — country, family or any other — not for itself, but because it is food for a certain number of human souls. . . .

The degree of respect owing to human collectivities is a very high one, for several reasons.

To start with, each is unique, and, if destroyed, cannot be replaced. One sack of corn can always be substituted for another sack of corn. The food which a collectivity supplies for the souls of those who form part of it has no equivalent in the entire universe.

Secondly, because of its continuity, a collectivity is already moving forward into the future. It contains food, not only for the souls of the living, but also for the souls of beings yet unborn which are to come into the world during the immediately succeeding centuries.

Lastly, due to this same continuity, a collectivity has its roots in the past. It constitutes the sole agency for preserving the spiritual treasures accumulated by the dead, the sole transmitting agency by means of which the dead can speak to the living. And the sole earthly reality which is directly connected with the eternal destiny of Man is the irradiating light of those who have managed to become fully conscious of this destiny, transmitted from generation to generation.

Because of all this, it may happen that the obligation towards a collectivity which is in danger reaches the point of entailing a total sacrifice. But it does not follow from this that collectivities are superior to human beings. It sometimes happens, too, that the obligation to go to the help of a human being in distress makes a total sacrifice necessary, without that implying any superiority on the part of the individual so helped.

Simone Weil   Mysticism   France   1943

in life and death

When our tears are dry on the shore
and the fishermen carry their nets home
and the seagulls return to bird island
and the laughter of the children recedes at night,
there shall still linger the communion we forged,
the feasts of oneness whose ritual we partook of.
There shall still be the eternal gateman
who will close the cemetery doors
and send the late mourners away.
It cannot be the music we heard that night
that still lingers in the chambers of memory.
It is the new chorus of our forgotten comrades
and the halleluyahs of our second selves.

    Kofi Awoonor   Poetry   Ghana   1964

past–future

A red glow in the sky, the dead night underground,
The pine trees imprison me in their dark density,
but unmistakably there comes the sound
of a far distant, undiscovered city.

You will make out houses in heavy rows,
and towers, and the silhouette of buttresses,
and gardens behind stone wall sombre with shadows,
and arrogant ramparts of ancient fortresses.

Unmistakably from submerged centuries
the piercing mind makes ready for dawning
the long forgotten roar of silted cities
and the rhythm of life returning.

    Alexander Blok   Poetry   Russia   1918

of the heart

Unity is substance of the heart
And not a chain that binds.

Sri Aurobindo   Yoga   India   1915

in conflict

If two horses are fighting, the grass underneath their hoofs will suffer.

Unknown   Proverb   Niger   Traditional

with intelligence   through community

We lie as Emerson said in the lap of an immense intelligence. But that intelligence is dormant and its communications are broken, inarticulate and faint until it possesses the local community as its medium.

John Dewey   Education   United States   1927

Nation

dream–action

The republic is a dream.
Nothing happens unless first a dream.

Carl Sandburg   Poetry   United States   1922

in national self-giving

Today I would like to speak about the ideal of the world-family.

Each nation is unique in its own way. Each nation has achieved something special, at least for itself. When a nation is ready to feel that other nations are an extension of its own being, when a nation becomes aware that all nations belong to one family, one source, and have one common goal, then that particular nation can easily teach or share its lofty achievements. Each nation knows inwardly that satisfaction and perfection lie only in self-giving, not in displaying grandiose achievements or in hoarding capacities.

Sri Chinmoy   Yoga   India   1974

of citizens

Remember that when you say, "I will have none of this exile and this stranger for his face is not like my face and his speech is strange," you have denied America with that word.

Stephen Vincent Benét   Poetry   United States   1943

with Earth

The Earth is the mother of all, and all ought to possess equal rights to her benefits. It is like expecting rivers to flow uphill to imagine that a man who was born free can be happy when he is confined to a given area and freedom to go wherever he fancies is taken from him.

Chief Joseph   Native America   America (Nez Perce)   1880

in love

If everyone adopts universal love and if everyone loves others as himself, will there still be those who are not dutiful? For in regarding the father and elder brother and the prince as oneself, who will be impious towards them? Will there still be those who are not well-disposed? For in regarding one's younger brother, one's son and one's subject as oneself, who will be ill-disposed towards them? Thus impiety and malevolence will no longer exist.

Will there still be burglars and bandits? In considering the house of another man as one's own house, who will burgle it? In regarding the body of another man as one's own body, who will attack that other man? Thus burglars and bandits will no longer exist.

Will there be a grand officer who disturbs the family of another grand officer and a lord who invades the State of another lord? In regarding the family of another grand officer as one's own family, who will disturb it? In regarding another State as one's own State, who will invade it? Thus grand officers causing trouble and aggressive lords will no longer exist.

Mo Tzu   Mohism   China   392 BCE

of humanity

From many people, one people.

Unknown   Proverb   Jamaica   Traditional

diversity into unity

E pluribus unum (out of many, one)

Pierre-Eugène du Simitière   Philosophy   Switzerland, United States   1776

in freedom

Freedom is an indivisible word. If we want to enjoy it, and fight for it, we must be prepared to extend it to everyone. . . .

Wendell L. Willkie   Politics   United States   1943

person—nation

O Russia beloved,
      all this is no trifle —
Each pain felt by you pierces me with pain, too.
O Russia,
   I am
      your capillary vessel,
Whatever hurts me, Russia,
        also pains you.

Andrei Voznesensky   Poetry   Russia   1963

with race

I am Black. This is a source of pride.
My hair is short and finely curled.
My skin is deep-hued, from brown to black.
My eyes are large, open to the world.
My lips are thick, giving resonance to my words.
My nose is broad to breathe freely the air.
My heritage is my experience in America . . . although not of it;
Seeking freedom that all life may be free.

I am Black, America has cause to be proud.

Barbara Buckner Wright   Poetry   United States   Unknown

of races in struggle

There is an old film called *The Defiant Ones*. In one scene, two convicts manacled together escape. They fall into a ditch with slippery sides. One of them claws his way to near the top and just about makes it. But he cannot. His mate to whom he is manacled is still at the bottom and drags him down. The only way they can escape to freedom is together. The one convict is black and the other white: a dramatic parable of our situation in South Africa. The only way we can survive is together, black and white; the only way we can be truly human is together, black and white.

Desmond Tutu   Christianity   South Africa   1989

ruler–nation

I have travelled over many lands and distant seas,
to India afar and China renowned.
I have touched the shores of Africa and the boundaries
  of Europe,
and I have met the great ones of all the lands.

As I stood at the side of heads of governments,
next to leaders proud of their rule, their authority
  over their own,
I realized how small and weak is the power I hold.
For mine is a throne established upon a heap of lava.
They rule where millions obey their commands.
Only a few thousands can I count under my care.

Yet one thought came to me of which I may boast,
that of all beauties locked within the embrace of
  these shores,
one is a jewel more precious than any owned by my
fellow monarchs.
I have nothing in my Kingdom to dread.

I mingle with my people without fear.
My safety is no concern, I require no bodyguards.
Mine is the boast that a pearl of great price has fallen to me
  from above.
Mine is the loyalty of my people.

King David Kalakaua   Politics   America (Hawaii)   1881

of a nation

Not life, liberty, and the pursuit of happiness, but peace, order and good government
are what the national government of Canada guarantees. Under these, it is assumed,
life, liberty, and happiness may be achieved, but by each according to his taste. For the
society of allegiance admits of a diversity the society of compact does not, and one of
the blessings of Canadian life is that there is no Canadian way of life, much less two,
but a unity under the Crown admitting to a thousand diversities.

H.L. Morton   Nationalism   Canada   1940

in family

A house is so important because it is the smallest example of how the nation works.

Maulana Karenga   Kwanzaa   United States   1960

of a nation

Canada has no cultural unity, no linguistic unity, no religious unity, no economic unity, no geographic unity. All it has is unity.

Kenneth Boulding   Economics   Canada   1957

in balance

When written in Chinese, the word "crisis" is composed of two characters - one represents danger and the other represents opportunity.

John F. Kennedy   Politics   United States   1959

in diversity

America is so vast that almost everything said about it is likely to be true, and the opposite is probably equally true.

James T. Farrell   Socialism   United States   1934

in bureaucracy

If a leader appointed by me commits an injustice toward a human being, and I learn thereof, if I do nothing to repair it, it is I who commit the injustice. . . . Anyone who is the victim of an unjust governor, let him complain to me!

Caliph Omar Ibn al-Khattab   Islam   Saudi Arabia (Persia)   644 *person–principle*

. . . law is not sufficient of itself, order does not perpetuate itself. When the right man comes, law succeeds, but not otherwise. When the saint rules, general laws will meet all cases; but when the ruler is not a saint, no amount of legislation can be properly applied.

Hsun-tzu   Confucianism   China   235 BCE

in politics slaves–nobles

Diop remarks that in Africa, all castes — including slaves — were associated with power. Thus in the Mossi country, although power was hereditary, it was not automatically transmitted from father to son. The emperor must belong to the family of the Mora Naba but he was chosen from among the possible candidates by a college of dignitaries presided over by the prime minister. The latter was not noble: he must be from the people. The chief of cavalry also was always a member of one of three ordinary Mossi families. Diop adds the following comments:

So the Ministers instead of coming from the aristocracy, were systematically chosen outside this class, from among the proletariat and slaves. . . . Such was the spirit of this constitution. To grasp its full originality, one must imagine that in the middle ages in the West (the time of the Hundred Years' War) the king of France or England — not just some proverbial lord — chose to share his power, electively, with county serfs tied to the soil, free peasants, town craftsmen organized in guilds, and merchants.

Cheikh Anta Diop   Anthropology   Senegal   1960

leader–citizens

We have already seen that we are all equal; that the power of the ruler was not given to him by nature, and that as a man he is on the same level as the rest. Hence, all power, in order to be reasonable and genuine, must be exercised for the benefit of the people from which it emanated.

Briefly, we must not recognize the superiority of the ruler as an attribute attached to him by nature. The obedience and respect due him are derived from the power which is the integration of the power of his people.

For this reason, he who obeys the power conferred by the people obeys the people and identifies himself with the will of all the citizens that compose the people, which identification or accord is necessary for the very life of the people.

Emilio Jacinto   Nationalism   The Philippines   1899

with language

Lexicon

I am a younger branch of the Russian tree,
I am her flesh, and up to my leaves
There lead the moist, steely,
Fibrous sinews, direct blood and bone
Extensions from the roots.

There is an enormous upward attraction,
And for this reason I am immortal as long
As there flows in my veins — my blessing and pain —
The icy liquid of subterranean springs,
All the R's and L's of the sacred tongue.

I was called to life by the blood of all births
And of all deaths, lived in the times
When the nameless genius of mankind
Breathed life into the mute dead flesh
Of things and happenings, granting them names.

His lexicon is opened out full page
From the clouds to the depths of the earth.
 — Teach the blue titmouse words of reason
And let fall a single leaf onto the wall,
Scarlet, russet, green and golden.

Arseny Tarkovsky   Poetry   Russia   1963

in individuality   person–nation

Either the State is founded on the personal identity of each of its children — manual labour, individual thought, self-fulfillment, respect for family honour and the self-fulfillment of others, in short, a passionate love of human dignity; or else the state is not worth a single tear shed by a single one of our women, nor a single drop of blood shed by our heroes.

José Marti   Revolution   Cuba   1891

through borders

The line that divides two countries also unites them.

William Leon   Geography   United States   1998

nature–nation

When you destroy a blade of grass,
You poison England at her roots.

Gordon Bottomley   Poetry   United Kingdom   1922

in freedom

Freedom, to be viable, has to be sincere and complete. If a republic refuses to open its arms to all, and move ahead with all, it dies.

José Marti   Revolution   Cuba   1870

in service to the United Nations   soul-reality

Each individual who has come to serve the United Nations represents his own country, his small world. But when he becomes part and parcel of the United Nations, the big world, at that time he is for all, for the entire humanity. He started his journey from his own country and then moved towards the goal of goals: universal oneness. . . .

At the General Assembly each individual nation comes to offer its light, truth, willingness, capacity and sense of oneness. Each country embodies truth and light in its own way. But each country feels and knows in the inmost recesses of its heart that the light and truth it embodies cannot be sufficient. Therefore, it tries to accept and receive light from other countries. Similarly, each flame that each individual embodies cannot be sufficient to solve any world-problem or to illumine world-ignorance. What is needed is the unification of all the flames that are here, there and everywhere. All the flames that are here have to be collected so that they can muster their joint strength. At that time, the ignorance-dream that separates one country from another, one man from another, can no longer last. It will be replaced by wisdom-reality. And what is wisdom-reality? Wisdom-reality is the song of oneness. This song of oneness is founded only on self-giving, which is nothing short of truth-becoming. And truth-becoming is oneness with the all-embracing, all-loving, all-illumining and all-fulfilling Reality.

The higher reality is the soul in us; the lower reality is the body-consciousness. The lower reality aspires to grow into the higher reality. The higher reality inspires us to move forward in our quest for truth, light and peace. Most people think only of the lower reality of the United Nations — the body-reality, the U.N. building, where thousands of human beings are serving one cause. The actual building, the body-reality of the United Nations, immediately captures their minds. The outside world does not easily think of the soul-reality, which is the real reality of the United Nations. But it is the loving soul, the illumining soul of the United Nations, that guides the body-reality, or tries to guide it. The day will come when the outer world will realise that looming large inside the famous body-reality is the precious soul-reality.

We, the seekers and members of the Meditation Group at the United Nations, are trying to serve both the soul-reality and the body-reality according to our limited capacity. Our capacity is limited, but our sincere efforts we place at the Feet of the Inner Pilot of the United Nations. This Inner Pilot is our fate-maker, the Author of all good, God.

Sri Chinmoy   Yoga   India   1976

between countries

Across the wall of the world,
A river sings a beautiful song. It says,
Come, rest here by my side.

Each of you, a bordered country,
Delicate and strangely made proud,
Yet thrusting perpetually under siege.
Your armed struggles for profit
Have left collars of waste upon my shore,
Currents of debris upon my breast.
Yet today I call you to my riverside,
If you will study war no more.
Come, clad in peace, and I will sing the songs
The Creator gave to me
When I and the tree and the rock were one.
Before cynicism was a bloody sear across your brow
And when you yet knew
You still knew nothing.
The river sang and sings on.

Maya Angelou   Poetry   United States   1993

with nation

But just to see a chapel like this room,
No bigger: there to watch Polish symbols loom
In warm expanding series which reveal
Once and for all the Poland that is real.
There the stone cutter, mason, carpenter,
Poet, and, finally, the knight and martyr
could re-create with pleasure, work and prayer.
There iron, bronze, red marble, copper could
Unite with native larches, stone with wood,
Because those symbols, burrowed by deep stains,
Run though us all as ores run through rock veins.

Cyprian Norwid   Poetry   Poland   1840

in balance

Every reform, however necessary, will by weak minds be carried to an excess, that itself will need reforming.

Samuel Taylor Coleridge   Romanticism   United Kingdom   1817

in revolution   in war   heart–will

And in just one day they did rise to the task, following no other voice or command but that of their unified spirit! Some today, others immediately thereafter, and then still others — all of them arguing the prime importance of enthusiasm — are proclaiming, with the fire that burns only when one is going to win, their determination to follow the personification of freedom and go to the war without hatred, thereby achieving an industrious and just Republic. In the presence of the flag that shelters within its folds the idea's master craftsman and the battle hero, these people are proclaiming their power of fusing heart and will in the determination to put into their lives all that has been vainly striving for peace, work and decency. They are not declaring war by wearing the frown of the conquistador, but with their arms held out to their brothers. Thus, from 12 years of silent and ceaseless effort, and purified by trials, the Cuban Revolutionary Party came into being.

José Marti   Revolution   Cuba   1892

leader–followers

Why is the sea king of a hundred streams?
Because it lies below them.
Therefore it is the king of a hundred streams.

If the sage would guide the people, he must serve with humility.
If he would lead them, he must follow behind.
In this way when the sage rules, the people will not feel oppressed;
When he stands before them, they will not be harmed.
The whole world will support him and will not tire of him.

Because he does not compete,
He does not meet competition.

Lao Tzu   Taoism   China   500 BCE

of freedom and harmony

Is liberty conceivable without perfect harmony? It soon turns into unavowed slavery: I become free by oppressing another. We can very quickly learn to avoid getting crushed, but it will need a new, unheard-of probation lasting unrelenting centuries before we lose the desire to crush others. . . . Mankind is now moving, not towards paradise, but towards the hardest, blackest and most burning of purgatories. The twilight of liberty is closing in. Assyria and Egypt will pale before a new, unprecedented bondage. But the galleys are an apprenticeship that will forerun freedom — a created freedom, impeccably equilibrated, in utmost harmony.

Ilya Ehrenburg   Journalism   Russia   1921

through internal persuasion

If government is merely external, the state may seem temporarily well ordered, but the hearts of men are not at peace. To govern according to my way of internal persuasion will bring the whole world into personal relations and so government will become unnecessary.

Lieh-tzu   Taoism   China   350 BCE

person–nation

Lay down your life in the interest of your land abnegating the little ego, and having thus loved the country, feel anything and the country will feel with you.

Sri Swami Sivananda   Yoga   India   1951

person–nation   micro–macro

Vladimir Mayakovsky, the greatest poet of the Revolution, wrote: "That's how it was with the soldiers, or perhaps with the country, or maybe that's how it was in my heart." This indivisibility of the macro world of ideas and the microworld of emotions, this merging of the interests of society with the individual's private interests, is reflected in our art not as mere declarations but as the norm in our way of life.

Vladimir Ognev   Poetry   Russia   1969

in sovereignty

Differences in ideology must not preclude unity. There are, and will be, socialists and non-socialists, democrats and non-democrats in Africa. Some of us may believe — indeed do believe — that others are compromising the future of Africa for the doubtful favour of imperialist powers; some will believe that others are using too short a spoon to sup with communists. Some Africans may believe that other leaders are exploiting their people; some of us may feel bitter hostility toward those who have seized power from the people's autocratic leaders. But whatever our feelings or private judgments, we have to accept the existing sovereignty of each African state. If the people of the state concerned acquiesce in the actions of their effective rulers, the rest of Africa does not have to rejoice; it merely cannot intervene. And it does have to accept that the country is still part of Africa. We have either to live with our neighbors or risk the whole future of a continent and its people. Our Brothers may be wrong, but they remain our brothers. This appears to be the only attitude open to us on our path to real unity.

Julius Nyerere   Nationalism   Tanzania   1965

in diversity

The only intelligible goal open to a nation proud of its human richness is that of unity in diversity.

J.W. Hanson   Christianity   United States   1981

ruler–ruled

In the happiness of his subjects lies the happiness of the king and in the good of his subjects his good. What is dear to himself does not constitute the good of the king; but what is dear to his subjects constitutes his good.

Kautilya   Economics   India   283 BCE

weakness–strength

Under heaven nothing is more soft and yielding than water.
Yet for attacking the solid and strong, nothing is better; it has no equal.
The weak can overcome the strong;
The supple can overcome the stiff.
Under heaven everyone knows this,
Yet no one puts it into practice.
Therefore the sage says:
He who takes upon himself the humiliation of the people is fit to rule them.
He who takes upon himself the country's disasters deserves to be king of the universe.
The truth often sounds paradoxical.

Lao Tzu   Taoism   China   500 BCE

with homeland

Isocrates argued powerfully for the importance of lineage and of having roots in the
land. Athens was great for many reasons, but its clearest title to distinction lay in this:
We did not become dwellers in this land by driving others out of it, nor by finding it
uninhabited, nor by coming together here a motley horde composed of many races;
but we are of a lineage so noble and so pure that throughout history we have continued
in possession of the very land that gave us birth.

Isocrates   Philosophy   Greece   338 BCE

person–epoch   with time

I've written everything the way I saw it,
The way I had imagined it, as best I could.
It pains me now that I've left out so much,
But I would need ten lifetimes at the very least
To paint in words the richness of our life,
And that which we have brought into the world
In this mid-century to take the place of old.
There's always something fabulous about the truth.
And I, I see the fabulous in everything:
In nature, and in the struggle, and in life itself.
And I am yours, my epoch, yours completely!

Vladimir Lugovskoy   Poetry   Russia   1957

in equality   in liberation

He is not well acquainted with our country if he overlooks the intimate harmony among Cubans of natural law, without history or books, and among Cubans who have put into their studies the passion they were unable to put into building their new country — that because of this unanimous and burning love of justice in those of one occupation and those of another; that due to this equally sincere human ardor of men who hold their necks erect because their heads are held high by natures and men whose necks are bent because fashion demands the display of a handsome back; because of this vehement country where those whom various states of culture might drive apart are drawn together by the same dreams and honesty — due to all this our Cuba, free in the harmony of equality, will tie down the colonial hand.

José Marti   Revolution   Cuba   1870

of self   in conflict

At the end of a talk someone from the audience asked the Dalai Lama, "Why didn't you fight back against the Chinese?"

The Dalai Lama looked down, swung his feet just a bit, then looked back up at us and said with a gentle smile, "Well, war is obsolete, you know." Then, after a few moments, his face grave, he said, "Of course the mind can rationalize fighting back, . . . but the heart, the heart would never understand. Then you would be divided in yourself, the heart and the mind, and the war would be inside you."

H.H. the 14th Dalai Lama   Tibetan Buddhism   Tibet   2001

in knowledge of others

Reverend Pinckney once said, "Across the South, we have a deep appreciation of history — we haven't always had a deep appreciation of each other's history." What is true in the South is true for America. Clem understood that justice grows out of recognition of ourselves in each other. That my liberty depends on you being free, too. That history can't be a sword to justify injustice, or a shield against progress, but must be a manual for how to avoid repeating the mistakes of the past — how to break the cycle. A roadway toward a better world. He knew that the path of grace involves an open mind — but, more importantly, an open heart.

Barack Obama   Politics   United States   2015

through different cultures

[The American Indians] have . . . a high poetry and art, which only a colonialist ideology could have blinded us into labeling "primitive" or "savage." You have also the great hidden accomplishment of our older brothers [Indians] in America, made clear in the poetry and yet of concern not only to poets but to all (red, white and black) who want to carry the possibilities of reality and personhood into any new worlds to come. The yearning to rediscover the Red Man is part of this. It acknowledges not only the cruelty of what's happened in this place (a negative matter of genocide and guilt) but leads as well to the realization that "we" in a larger sense will never be whole without a recovery of the "red power" that's been here from the beginning. The true integration must begin and end with a recognition of all such powers. That means a process of translation and of mutual completion. Not a brotherhood of lies this time but an affiliation based on what the older had known from the start: that we're doomed without his tribal and matrilocal wisdom, which can be shared only among equals who have recognized a common lineage from the Earth.

Jerome Rothenberg   Poetry   United States   1971

in the journey to world-perfection

The United Nations is the seed. World-union is the fruit. Both are of supreme importance. God-Vision embodies the seed. God-Reality reveals the fruit. . . .

The United Nations is a group of pilgrims on a journey. As the pilgrims walk along the path of light towards the same destination, they feel mutual appreciation. From appreciation they go one step ahead to love. Then from love they move to oneness. Oneness is the perfection of man in God and the satisfaction of God in man.

He who is a true member of the United Nations treasures a shared life in a shared world. A divided mind and a separated heart cannot quench the inner thirst of either the United Nations or the world. We must cultivate a new type of reality, a new type of truth. This truth is creative, illumining and fulfilling. This truth must awaken the dormant physical in us, marshal the unruly vital in us, illumine the doubtful and suspicious mind in us, and strengthen and immortalise the insecure heart in us. This truth is world-union. . . .

The United Nations and world-union have an evolutionary faith and a revolutionary life. This revolutionary life wants to challenge the untold poverty and teaming ignorance of the world. The golden day is bound to dawn when this world of ours will be totally freed from poverty. But the outer poverty can be transformed only when the inner poverty is removed. Inner poverty is our lack of faith in our divine reality, our lack of faith in our capacity to realise the ultimate Truth. Unless and until we have put an end to our inner poverty, the problem of outer poverty cannot be solved. . . .

Each nation has the strength and willpower of the Absolute. Each nation has the golden opportunity in the inner world to offer to the outer world a living hope and a living promise. This hope and this promise are not mental hallucinations or false aggrandisements of ego. They are an inner reality that the nation can easily bring to the fore. In the inner world all nations are equally important, for in the inner world each nation has a free access to world-peace, world-light, world-harmony and world-perfection. But in the outer life the nations that consciously aspire and cry for light are in a position to help the less advanced nations that are walking behind.

In the evolutionary process of human life, the first rung of the ladder is the United Nations, the second rung is world-union and the third rung is man's total and perfect Perfection. If we do not place our foot on the first rung and then on the second, it will be simply impossible for us to climb up to the highest rung.

Each nation is a promise of God for God Himself. What we call world-union today has to be surpassed tomorrow by something else, and that something else is world-perfection. Union as such is not enough; the perfection of union is what we actually want. We may stay in a family even though we quarrel, fight and kill one another. Only if we can establish the sweetest feeling of oneness, does our union reach the acme of perfection.

Sri Chinmoy   Yoga   India   1974

Humanity

person—humanity

I celebrate myself, and sing myself,
And what I assume you shall assume,
For every atom belonging to me as good belongs to you.

Walt Whitman   Mysticism   United States   1855

in the modern world

We have been seeded far and wide across the continents of the world. We listen to the same music as we drive to work in Hong Kong, London, Tokyo and New York. We cherish the same vision of peace and disarmament as we watch children play in the parks of Cape Town, Paris, Singapore and Rome. We dream the same dreams as evenings slide across Adelaide, Tel Aviv, Rio and Leningrad. We witness the same events from Mexico City, Los Angeles, Toronto and Berlin — even as they are occurring, broadcast live, we watch them. Together. We open our eyes in the deserts, in the mountains, in the forests, in the jungles and cities of every nation. We are today's people.

Ken Carey   Mysticism   United States   1988

in matter

All men are baked of the same dough.

Unknown   Proverb   Romania   Traditional

beyond race

Ashamed of my race? And of what race am I? I am many in one.

Joseph S. Cotter   Poetry   United States   1920

of humanity

There is only one caste — humanity.

Pampa   Jainism   India   950

in geometry

Once you see that the world is round, it's impossible to choose sides.

Wayne W. Dyer   Psychology   United States   1989

with humanity

My family is the world.

Maha Upanishad   Hinduism   India   Unknown

in truth

For those who love God-the-Truth with a real love, the inhabitants of the whole world are as real brothers.

Yunus Emre   Sufism   Turkey   1321

person–God   person–humanity

Swiftly arose and spread around me the peace and knowledge that pass all the
    argument of the earth,
And I know that the hand of God is the promise of my own,
And I know that the spirit of God is the brother of my own,
And that all the men ever born are also my brothers, and the women my sisters
    and lovers.

Walt Whitman   Mysticism   United States   1855

women's rights–human rights

Human rights are women's rights and women's rights are human rights. . . .

Hillary Clinton   Politics   United States   1995

struggle for human rights   through education

Malala day is not my day. Today is the day of every woman, every boy and every girl who have raised their voice for their rights. There are hundreds of human rights activists and social workers who are not only speaking for human rights, but who are struggling to achieve their goals of education, peace and equality. Thousands of people have been killed by the terrorists and millions have been injured. I am just one of them.

So here I stand . . . one girl among many.
I speak – not for myself, but for all girls and boys.
I raise up my voice – not so that I can shout, but so that those without a voice
    can be heard.
Those who have fought for their rights:
Their right to live in peace.
Their right to be treated with dignity.
Their right to equality of opportunity.
Their right to be educated. . . .

Dear brothers and sisters, we want schools and education for every child's bright future. We will continue our journey to our destination of peace and education for everyone. No one can stop us. We will speak for our rights and we will bring change through our voice. We must believe in the power and the strength of our words. Our words can change the world.

Because we are all together, united for the cause of education. And if we want to achieve our goal, then let us empower ourselves with the weapon of knowledge and let us shield ourselves with unity and togetherness.

Dear brothers and sisters, we must not forget that millions of people are suffering from poverty, injustice and ignorance. We must not forget that millions of children are out of schools. We must not forget that our sisters and brothers are waiting for a bright peaceful future.

So let us wage a global struggle against illiteracy, poverty and terrorism and let us pick up our books and pens. They are our most powerful weapons.

One child, one teacher, one pen and one book can change the world.

Education is the only solution. Education First.

Malala Yousafzai   Youth   Pakistan   2013

in international relations

WE THE PEOPLES OF THE UNITED NATIONS DETERMINED
* to save succeeding generations from the scourge of war, which twice in our lifetime
    has brought untold sorrow to mankind, and
* to regain faith in fundamental human rights, in the dignity and worth of the human
    person, in the equal rights of men and women and of nations large and small, and
* to establish conditions under which justice and respect for the obligations arising
    from treaties and other sources of international law can be maintained, and
* to promote social progress and better standards of life in larger freedom,
AND FOR THESE ENDS
* to practice tolerance and live together in peace with one another as good
    neighbours, and
* to unite our strength to maintain international peace and security, and
* to ensure, by the acceptance of principles and the institution of methods, that armed
    force shall not be used, save in the common interest, and
* to employ international machinery for the promotion of the economic and social
    advancement of all peoples,
HAVE RESOLVED TO COMBINE OUR EFFORTS TO ACCOMPLISH THESE AIMS
Accordingly, our respective Governments, through representatives assembled in the
city of San Francisco, who have exhibited their full powers found to be in good and due
form, have agreed to the present Charter of the United Nations and do hereby
establish an international organization to be known as the United Nations.

United Nations Charter Commission   International Relations   United Nations   1945

in the oneness of nations

The inner role of the United Nations helps us discover a unique prayer, the prayer of
prayers. At each moment, we have to pray not to conquer but to serve, and while
serving, to free the oneness-reality in and around the world. We have to pray not to
lead and again not merely to follow, but to become inseparably one with the comity of
nations. Together, all the nations will dive the deepest, march the farthest and fly the
highest.

Sri Chinmoy   Yoga   India   1993

in responsibility   in problems

As the twentieth century draws to a close, we find that the world has grown smaller and the world's people have become almost one community. Political and military alliances have created large multinational groups, industry and international trade have produced a global economy, and worldwide communications are eliminating ancient barriers of distance, language and race.

We are also being drawn together by the grave problems we face: overpopulation, dwindling natural resources, and an environmental crisis that threatens our air and water, along with the vast number of beautiful life forms that are the very foundation of existence on this small planet we share.

I believe that to meet the challenge of our times, human beings will have to develop a greater sense of universal responsibility. Each of us must learn to work not just for his or her own self, family or nation, but for the benefit of all. Universal responsibility is the key to human survival. It is the best foundation for world peace, the equitable use of natural resources and the proper care of the environment.

Whether we like it or not, we are all part of one great human family. Rich or poor, educated or uneducated, belonging to one nation or another, to one religion or another, adhering to this ideology or that — ultimately, each of us is just a human being like everyone else: we all desire happiness and do not want suffering. Furthermore, each of us has an equal right to pursue these goals.

Today's world requires that we accept the oneness of humanity.

H.H. the 14th Dalai Lama   Tibetan Buddhism   Tibet   1992

of humanity

Rabbi Meir said: "The dust from which the first man was made was gathered in all the corners of the world."

Unknown   Judaism   Israel   500

of humanity

God hath made of one blood all nations that dwell upon the face of the earth.

Saint Luke   Christianity   Palestine (Judea)   Traditional

person—humanity

I am because we are.

Unknown   Unknown   Malawi   Traditional

in humanity

Human beings, all, are as head, arms, trunk, and legs unto one another.

The Vedas   Hinduism   India   1500 BCE

of humanity

We should think of humanity as a body and of a nation as one of its limbs. Pain in a finger-tip affects the whole system. If there is disorder anywhere in the world, we cannot shrug it off. We must deal with it as if it had made itself felt in our midst. However distant an event, we must never forget this principle.

Kemal Pasha Atatürk   Nationalism   Turkey   1937

in stories   in mischief

Are the dreams of other men so different from those of Africans? The similarity between other people's stories and ours is such that it is difficult to speak of a black or a white soul. Souls are seen to be the same in their aspirations. The adventures of Tom Thumb resemble those of the young Soudanese Marandenboué; the tricks of the fox are like those of the hare; indiscretion is punished in the bee-woman of Borneo as in the yam-woman of the Ivory Coast; the bee and the toad of Senegal, and the fox and the stork of France play the same tricks on each other.

Bernard Dadíe   Literature   Ivory Coast   1950

in religion

[A good Minister] should get religion like a Methodist; experience it like a Baptist; be sure of it like a Disciple; stick to it like a Lutheran; pray for it like a Presbyterian; conciliate like a Congregationalist; glorify it like a Jew; be proud of it like an Episcopalian; practice it like a Christian Scientist; propagate it like a Roman Catholic; work for it like a Salvation Army lassie; enjoy it like a colored man.

Edgar Dewitt Jones   Christianity   United States   1916

of humanity

Those born of illustrious fathers we respect and honour, whereas those who come from an undistinguished house we neither respect nor honour. In this we behave like barbarians towards one another. For by nature we all equally, both barbarians and Greeks, have an entirely similar origin: for it is fitting to fulfill the natural satisfactions which are necessary to all men: all have the ability to fulfill these in the same way, and in all this none of us is different either as barbarian or as Greek; for we all breathe into the air with mouth and nostrils and we all eat with the hands.

Antiphon   Sophism   Greece   400 BCE

of time

The artist cannot get along without a public; and when the public is absent, what does he do? He invents it, and turning his back on his age, he looks toward the future for what the present denies.

André Gide   Moralism   France   1903

with the oppressed

I want you to understand, gentlemen, that I respect the rights of the poorest and weakest of the colored people, oppressed by the slave system, just as much as I do those of the most wealthy and powerful. That is the idea that has moved me, and that alone.

John Brown   Abolitionism   United States   1855

in response to injustice

I am cognizant of the interrelatedness of all communities and states. I cannot sit idly by in Atlanta and not be concerned about what happens in Birmingham. Injustice anywhere is a threat to justice everywhere. We are caught in an inescapable network of mutuality, tied in a single garment of destiny. Whatever affects one directly, affects all indirectly. Never again can we afford to live with the narrow, provincial "outside agitator" idea. Anyone who lives inside the United States can never be considered an outsider anywhere within its bounds.

Martin Luther King, Jr.   Social Justice   United States   1963

with life   with all humans

Each man carries the vestiges of his birth — the slime and eggshells of his primeval past — with him to the end of his days. Some never become human, remaining frog, lizard, ant. Some are human above the waist, fish below. . . . We all share the same origin, our mothers; all of us come in at the same door. But each of us — experiments of the depths — strives toward his own destiny. We can understand one another; but each of us is able to interpret himself to himself alone.

Hermann Hesse   Literature   Germany   1925

in freedom

Nature hath placed us in the world free and unbound; we imprison ourselves into certain straits, as the kings of Persia, who bound themselves never to drink other water than of the river Choaspez, foolishly renouncing all lawful right of use in all other waters, and for their regard dried up all the rest of the world. . . .

Michel de Montaigne   Skepticism   France   1580

nature–humans

I have no patience with people who say they love nature and go out to look at a field on Sunday afternoon. Our families, the way we live with our fellowmen, are a part of nature, too.

Thornton Wilder   Drama   United States   1920

in tai chi   with humanity   in movement

Tai Chi Song

Stance upon a knoll of grass under summer sun.
Motion coming — slow and soft, a flow of secrets hidden
in the body limbs — some will name "The Crane Spreads
Its Wings" a curve like that. Or Fibonacci's grace. What matters
not are names but planes descried by fingertips of you
or me that, look! identically descry the brow of line
hovering above the plains of Iraq, Afghanistan
and Israel, India, Pakistan, United States of America.

Who can see the beauty of body's motion,
then scan the planet and say there's no hope?

Ronald Jorgensen   Tai Chi   United States   2002

in happiness   with humanity

If only men would see each other as agents of each other's happiness, they could
occupy the earth, their common habitation, in peace, and move forward confidently
together to their common goal.

Abbe Siéyés   Politics   France   1799

in music

My real governing idea, the idea which has completely dominated me ever since I have
been a composer, is that of the brotherhood of all peoples, their brotherhood in the
face of, and against, all war or conflict of any kind. This is the idea which, to the
utmost of my strength, I try to serve through my work. It is for this reason that I do
not set my face against any influence, whether its source be Slovak, Romanian, Arab or
any other. All that matters is that the source shall be pure, fresh and healthy!

Bela Bartok   Music   Hungary   1931

in poetry

The messages of great poems to each man and woman are, Come to us on equal terms, only then can you understand us. We are no better than you, what we inclose you inclose, what we enjoy you may enjoy.

Walt Whitman   Mysticism   United States   1855

through poetry

The poet is the child of harmony; and he is given a part to play in world culture. His mission is three-fold; firstly, to free sounds from the original, primeval element wherein they are submerged; secondly, to imbue them with harmony and form; thirdly, to bring this harmony into the external world.

   The sounds, reft from the elements and transformed into harmony, themselves begin to work their effect when introduced into the world. "The poet's words are his deeds."

Alexander Blok   Poetry   Russia   1921

in goodness

Look for your good in the good of all.

Swami Dayananda Saraswati   Nationalism   India   1883

in opposition   in diversity   in balance

If all pulled in one direction the world would keel over.

Unknown   Judaism   Israel   Traditional

in being human

Africans believe in something that is difficult to render in English. We call it ubuntu, botho. It means the essence of being human. You know when it is there and when it is absent. It speaks about humaneness, gentleness, hospitality, putting yourself out on behalf of others, being vulnerable. It embraces compassion and toughness. It recognizes that my humanity is bound up in yours, for we can only be human together.

Desmond Tutu   Christianity   South Africa   1989

in education

He who receives an idea from me receives instructions himself without, lessening mine; as he lights his taper at mine, receives light without darkening me. That ideas should freely spread from one another over the globe, for the moral and mutual instruction of man, and improvement of his condition, seems to have been peculiarly and benevolently designed by nature, when she made them, like fire, expansible over all space, without lessening their density in any point; and like the air which we breathe, move, and have our physical being, incapable of confinement, or exclusive approbation.

Thomas Jefferson   Government   United States   1813

with humanity

I sought my soul — but my soul I could not see;
I sought my God — but my God eluded me;
I sought my brother and found all three.

Baba Amte   Social Work   India   1942

of humanity

Until you have become really, in actual fact, a brother to every one, brotherhood will not come to pass.

Fyodor Dostoyevsky   Literature   Russia   1880

with the unwanted

When we think of helping the world, of being brothers to all, we should remember that the world means also the unwanted who knock at our door at an inopportune moment, the people whom we may dislike for some reason, physical or mental, those whose appearance or ways may be disagreeable to our tastes, and those whom we might be ashamed of, if we were of that company.

N. Sri Ram   Theosophy   India   1973

with the oppressed

[Said at his sentencing for opposing war and supporting socialist reforms]

Your Honor, years ago I recognized my kinship with all living beings, and I made up my mind that I was not one bit better than the meanest on earth. I said then, and I say now, that while there is a lower class, I am in it. While there is a criminal class I am in it. While there is a soul in prison I am not free.

Eugene V. Debs   Socialism   United States   1918

in collectivity

We are members one of another.

Raynor C. Johnson   Metaphysics   United Kingdom   1963

person—world   crime—thought   in virtue   in thoughts

We cannot any longer say, as we are tempted to do, that our thoughts at least are our own, and affect none but ourselves, so while we should certainly be careful about our words and actions, it does not matter so much about our thoughts. As a matter of fact, our thoughts are even less our own than either our words or our actions; for they travel to far greater distances from us, and their influence is not only far more widely spread, but is stronger, for it works directly on the minds of others.

No crime is ever committed on earth that we may not have made a little easier to do, if we have cherished thoughts of enmity, hatred, or violence. But, on the other hand, no deed of virtue or heroism is ever done that we may not have helped to bring about by our thoughts of love to others. At all times, for we are always thinking, we are either increasing the virtue of the world, or else adding to the evil that is in it.

Lilian Edgar   Theosophy   New Zealand   1903

of humanity   in literature

It may be glorious to write
  Thoughts that shall glad the two or three
High souls, like those far stars that come in sight
  Once in a century;
But better far it is to speak
  One simple word, which now and then
Shall waken their free nature in the weak
  And friendless sons of men;
To write some earnest verse or line,
  Which, seeking not the praise of art,
Shall make a clearer faith and manhood shine
  In the untutored heart.

James Russell Lowell   Literature   United States   1848

beyond religion

As Muhammad hoped for the day when all who shared the common belief in God would exist together in peace he invited a visiting deputation of Christians, "Conduct service here in the mosque. It is a place consecrated to God."

Mohammed   Islam   Saudi Arabia   632

of forms of traditions

Fu-hsi, a Ch'an (Zen) Buddhist sage was discovered in the court wearing a monk's robe, a Taoist hat, and the shoes of a common laborer.

The emperor, seeing him, asked, "Is that a Buddhist costume you are wearing?"

Fu-hsi pointed to his Taoist hat.

The Emperor asked, "Are you a Taoist?"

Fu-hsi pointed to his laborer's shoes.

"Are you a common man?" asked the Emperor.

Fu-hsi pointed to his fine Buddhist robes.

Chang Chung-yuan   Taoism   China   1963

of humanity   beyond race   in nakedness

Ut omnes unum sint',
The point is obtuse, I think,
That all men may be one!
The black and white keys won
Into harmony to settle
A matter man has scuttled.
The division is not there.
If you look everywhere,
No man is black or white;
I may be black, but not quite:
My teeth are perhaps white, my skin somewhat dark,
Your skin somewhat white, your hair perhaps dark.
The trouble is in the mind,
It is not a matter of kind.
Creature comfort and security breed fear,
They cause the philosophy some hold dear.
Let everybody have them and man is naked;
The thinking and the psychology, too, will be naked.
And when everybody is naked, we shall all join
In a global dance forgetting the old facile motto.

Amu Djoleto   Poetry   Ghana   1971

with humanity

Your own,
        your private
                immortality
is not
    in station
            rank or birth:
your this, your that —
            what triviality —
it's in the future
            of your earth!
And since
        the earth began its spinning,
since man
        upon his feet first stood,
we see at last,
            the faint beginning
of universal
        brotherhood.
May every
        colour
            be invited,
to share
    the world's
            abundant good,
to come together,
            live united
as decent human beings should.

Nikolai Aseyev   Poetry   Russia   1963

in viewpoint   in heart

When someone said to Majnun, "Leila, your beloved, is not so beautiful as you think," he said, "My Leila must be seen with my eyes. If you wish to see how beautiful Leila is, you must borrow my eyes." Therefore if we wish to regard the object of devotion of whatever faith, of whatever community, of whatever people, we have to borrow their eyes, we have to borrow their heart.

Hazrat Inayat Khan   Sufism   India   1927

in conflict   in politics

Two thousand years ago, the proudest boast was "civis Romanus sum." Today, in the world of freedom, the proudest boast is "Ich bin ein Berliner." . . .

Freedom is indivisible, and when one man is enslaved, all are not free. When all are free, then we look — can look forward to that day when this city will be joined as one and this country and this great Continent of Europe in a peaceful and hopeful globe. When that day finally comes, as it will, the people of West Berlin can take sober satisfaction in the fact that they were in the front lines for almost two decades.

All — All free men, wherever they may live, are citizens of Berlin.

And, therefore, as a free man, I take pride in the words "Ich bin ein Berliner."

John F. Kennedy   Politics   United States   1963

in aspiration for the ideals of the United Nations

Inner flames signify aspiration. Aspiration illumines the undivine in us and fulfils the divine in us. Our doubting mind is the undivine in us. Our loving heart is the divine in us. The doubting mind unconsciously and consciously tries to destroy the whole world. The loving heart consciously and unreservedly creates a new world: a world of hope, a world of light, a world of delight.

Aspiration is the inner cry. Both God and man have this inner cry. With His inner Cry, God claims us. With our inner cry, we follow God. God's inner Cry is for our perfection, and our inner cry is for God's Satisfaction.

We, the members of the Meditation Group of the United Nations, are all inner flames. We are trying, with utmost humility and sincerity, to be of service to each member of the United Nations, to the dream of the United Nations, to the pristine purity of the United Nations. Our capacity may be limited, but our willingness and eagerness to be of service to each member, to each ideal of the United Nations, is most sincere.

Sri Chinmoy   Yoga   India   1976

through time

An everlasting Now reigns in nature, which hangs the same roses on our bushes which charmed the Roman and the Chaldean in their hanging gardens.

Ralph Waldo Emerson   Transcendentalism   United States   1870

in the crucifix   in sacrifice   the godhead–humanity

In tracing the symbolism of this Latin cross, or rather of the crucifix, back into the night of time, the investigators had expected to find the figure disappear, leaving behind what they supposed to be the earlier cross-emblem. As a matter of fact, exactly the reverse took place, and they were startled to find that eventually the cross drops away, leaving only the figure with uplifted arms. No longer is there any thought of pain or sorrow connected with that figure, though still it tells of sacrifice; rather is it now the symbol of the purest joy the world can hold — the joy of freely giving — for it typifies the Divine Man standing in space with arms upraised in blessing, casting abroad his gifts to all humanity, pouring forth freely of himself in all directions, descending into the "dense sea" of matter, to be cribbed, cabined and confined therein, in order that through the descent we may come into being.

C.W. Leadbeater   Theosophy   United Kingdom   1904

with God

"Who hates his neighbour has not the rights of a child." And not only has he no rights as a child, he has no "father."
God is not my father in particular, nor any man's father (horrible presumption and madness!), no, he is only my father in the sense of father of all and consequently only my father in so far as he is the father of all. When I hate someone or deny that God is his father — it is not he who loses, but me: for then I have no father.

Søren Kierkegaard   Existentialism   Denmark   1848

in the godhead

There is neither Jew nor Greek, there is neither bond nor free, there is neither male nor female; for ye are all one in Christ Jesus.

Saint Paul   Christianity   Palestine (Judea)   50

of humanity

Independence? That's middle class blasphemy. We are all dependent on one another, every soul of us on earth.

George Bernard Shaw   Drama   Ireland   1912

with humanity   in helping

There is a marvellous clearness, or as I may term it, an enlightening of man's judgement drawn from the commerce of men, and by frequenting abroad in the world; we are all so contrived and compact in ourselves, that our sight is made shorter by the length of our nose. When Socrates was demanded whence he was, he answered, not of Athens, but of the world; for he, who had his imagination more full and farther stretching, embraced all the world for his native city, and extended his acquaintance, his society, and affections to all mankind; and not as we do, that look no further than our feet. . . .

Michel de Montaigne   Skepticism   France   1580

through compassion

Compassion can be put into practice if one recognizes the fact that every human being is a member of humanity and the human family regardless of differences in religion, culture, color, and creed. Deep down, there is no difference.

H.H. the 14th Dalai Lama   Tibetan Buddhism   Tibet   1989

in helping

The Stoics say that there is so great an affinity and mutual relation between wise men that he who dineth in France feedeth his companion in Egypt; and if one of them do but hold up his finger, wherever it be, all the wise men dispersed upon the habitable land feel a kind of aid thereby.

Michel de Montaigne   Skepticism   France   1580

in the godhead   with humanity

But John rightly says that the Word dwelt among us in order to reveal to us another profound mystery, that is, that we were all in Christ and that through Him the common person of mankind came back to life.

Cyril of Alexandria   Christianity   Egypt (Rome)   444

in service

A call resounds throughout the realms,
   We wait, we long for thee!
The call is heard, the souls respond, echoing through eternity:
   Bind us to the breast of service.
   Purge us with the fire of affliction.
   Forge us to Thy Will!
And let us serve humankind, our hands in soil and grime!
   Let us go to render this. Oh how our hearts ache so!
Desirous of reunion, of innate association. Bring us close! they cry.

With ardor each piercing cry is heard
by the songbirds of these souls.
Yet how these songbirds languished,
   their pleas so long denied.

Weary they returned to wait, till time and space would merge.
   To take melodious flight on love's two wings . . .
      to the realm of Kings.
Where merged as one, with the One, their songs would coincide.
   Entwined beyond the realms of time
   as willing captives in His Love,
    within the Celestial Nest,
   their pleas were put to rest.

Cherlynn A. Rush   Bahá'í   United States   1988

in pity

Pity is the feeling which arrests the mind in the presence of
whatsoever is grave and constant in human sufferings and unites
it with the human sufferer.

James Joyce   Literature   Ireland   1916

in sorrow   in death

Buddha's favourite method of curing sorrow was to bring home to the mourner the fact that his or her case was but the case of all mankind. The story of Kisagotami, whom the Master sent in quest for five grains of mustard seed from a house where no one had ever died, when she came to him praying that he would call her dead child to life, is familiar to readers of Light of Asia. Kisagotami came back empty-handed because though everyone in the town was greatly moved by the sight of the dead babe in her arms and made haste to bring her the mustard seed she begged of them, when Kisagotami enquired if a parent or child or slave had died in the house every one said that the family history bore record of the death of some body or other. So she came back, having left the dead child in the woods, to Buddha who heard her story with the calm compassion which has come down to us in the many images of his face.

"My Sister! Thou hast found", the Master said, "searching for what none finds — that bitter balm I had to give thee. He thou lovedst slept dead on thy bosom yesterday: today thou know'st the whole wide world weeps with thy woe. The grief which all hearts share grows less for one. Lo! I would pour my blood if it could stay thy tears and win the secret of that curse which makes sweet love our anguish. . . . I seek that secret: bury thou thy child."

   Gautama Buddha   Buddhism   Nepal, India (Kapilavastu)   483 BCE

in death and life

Hey! You there, man of the future! Listen to what I say! Don't forget to remember me on that quiet summer evening. Look, I'm smiling at you, I'm smiling in you, I'm smiling through you. How can I be dead if I breathe in every quiver of your hand?

   Here I am! You think I don't exist? You think I've disappeared forever? Wait! The dead are singing in your body; dead souls are drowning in your nerves. Just listen! It's like bees buzzing in a hive or the hum of telegraph wires carrying news around the world. We were people too; we also laughed and cried. So look back at us!

   I want to warn you, not out of malice or envy, but only out of friendship — and fellow feeling, that you too will die. And you will come to us as an equal to equals and we shall fly on and on into unknown reaches of time and space!

   Abram Terts (Andrei Donatovich Sinyavsky)   Literature   Russia   1963

with liberty

Not a grave of the murder'd for freedom but grows seed for
  freedom in its turn to bear seed,
Which the winds carry afar, and re-sow, and the rains and the
  snows nourish.
Not a disembodied soul can the weapons of tyrants let loose,
But it stalks invisibly over the earth, whispering, counseling,
  cautioning.
Liberty, let others despair of you — I never despair of you.

Walt Whitman   Mysticism   United States   1855

of thought

As certainly as water falls in rain on the tops of mountains and runs down into valleys,
plains and pits, so does thought fall first on the best minds, and run down, from class
to class, until it reaches the masses, and works revolution.

Ralph Waldo Emerson   Transcendentalism   United States   1882

of humanity

I represent a party which does not yet exist: the Party of revolution, civilization. This
party will wake the twentieth century. There will issue from it first the United States of
Europa, then the United States of the World.

Victor Hugo   Romanticism   France   1885

in spirit

The spirit has no race, no nationality, no religion. It is outside all identifications. He
who is spiritual feels free to look at things from any point of view, and is committed to
nothing partial or exclusive.

N. Sri Ram   Theosophy   India   1973

in contrast

I think the world's future depends upon the emergence of men who combine within themselves the insight of the mystic and the practical concern of the reformer.

   Raynor C. Johnson   Metaphysics   United Kingdom   1963

in service

Humankind demonstrates two aspects:
   the singing of praise to God,
   and the doing of good works.

God is made known through praise,
And in good works
   the wonders of God can be seen.

In the praise of God
a person is like an angel.
But it is the doing of good works
that is the hallmark of humanity.

This completeness
makes humankind the fullest creation
   of God.

It is in praise and service
that the surprise of God is consummated.

   Hildegard of Bingen   Mysticism   Germany   1163

in heart

In every heart is hidden the myriad One.

   Sri Aurobindo   Yoga   India   1950

with enemies

Again I see it all noble
like a painting by Millais —
one day in the desolate battle field,
you had found an enemy's body, and
dug a grave while the sun was setting
and then put a cross before it.

To you who came across the rough ocean
a thousand miles away to a foreign land,
leaving everything lovely far behind,,
the enemy must have meant to be
what should be hated and burned up. . . .

For all, you said,
"I love North Koreans,
I only hate communism."
You buried the enemy's body
and prayed before a cross.

When you and the cross stood together
casting shadows in the bright sunset
no fight between the Free and Communists
was in your peaceful mind;
you were hearing the cathedral bell
ringing out far from your home.
Your prayer for the peace of the world
was beautiful as the early morning star.
"I love North Koreans,
I only hate Communism."

How many times I have muttered
to myself the words you said,
the warm tears trickling down,
thinking of you chanting "Hallelujah."

Yi Yong-Sang   Poetry   Korea   1950

of events   in war

The bomb that fell on Hiroshima fell on America too.
It fell on no city, no munition plants, no docks.
It erased no church, vaporized no public buildings,
  reduced no man to his atomic elements.
But it fell, it fell.
It burst. It shook the land.
God have mercy on our children.
God have mercy on America.

Hermann Hagedorn   History   United States   1950

of the world   in war

War is only a vast manifestation in dramatic style of the sham, hollow, mock conflicts which take place daily everywhere even in so-called times of peace. Every man contributes his bit to keep the carnage going, even those who seem to be staying aloof. We are all involved, all participating, willy-nilly. The earth is our creation and we must accept the fruits of our creation. As long as we refuse to think in terms of world good and world goods, of world order, world peace, we shall murder and betray one another. It can go on till the crack of doom, if we wish it to be thus. Nothing can bring about a new and better world but our own desire for it.

Henry Miller   Literature   United States   1941

of traditions

"Then I was standing on the highest mountain of them all, and round about beneath me was the whole hoop of the world. And while I stood there I saw more than I can tell and I understood more than I saw; for I was seeing in a sacred manner the shapes of all things in the spirit, and the shape of all shapes as they must live together like one being. And I saw that the sacred hoop of my people was one of many hoops that made one circle, wide as daylight and as starlight, and in the center grew one mighty flowering tree to shelter all the children of one mother and one father. And I saw that it was holy."

  Black Elk said that the mountain he stood upon in that vision was Harney Peak in the Black Hills. "But anywhere," he then added, "is the center of the world."

Black Elk   Native America   America (Sioux)   1872

with enemies

[The following is an extract from a letter received from an Austrian Jew now in the British Pioneer Corps . . . attached to a hospital receiving German wounded. He had been for nine months in the concentration camps of Dachau and Buchenwald [where] he had been hung by the wrists to a tree and nearly died of gangrene, Jews at that time not being allowed medical attention in concentration camps.]

This is being written in the solitude of a ward in which I am guarding wrecked soldiers from the Herrenvolk. It is so strange a situation that I can hardly describe what I am feeling. Loneliness is perhaps the only word for it. These are men who set out to conquer the world, and they and their kind have done unspeakable things to me and my kind, and I am supposed to hate them with all my strength, and would be right to do so according to recognized standards of human behavior. But I cannot hate, or is it that in the face of suffering hatred is silent? So it happens that the guard is turned into a nurse, and if a man, from losing too much blood, goes out of his mind and stammers incoherently, I have to talk him to sleep again. And it sometimes happens that men try to hold my hand when I have helped them. That makes me feel lonely.

Unknown   Judaism   Austria   1944

person–humanity   person–God

Our existence as embodied beings is purely momentary; what are a hundred years in eternity? But if we shatter the chains of egotism, and melt into the ocean of humanity, we share its dignity. To feel that we are something is to set up a barrier between God and ourselves; to cease to feel that we are something is to become one with God.

Mahatma Gandhi   Nationalism   India   1932

in murder

Brethren! If, indeed, the robbers cross you on the way,
And with a two-handed saw,
Carve you in pieces, limb by limb,
And you harbour for them hatred in your hearts,
Know, then, you are not worthy of me,
Nor of the message I come to give!

Gautama Buddha   Buddhism   Nepal, India (Kapilavastu)   483 BCE

with all

From all, one; and from one, all.

   Heraclitus of Ephesus   Philosophy   Greece   500 BCE

of cultures

The difference between black and white, between civilized and primitive, disappears when one talks to the inhabitants of the primeval forest about questions concerning our relations with ourselves, with other people, with the world and with eternity.

   Albert Schweitzer   Philosophy   Germany (France)   1900

in knowledge

Simple as it seems, it was a great discovery that the key of knowledge could turn both ways, that it could open, as well as lock, the door of power to the many.

   James Russell Lowell   Literature   United States   1870

through God

The image of God is found essentially and personally in all mankind. Each possesses it whole, entire and undivided, and all together not more than one alone. In this way we are all one, intimately united in our eternal image, which is the image of God and the source in us of all our life.

   Jan Van Ruysbroeck   Mysticism   Belgium   1321

in service

I always insist on people doing the work with us, and for us, and for the people. I never speak to them of money or ask for things from them. I just ask them to come and love the people, to give their hands to serve them and their hearts to love them. And when they come in touch with them, then their first impulse is to do something for them. And next time they come, they're already involved. When they have been for some time in Calcutta or in any other place, they feel that they are part of the people.

   Mother Theresa   Christianity   Macedonia, Albania   1976

in death   in decay

Moon shines while billions
of corpses rot
beneath earth's crust.
I who rise from them,
soon to join them — all.
Where does moon float?
In the waves of my brain.

Shinkichi Takahashi   Zen Buddhism   Japan   1970

in science   in knowledge

Ideally, the perfect ethnology should make a synthesis of all human activities, all
cultures, all periods.

Jacques Soustelle   Anthropology   France   1930

person–humanity   individuality–unity

The idea of the perfect unity of all can finally be realized, or incarnated, only through
the fullness of perfect individualities. Therefore the ultimate goal is inseparably
twofold: namely the highest development of every individuality, and every
individuality's fullest union with all.

Vladimir Soloyov   Philosophy   Russia   1870

humanity–God

The rights of Man are the Rights of God and to vindicate the one is to maintain the
other. We must be free in order to serve Him whose service is perfect freedom.

Wolfe Tone   Politics   Ireland   1791

in contradiction

To think ill of mankind, and not wish ill to them, is perhaps the highest wisdom and virtue.

William Hazlitt   Liberalism   United Kingdom   1823

in death

[by a child in Terezin concentration camp]
It All Depends on How You Look at It

Terezin is full of beauty
It's in your eyes now clear
And through the street the tramp
Of many marching feet I hear.

In the ghetto at Terezin,
It looks that way to me,
It's a square kilometer of earth
Cut off from the world that's free.

Death, after all, claims everyone,
You find it everywhere.
It catches up with even those
Who wear their noses in the air.

The whole, wide world is ruled
With a certain justice, so
That helps perhaps to sweeten
The poor man's pain and woe.

Miroslav Kosek   Childhood   Czech Republic   1943

of war   with nature

The war spirit is essentially one and indivisible, however it is expressed. We may denounce it as expressed in one form and take part in it when in another form. But as we vitalize it in one direction it becomes increasingly potent in all directions.

Theosophy does not condemn the war spirit lock, stock and barrel. Theosophy recognizes that the war spirit is an evolutionary stage. It has its work to do, and it will not disappear until its work is done. It will not disappear until the spirit of war ceases to exist altogether. It will not disappear, so far as human kingdom is concerned, until humanity has learned to transcend it, not only within its own kingdom, but no less in humanity's relations to all other kingdoms. So long as humanity, as a whole, is at war with the sub-human kingdoms of nature, so long is it fostering war within its own ranks.

G.S. Arundale   Theosophy   United Kingdom   1935

past—present   in poetry

The world is incomprehensible.
All right, let the world be incomprehensible!
Everything returns and is completed.
But to return is to be transformed.
Ages pass each other within ages.
The echo is mixed with the echo.
Now his poems are thousands of years old
Alien and therefore intimate with everyone.
Belonging to no one and therefore present in us all.
Like a servant in an ancient, half overgrown castle
This strangely costumed and nearly invisible man
Who shows us around in the echoing halls,
And whose voice finally cannot be distinguished
From the voices of Egyptian urns.

Werner Aspenstrom   Poetry   Sweden   1950

in transformation

If all who feel we are connected to each other, to nature, and to God join in a planetary Pentecost, we shall be transformed together in this lifetime. I believe in the peaceful Second coming as the solution to the world - not the exclusive Coming in which people will be destroyed, but the inclusive Coming in which God in the heart of everyone will gently rise and we shall all be changed.

Barbara Marx Hubbard   Futurism   United States   1990

of diversity

Critics seem often ill at ease in the bad company of this every-day world. . . . Were it not for the presence of the unwashed and the half-educated, the formless, queer and incomplete, the unreasonable and absurd, the infinite shapes of the delightful human tadpole, the horizon would not wear so wide a grin.

Frank Moore Colby   Literature   United States   1904

of humanity   through time

There is no difference between the man who appeared when the world was first created and the man who will be born at the end of everything; all alike bear the divine image . . . Thus the whole of nature, from the beginning right until the end, constitutes a single image of Him who is.

Bishop Gregory of Nyssa   Christianity   Turkey   394

evolution—opposites

A traveller new-discovering himself,
One made of Matter's world his starting-point,
He made of Nothingness his living-room
And Night a process of the eternal light
And death a spur towards immortality.
God wrapped his head from sight in Matter's cowl,
His consciousness dived into inconscient depths,
All-Knowledge seemed a huge dark Nescience;
Infinity wore a boundless zero's form.
His abysms of bliss became insensible deeps,
Eternity a blank spiritual Vast.
Annulling an original nullity
The Timeless took its ground in emptiness
And drew the figure of a universe,
That the spirit might adventure into Time
And wrestle with adamant Necessity
And the soul pursue a cosmic pilgrimage.
A spirit moved in black immensities
And built a Thought in ancient Nothingness;
A soul was lit in God's tremendous Void,
A secret labouring glow of nascent fire.
In Nihil's gulf his mighty Puissance wrought;
She swung her formless motion into shapes,
Made Matter the body of the Bodiless.
Infant and dim the eternal Mights awoke.
In inert Matter breathed a slumbering Life,
In a subconscient Life Mind lay asleep;
In waking Life it stretched its giant limbs
To shake from it the torpor of its drowse;
A senseless substance quivered into sense,
The world's heart commenced to beat, its eyes to see,
In the crowded dumb vibrations of a brain
Thought fumbled in a ring to find itself,
Discovered speech and fed the new-born Word
That bridged with spans of light the world's ignorance.
In waking Mind, the Thinker built his house.
A reasoning animal willed and planned and sought;
He stood erect among his brute compeers,
He built life new, measured the universe,
Opposed his fate and wrestled with unseen Powers,

Conquered and used the laws that rule the world,
And hoped to ride the heavens and reach the stars,
A master of his huge environment.
Now through Mind's windows stares the demigod
Hidden behind the curtains of man's soul:
He has seen the Unknown, looked on Truth's veilless face;
A ray has touched him from the eternal sun;
Motionless, voiceless in foreseeing depths,
He stands awake in Supernature's light
And sees a glory of arisen wings
And sees the vast descending might of God.

Sri Aurobindo   Yoga   India   1950

with humanity

Abou Ben Adhem (may his tribe increase!)
Awoke one night from a deep dream of peace,
And saw, within the moonlight in his room,
Making it rich, and like a lily in bloom,
An angel writing in a book of gold: —
Exceeding peace had made Ben Adhem bold,
And to the Presence in the room he said
"What writest thou?" — The vision raised its head,
And with a look made of all sweet accord,
Answered "The names of those who love the Lord."
"And is mine one?" said Abou. "Nay, not so,"
Replied the angel. Abou spoke more low,
But cheerly still, and said "I pray thee, then,
Write me as one that loves his fellow men."

The angel wrote, and vanished. The next night
It came again with a great wakening light,
And showed the names whom love of God had blessed,
And lo! Ben Adhem's name led all the rest.

James Henry Leigh Hunt   Poetry   United Kingdom   1838

East–West   in balance

The West needs to learn more detachment as perhaps the East needs to learn a little more attachment.

Raynor C. Johnson   Metaphysics   United Kingdom   1963

in love   beyond religion   beyond nation

He who savours the fragrance of love has no further need of religion or of nation. He who holds his own being to be of no account, can he distinguish between religions and sects?

Yunus Emre   Poetry   Turkey   1250

person–humanity

Our true nationality is mankind.

H.G. Wells   History   United Kingdom   1920

human unity   with the divine consciousness

Auroville's Charter

1. Auroville belongs to nobody in particular. Auroville belongs to humanity as a whole. But to live in Auroville, one must be a willing servitor of the Divine Consciousness.

2. Auroville will be the place of an unending education, of constant progress, and a youth that never ages.

3. Auroville wants to be the bridge between the past and the future. Taking advantage of all discoveries from without and from within, Auroville will boldly spring towards future realisations.

4. Auroville will be a site of material and spiritual researches for a living embodiment of an actual Human Unity.

The Mother   Yoga   France   1968

through respect   through change

If we understand the oneness of humankind, then we realize the differences are secondary. With an attitude of respect and concern for other people, we can experience an atmosphere of happiness. That way we can create real harmony, real brotherhood. Through your own experience, try to be patient. You can change your attitude. If you practice continuously, you can change. The human mind has such potential — learn to train it.

H.H. the 14th Dalai Lama   Tibetan Buddhism   Tibet   1989

in life

Hear, O Humankind, the prayer of my heart.

For are we not One, have we not one desire,
to heal our Mother Earth, and bind her wounds?
And still to be free as the spotted Eagle climbing
the laughing breath of our Father Sky,
to hear again from dark forests and flashing rivers
the varied ever-changing Song of Creation?

O Humankind, are we not all brothers and sisters?
are we not all grandchildren of the Great Mystery?
Do we not all want to love and be loved, to work
and play, to sing and dance together? . . .

O Humankind, life is the only treasure.
We are the custodians of it, it is our sacred trust.
Life is wondrous, awesome, and holy, a burning glory,
and its price is simply this: courage . . .
we must be brave enough to love.

Manitonquat   Native America   America (Wampanoag)   1973

Life

of knowledge   of science

The time cannot be too far distant when physical science, the science of the mind and the science of the soul will all be seen as parts of a yet greater science, the science of life.

Ian Gordon-Brown   Transpersonal Psychology   United States   1964

mineral, vegetable, animal and human

Consciousness claims the totality of the sensible universe as the indispensable realm of the me. The visible world is but man turned inside out that he may be revealed to himself. All that sensibly exists is but the mind's furniture. . . . Man reproduces in himself all mineral, all vegetable, and all animal forms. His is fixed as the rock, unstable as the water; hard as the iron, sensitive as the flower; indolent as the sloth, busy as the bee; blind as the bat, far-sighted as the eagle; venomous as the serpent, harmless as the dove. All the antagonisms of nature are united in his form.

Henry James, Sr.   Swedenborgianism   United States   1869

nature—center in life

Almost every great discovery of modern biology, every breakthrough to a new scale of size and time, reveals that life exists within life, and worlds exist within worlds. Every structure and process have shown themselves to be involved with the whole of life: from the digestion of food to the exchange of neuronal energies, to the patterns of insect communication, biological rhythms or bird migration. Whenever we have looked to a part for the sake of understanding the whole, we have eventually found that the part is a living component of the whole. In a universe without a visible center, biology presents a reality in which the existence of a center is everywhere implied.

Life inevitably is discovered to be composed of life. We always think we have finally isolated the mechanism (cell, chromosome, gene, DNA) only to find the mechanism is an organism.

Jacob Needleman   Philosophy   United States   1965

233

in genetics

. . . I learned in biology class that more bacteria live and work in one centimeter of my colon than the number of people who have ever existed in the world. That kind of information makes you think twice about who — or what — is actually in charge.

From that day on, I began to think of people not as the masters of space and time but as participants in a great cosmic chain of being, with a direct genetic link across species, both living and extinct, extending back nearly four billion years to the earliest single-celled organism on Earth.

Neil deGrasse Tyson   Physics   United States   2012

in life

What a pity that too, too seldom
in our lives is it given to us
to look upon the world without a screen,
as through an open window.

The fog disperses — what then?
For an instant you will see
that people resemble one another —
all clear and simple.

In that cosmic expanse,
born of fire,
there throbs an ocean of life,
and you — are a drop in it.

Mirtala Kadinalovska   Poetry   Russia   1972

in peace

It is only when there is a condition of peace in ourselves that the richness and beauty of life all around can flow into our hearts.

N. Sri Ram   Theosophy   India   1973

in life

Never think of any creature as mean. Never think of anyone as inferior to thee. Open the inner eye that beholdeth the Countenance of God and thou wilt see that in all creatures shineth the One Glory!

Dhul-Nun al-Misri   Sufism   Egypt   859

in orchestration

We are members of a vast cosmic orchestra, in which each living instrument is essential to the complementary and harmonious playing of the whole.

J. Allen Boone   Communication   United States   1954

in humanity   high—low

Where there are humans
you'll find flies,
and Buddhas.

Kobayashi Issa   Zen Buddhism   Japan   1827

person—whole

Thou shalt not separate thy being from Being and the rest, but merge the ocean in the drop, the drop within the ocean.
So shalt thou be in full accord with all that lives; bear love to men as though they were thy brother-pupils, disciples of one Teacher, the sons of one sweet mother.

Unknown   Buddhism   India   Traditional

life—God   inner—outer

Life is the external text, the burning bush by the edge of the path from which God speaks.

José Ortega y Gasset   Philosophy   Spain   1900

in life and death

Our life is made by the deaths of others. In dead matter insensible life remains, which, reunited to the stomachs of living beings, resumes life, both sensual and intellectual.

Leonardo da Vinci   Art   Italy   1519

with life

And when you crush an apple with your teeth, say to it in your heart,
"Your seeds shall live in my body,
And the buds of your tomorrow shall blossom in my heart,
And your fragrance shall be my breath,
And together we shall rejoice through all the seasons."

Kahlil Gibran   Mysticism   Lebanon   1923

through generations

There are some creatures that do not seem to die at all; they simply vanish totally into their own progeny. Single cells do this. The cell becomes two, then four, and so on, and after a while the last trace is gone. It cannot be seen as death; barring mutation, the descendants are simply the first cell, living all over again.

Lewis Thomas   Biology   United States   1974

with life

To be happy in this world, especially when youth is past, it is necessary to feel oneself not merely an isolated individual whose day will soon be over, but part of the stream of life flowing on from the first germ to the remote and unknown future.

Bertrand Russell   Mathematics   United Kingdom   1930

through love

No, the heart that has truly lov'd never forgets,
But as truly loves on to the close;
As the sunflower turns on her god, when he sets,
The same look which she turn'd when he rose.

Thomas Moore   Music   Ireland   1852

with your path

When hot and cold combine,
When greed and desire have faded out,
When all wanting melts like wax,
Then your road will be like glass, like smooth stone

Hamzah Pansuri   Poetry   Indonesia   1590

of life   through touch

Place your hands on the Earth Mother. Try to feel the natural life force surging within.
Embrace a tree until you can feel the life force within it. A tree is like a pipeline or
conductor bringing energy from the sky to the earth. The same life force energy surges
through all life. When you embrace someone and you feel good energy surging
between you, that is the same life force energy that is in the trees and the other
creatures.

Sun Bear and Wabun   Native America   America (Chippewa)   1980

with life

The noise of clapping of hands is never heard
From one of thy hands unaided by the other hand
The man athirst cries, 'Where is delicious water?'
Water too cries, 'Where is the water-drinker?'
This thirst in my soul is the attraction of the water
I am the water's and the water is mine.

Jalal ad-Din Rumi   Sufism   Tajikistan, Turkey (Persia)   1230

in life and Earth

Nothing originates in a spot where there is no sentient, vegetable and rational life; feathers grow upon birds and are changed every year; hairs grow upon animals and are changed every year, except some parts, like the hairs of the beard of lions, cats, and their like. The grass grows in the fields, and the leaves on the trees, and every year they are, in great part, renewed. So that we might say that the earth has a spirit of growth; that its flesh is the soil, its bones the arrangement and connections of the rocks of which the mountains are composed, its cartilage the tufa, and its blood the springs of water. The pool of blood which lies round the heart is the ocean, and its breathing, and the increase and decrease of the blood in the pulses, is represented in the earth by the ebb of the sea; and the heat of the spirit of the world is the fire which pervades the earth, and the seat of the vegetative soul is the fire, which in many parts of the earth find vent in baths and mines of sulpher, and in volcanoes, as at Mount Etna in Sicily, and in many other places.

Leonardo da Vinci   Art   Italy   1519

life–nature

The young science of Ecology has been built up since Darwin's time and is based on the recognition of this fact, that in addition to the operation of Natural Selection, the environment has a silent, assimilative, transformative influence of a very profound and enduring character on all organic life. In the subtle ways of Nature, sun and earth, night and day, and all the things of earth and air and sun mingle silently with life, sink into it and become part of its structure. And in response to this profound stimulus, life grows and evolves, the less whole in harmony with the greater whole of Nature.

Jan C. Smuts   Science   South Africa   1926

through yoga

The man whose self is in yoga, sees the self in all beings and
all beings in the self, he is equal-visioned everywhere.

Unknown   Yoga   India   600 BCE

humanity—life

Humanity finds itself in the midst
of the world.

In the midst of all other creatures
humanity is the most significant
and yet the most dependent upon
the others.

Humanity is small in stature,
but powerful in strength of soul.

With head directed upward,
with feet on firm ground,
humanity can set all things in motion,
   things above as well as
   things below.

   Hildegard of Bingen   Mysticism   Germany   1163

of life

The tendency to unite, the attraction of atom to atom, molecule to molecule or cell to
cell is the universal property of all life.

   Pierre Teilhard de Chardin   Christianity   France   1955

in altruism

Various arguments have been presented to indicate that voluntarism is built directly
into the fabric of social life. Scientist Warren Weaver for example points to the
widespread presence of cooperative behavior among animal species and observes that
"altruistic behavior is an invention of nature herself." And physician Lewis Thomas
arguing from a sociobiological position claims "a biological mandate for each of us to
do whatever we can to keep the rest of the species alive." "Altruism," writes Thomas,
"in its biological sense is required of us".

   Jon Van Til   Sociology   United States   1988

in pregnancy

In pregnancy, one is unusually aware of individuality — one's own, one's husband's, one's baby's — and of the way individuality is inextricably grounded in particular, unalterable time; time, which can so often seem like a great, undifferentiating river on which one is helplessly adrift, becomes instead a very local force in league with individual life. Yet pregnancy is also a state in which one feels a part of the grand, timeless, archetypal forces of nature. So during pregnancy one senses a profound harmony with the universe, an interchange between the grand and the particular which endows every detail of life with a new vividness and meaning.

Unknown   Popular Culture   United States   1980

with life   with humanity

My mission is not merely brotherhood of Indian humanity. . . . But through realization of freedom of India I hope to realize and carry on the mission of the brotherhood of man. I want, if I don't give you a shock, to realize identity with even the crawling things upon earth, because we claim descent from the same God, and that being so, all life in whatever form it appears must be essentially one.

Mahatma Gandhi   Nationalism   India   1929

with animals   in death

For the fate of the sons of men and the fate of the beasts is the same; as one dies, so dies the other. They all have the same breath, and man has no advantage over the beasts; for all is vanity. All go to one place; all are from the dust, and all turn to dust again. Who knows whether the spirit of man goes upward and the spirit of the beast goes down to the earth?

Unknown   Judaism   Israel   200 BCE

with beauty

I find, under the boughs of love and hate,
In all poor foolish things that live a day,
Eternal beauty wandering on her way.

William Butler Yeats   Poetry   Ireland   1900

with Martians

Yes we are stardust. But we may not be of this Earth. Several separate lines of research, when considered together, have forced investigators to reassess who we think we are and where we think we came from.

First, computer simulations show that when a large asteroid strikes a planet, the surrounding areas can recoil from the impact energy, catapulting rocks into space. From there they can travel to — and land on — other planetary surfaces. Second, microorganisms can be hardy. Some survive the extremes of temperature, pressure, and radiation inherent in space travel. If the rocky flotsam from an impact hails from a planet with life, microscopic fauna could have stowed away in the rocks' nooks and crannies. Third, recent evidence suggests that shortly after the formation of our solar system, Mars was wet, and perhaps fertile, even before Earth was.

Those findings mean it's conceivable that life began on Mars and later seeded life on Earth, a process known as panspermia. So all earthlings might — just might — be descendants of Martians.

Neil deGrasse Tyson   Physics   United States   2012

of time   in evolution

The sensible organism is only a point, a sort of transit station which stands for an infinite past of development, for the history and experience of untold millions of ancestors, and in a vague, indefinite way, for the future which will include an indefinite number of descendants. The past, the present, the future all meet in that little structural center, that little way-side station on the infinite trail of life. But they only meet there, without its being able to contain them all. From that center radiates off a field of ever decreasing intensity of structure or force, which represents what has endured of that past, and what is vaguely anticipated of the future. The organism and its field is one continuous structure which, beginning with an articulated sensible central area, gradually shades off into indefiniteness. In this continuum is contained all of the past which has been conserved and still operates to influence the present and the future of the organism; in it also is contained all that the organism is and does in the present; and finally, in it is contained all that the organism vaguely points to in its own future development and that of its offspring. In other words, the organism and its field, or the organism as a "whole" — the holistic organism — contain its past and much of its future in its present. These elements are in it as active factors, the future and the past interacting with the present. The whole is there, carrying all its time with it, but clear and definite only for a small central area, and beyond that more and more fading away in respect of the dim past and the dimmer future.

Jan C. Smuts   Science   South Africa   1926

of phenomena and cosmos

The tree and its process would not be what they are, could not indeed exist, if it were a separate existence; forms are what they are by the force of the cosmic existence, they develop as they do as a result of their relation to it and to all its other manifestations. The separate law of their nature is only an application of the universal law and truth of all Nature; their particular development is determined by their place in the general development. The tree does not explain the seed, nor the seed the tree; cosmos explains both and God explains cosmos. The Supermind, pervading and inhabiting at once the seed and the tree and all objects, lives in this greater knowledge which is indivisible and one though with a modified and not an absolute indivisibility and unity. In this comprehensive knowledge there is no independent centre of existence, no individual separated ego such as we see in ourselves; the whole of existence is to its self-awareness an equable extension, one in oneness, one in multiplicity, one in all conditions and everywhere. Here the All and the One are the same existence; the individual being does not and cannot lose the consciousness of its identity with all beings and with the One Being; for that identity is inherent in supramental cognition, a part of the supramental self-evidence.

Sri Aurobindo   Yoga   India   1940

in natural action

The breeze from the pine woods blows my sash;
The mountain moon shines upon my harp.
You ask me to explain the reason of failure or success.
The fisherman's song goes deep into the river.

Wang Wei   Taoism   China   700

bliss

Now may every living thing, feeble or strong, omitting none, or tall or middle-sized or short, subtle or gross of form, seen or unseen, those dwelling near or far away, — whether they be born or yet unborn — may every living thing be full of bliss.

Gautama Buddha   Buddhism   Nepal, India (Kapilavastu)   483 BCE

Earth

in discovery

The world cannot be discovered by a long journey of miles, no matter how long, but only by a spiritual journey of one inch, very arduous and humbling and joyful, by which we arrive at the ground of our feet, and learn to be at home.

Wendell Berry   Agriculture   United States

with nature

Today we tend to see the earth as a stable backdrop for all of the affairs of humankind. We see the minerals, the plants and the animals as servants of man. We have forgotten that they can be our teachers as well; that they can open us to ideas and emotions that have been blocked from the human heart for too long a time.

We have forgotten that we are all connected to all of our relations on the earth, not just our human family. We have forgotten that we have responsibilities to all these relations, just as we have them to our human families. We have imprisoned ourselves in tight little worlds of man-made creations.

We have forgotten how to hear the stories and songs that the winds can bring us. We have forgotten to listen to the wisdom of the rocks that have been here since the beginning of time. We have forgotten how the water refreshes and renews us.

We have lost the ability to listen to the plants as they tell us which ones of them we should eat to live well. We have lost the ability to listen to the animals as they give us their gifts of learning, laughter, love and food. We have cut ourselves off from all these relations, and then we wonder how we can so often be bored and lonely.

Sun Bear and Wabun   Native America   America (Chippewa)   1980

with the world

O world, I cannot hold thee close enough!

Edna St. Vincent Millay   Poetry   United States   1917

nations—world

My country is the world.

Thomas Paine   Nationalism   United Kingdom, United States   1792

of countries

It is not for him to pride himself who loveth his own country, but rather for him who loveth the whole world. The earth is but one country, and mankind its citizens.

Bahá'u'lláh   Bahá'í   Iran (Persia)   1892

in the politics of ecology

We stand at a critical moment in Earth's history, a time when humanity must choose its future. As the world becomes increasingly interdependent and fragile, the future at once holds great peril and great promise. To move forward we must recognize that in the midst of a magnificent diversity of cultures and life forms we are one human family and one Earth community with a common destiny. We must join together to bring forth a sustainable global society founded on respect for nature, universal human rights, economic justice, and a culture of peace. Towards this end, it is imperative that we, the peoples of the Earth, declare our responsibility to one another, to the greater community of life, and to future generations.

The Earth Charter Commission   Ecology   United Nations   2000

of the cosmos of the Earth

There is only one heaven, one earth, the wheat belongs to all, and the water also.

Avvakum Petrov   Christianity   Russia   1682

with land

Sell a country! Why not sell the air, the clouds and the great sea, as well as the earth? Did not the Great Spirit make them all for the use of his children?

Tecumseh   Native America   America (Shawnee)   1790

with nature

In times past, our Native people had a very strong contact with the natural forces. When we would make prayers for rain, the rain would come. When we were hungry, we held a buffalo dance and sang to the buffalo, and they heard our songs and came. It's possible to re-establish that relationship, but people must stop and put aside their haughty ways and learn to seek harmony with the rest of Creation. They must seek to blend with nature rather than to conquer her. When a person is a true seeker, the universe will open up to him or her.

Sun Bear and Wabun   Native America   America (Chippewa)   1980

day and night

That hour of the day when, face to face, the rising moon beholds the setting sun.

Henry Wadsworth Longfellow   Poetry   United States   1839

of nature

The sun is coming down to earth, and the fields and the waters shout to him golden shouts.

George Meredith   Romanticism   United Kingdom   1859

sky–soul

The world stands out on either side
No wider than the heart is wide;
Above the world is stretched the sky,
No higher than the soul is high.

Edna St. Vincent Millay   Poetry   United States   1917

in nature

Is there a great green commonwealth of Thought
Which ranks the yearly pageant, and decides
How Summer's royal progress shall be wrought
By secret stir which in each plant abides?

John Masefield   Naturalism   United Kingdom   1913

in nature   in seasons

Why should flowers mind
   what the wind is trying?
They know well they will fall
   when the time comes, not forced.

No trees have flowers anymore,
   leaves alone are left,
Yet the wind still insists —
   unsatisfied with what?

Flowers do not seem, while leaving,
   to blame anybody for a cause,
Instead, they are dancing joyfully,
   fluttering in the air.

Kim Ŏk   Poetry   Korea   1929

in death and life   in nature

Earth knows no desolation,
She smells regeneration
In the moist breath of decay.

George Meredith   Romanticism   United Kingdom   1850

in day and night

What death more wonderful
Than day's in winter?
All the cold west burns,
Burns to be near its insatiable lover,
The dark.

     Mark Van Doren   Poetry   United States   1935

of time

'T is always morning somewhere in the world.

     Richard Hengist Horne   Poetry   United Kingdom   1820

of Earth   through oceans

How can they feel
The exhilaration of tall brown spray
Reaching high to the bare cliff edge,
Bringing the kiss of a distant shore
To touch the cheek in gentle salutation?

     Ellis Ayitey Komey   Poetry   Ghana   1964

micro–macro

I still believe that I shall return to life,
shall wake early one day, at dawn
in the light, early hours, in the transparent dew,
where the branches are studded with drops,
and a small lake stands in the sundew's bowl
reflecting the swift flight of the clouds.
And, inclining, my young face, I shall gaze
at a drop of water as on a miracle,
and tears of rapture will flow, and the world,
the whole world will be seen, wide and far.

     Olga Bergholz   Poetry   Russia   1949

in nature

mountain's morning cloud
caresses cedar's crown

a

dew

drop

drops

and is the sea

William Leon   Geography   United States   1996

in contrast

The land is dearer for the sea,
The ocean for the shore.

Lucy Larcom   Poetry   United States   1875

of beauty

Then in the sunset's flush they went aloft,
And unbent sails in that most lovely hour,
When the light gentles and the wind is soft,
And beauty in the heart breaks like a flower.

John Masefield   Naturalism   United Kingdom   1913

in sound

Today, however the satellites and microwave transmitters make it possible for all
cultures to hear one another simultaneously. The planet earth is truly an amplified
sound sphere.

Willard Von DeBogart   Science   The Netherlands   1976

with sound   with nature

She shall lean her ear
In many a secret place
Where rivulets dance their wayward round,
And beauty born of murmuring sound
Shall pass into her face.

William Wordsworth   Mysticism   United Kingdom   1800

with all

I am the wind which blows over the sea,
I am the wave of the sea,
I am lowing of the sea,
I am the bull of seven battles,
I am bird of prey on the cliff-face,
I am sunbeam,
I am skillful sailor,
I am a cruel boar,
I am lake in the valley,
I am word of knowledge,
I am a sharp sword threatening an army,
I am the god which gives fire to the head,
I am he who casts light between the mountains,
I am he who foretells ages of the moon,
I am he who teaches where the sun sets.

Áed Ua Crimthainn   Mythology   Ireland   1160

in ecology

The creative intensified Field of Nature, consisting of all physical organic and personal wholes in their close interactions and mutual influences, is itself of an organic or holistic character. That Field is the source of the grand Ecology of the universe. It is the environment, the Society — vital, friendly, educative, creative — of all wholes and souls. It is not a mere figure of speech or figment of imagination, but a reality with profound influence of its own on all wholes and their destiny.

Jan C. Smuts   Science   South Africa   1926

in decay

When I die, I want to be buried, not cremated. Whenever you burn organic matter, including human corpses, the chemical energy content of the body's quadrillion cells converts entirely into heat energy, which raises the atmospheric temperature near the crematorium, and eventually radiates back into space. When deposited into the universe, this low energy thermal radiation increases cosmic entropy and is largely unrecoverable to perform any other further work.

I owe Earth (and the universe) much more than this. For my entire omnivorous life I have eaten of its flora and feasted on its fauna. Countless plants and animals have sacrificed their lives and unwillingly donated their energy content to my sustenance. The least I can do is donate my body back to this third rock from the Sun. I want to be buried, just like in the old days, where I decomposed by the action of microorganisms, and I am dined upon by any form of creeping animal or root system that sees fit to do so. I would become their food, just as they had been food for me. I will have recycled back to the universe at least some of the energy that I have taken from it. And in doing so, at the conclusion of my scientific adventures, I will have come closer to the heavens than to Earth.

Neil deGrasse Tyson   Physics   United States   2004

pollution–resources

Pollution is nothing but resources we're not harvesting. We allow them to disperse because we've been ignorant of their value. But if we got onto a planning basis, the government could trap pollutants in the stacks and spillages and get back more money than this would cost out of the stockpiled chemistries they'd be collecting.

Buckminster Fuller   Geometry   United States   1971

with nature

When I came to life,
my creator fashioned me
from the fruit of fruits
from the fruit of the primordial god
from the primroses and the hill-flowers
from the flowers of trees and bushes
from the earth and its terrestrial course.
I have been shaped
from the flowers of the nettle
from the water of the ninth wave.

Taliesin   Mythology   United Kingdom   599

in running

While running from one country to another in this Peace Run, we are transcending our capacities and at the same time, we are inviting the whole world to feel the supreme importance of oneness.

Sri Chinmoy   Yoga   India   2011

God—world

And if you would know God, be not therefore a solver of riddles.
Rather look about you and you shall see Him playing with your children.
And look into space; you shall see Him walking in the cloud, outstretching His arms in the lightning and descending in rain.
You shall see Him smiling in flowers, then rising and waving His hands in trees.

Kahlil Gibran   Mysticism   Lebanon   1923

in mind

To the dull mind all nature is leaden. To the illumined mind the whole world burns and sparkles with light.

Ralph Waldo Emerson   Transcendentalism   United States   1882

in stillness

The water is still,
I wait and my friend comes.
In the sky the fish swim,
In the water the birds fly —
And I sit on a rock.

Unknown Child   Poetry   United States   1979

with nature

And one lone watcher draws in all he sees,
half-waking vision of tranquility
impresses itself on the retina of his inner eye
so that he feels time will not dim the details
or the rough thumb of death erase the scene.

Then a soft murmuring moves toward him
across the vast face of the continent,
until around him the leaves of ancient trees
that lean out over the starlit river
whisper with the faint voice of the night breeze.

Ian Mudie   Poetry   Australia   1975

micro—macro

I have been trying to think of the earth as a kind of organism, but it is no go. I cannot think of it this way. It is too big, too complex, with too many working parts lacking visible connections. The other night, driving through a hilly, wooded part of southern New England, I wondered about this. If not like an organism, what is it like, what is it most like? Then, satisfactorily for that moment, it came to me: it is most like a single cell.

Lewis Thomas   Biology   United States   1974

micro–macro

In a single handful of fertile soil, there are as many living micro-organisms as there are people on the planet. The Earth's soil is alive.

Unknown   Organic Gardening   Canada   1993

with nature

Beside the house in the damp rich earth I played
I gently thrust my hands into the Earth
And we are intimate friends.

Brooke Medicine Eagle Edwards   Native America   America (Sioux, Nez Perce)   1970

humanity–Earth

Your Mother is in you, and you in her. . . .
    The blood which runs in us is born of the blood of our Earthly Mother. Her blood falls from the clouds; leaps up from the womb of the earth; babbles in the brooks of the mountains. . . .
    The air which we breathe is born of the breath of our Earthly Mother. Her breath is azure in the heights of the heavens; soughs in the tops of the mountains; whispers in the leaves of the forest. . . .
    The hardness of our bones is born of the bones of our Earthly Mother, of the rocks and of the stones. They stand naked to the heavens on the tops of the mountains . . . and are hidden in the deepness of the earth.
    The tenderness of our flesh is born of the flesh of our Earthly Mother; whose flesh waxes yellow and red in the fruits of the trees, and nurtures us in the furrows of the fields. Our bowels are born of the bowels of our Earthly Mother, and are hid from our eyes, like the invisible depths of the earth. . . .
    The light of our eyes, the hearing of our ears, both are born of the colours and the sounds of our Earthly Mother; which encloses us about, as the waves of the sea a fish, as the eddying air a bird. . . .
    Man is the son of the Earthly Mother, and from her did the Son of Man receive his whole body, even as the body of the newborn babe is born of the womb of his mother. I tell you truly, you are one with the Earthly Mother; she is in you, and you in her.

Jesus Christ   Christianity   Palestine (Judea)   33

with things

The moon's the same old moon,
The flowers exactly as they were,
Yet I've become the thingness
Of all the things I see!

    Bunan   Zen Buddhism   Japan   1676

in death and life   ancestors and nature

Listen to Things
More often than Beings,
Hear the voice of fire,
Hear the voice of water.
Listen in the wind,
To the sighs of the bush;
This is the ancestors breathing.

Those who are dead are not ever gone;
They are in the darkness that grows lighter
And in the darkness that grows darker.
The dead are not down in the earth;
They are in the trembling of the trees,
In the groaning of the woods,
In the water that runs,
In the water that sleeps,
They are in the hut, they are in the crowd:
The dead are not dead.

. . .

Spirits inhabit
The darkness that lightens, the darkness that darkens,
The quivering tree, the murmuring wood,
The water that runs and the water that sleeps:
Spirits much stronger than we,
The breathing of the dead who are not really dead,
Of the dead who are not really gone,
Of the dead now no more in the earth.

    Birago Diop   Poetry   Senegal   1930

with the godhead

Cleave a piece of wood, I am there; lift up the stone and you will find me there.

Jesus Christ   Christianity   Palestine (Judea)   33

with land

No house should ever be *on* a hill or *on* anything. It should be *of* the hill. Belonging to it. Hill and house could live together each the happier for the other.

Frank Lloyd Wright   Architecture   United States   1914

among nations

The same sun is newly born in new lands, in a ring of endless dawns.

Rabindranath Tagore   Poetry   India   1931

with nature

Oh our Mother the Earth oh our Father the Sky
Your children are we
   with tired backs we bring you the gifts you love

So weave for us a garment of brightness

May the warp be the white light of the morning
May the weft be the red light of evening
May the fringes be the falling rain
May the border be the standing rainbow

Weave for us this bright garment
that we may walk where birds sing
   where grass is green

Oh our Mother the Earth oh our Father the Sky

Unknown   Native America   America (Tewa)   Traditional

in marveling at the Earth

If the Earth
were only a few feet in diameter,
floating a few feet above a field somewhere,
people would come from everywhere to marvel
at it. People would walk around it marveling at its
big pools of water, its little pools and the water flowing
between. People would marvel at the bumps on it and the
holes in it. They would marvel at the very thin layer of gas
surrounding it and the water suspended in the gas. The people
would marvel at all the creatures walking around the surface of
the ball and at the creatures in the water. The people would
declare it as sacred because it was the only one, and they would
protect it so that it would not be hurt. The ball would be the
greatest wonder known, and people would come to pray to
it, to be healed, to gain knowledge, to know beauty and to
wonder how it could be. People would love it and defend
it with their lives because they would somehow
know that their lives would be nothing
without it. If the Earth were only
a few feet in diameter.

Joe Miller   Art   United States   1975

in nature

My heart is joyful,
My heart flies away, singing,
Under the trees of the forest,
Forest our home and our mother,
In my net I have caught
A little bird.
My heart is caught in the net, in the net with the bird

Unknown   Pygmy Poetry   Congo (Efe Pygmy)   Traditional

in light

I, Djanggawul, look back; and see the rays of light leading back to our island of Bralgu
Shine that falls on the paddle as it's dipped into and drawn from the sea:
Shine that spreads from the star's rays, from Bralgu.
The Morning Star skimming the sea's surface, sent by the dancing spirits there,
Shine following us from Bralgu, like a feathered ball with string attached.
Foam and bubbles rise to the sea's surface: a large wave carries us on its crest.
The roar of the sea, the sound of our paddling, the spray of the waves, its salty smell!
We carry with us the sacred mat within which lie the sacred rangga objects.

    Unknown   Wulamba Mythology   Australia (Wulamba Tribe)   Traditional

with nature

let this water
this sea
seep into me own me
and break my face into its moods
break my chest
break my heart into its fathoms where no hands reach
let the salt of the sea
settle down like a dove comes home into the wounds
that this earth made in my bosom
ah
let this water, this sea
these waves
these colors
this movement
this wide deep blue solid reality break me down
like it has rocks
let me seep into africa
africa

    Mongane (Wally Serote)   Poetry   South Africa   1970

change—loss—delight

Loss is nothing else but change, and change is Nature's delight.

  Marcus Aurelius   Stoicism   Italy   180

with Earth   in connections

This we know: The Earth does not belong to man, man belongs to the Earth. All things are connected like the blood, which unites one family. Man did not weave the web of life: he is merely a strand in it. Whatever he does to the web he does to himself.

  Chief Seattle   Native America   America (Suquamish)   1866

with nature

Because of the powerful love, I have become an integral part of my environment, bird, animal, forest, desert, rock, water — everything, everywhere, at one time. I am linked indivisibly with all of them. In this way I have come to know that separateness is the enemy of true religion.

  William Rickels   Religion   Australia   1981

with nature

The great sea
Has set me adrift
It moves me as the weed in a great river,
Earth and the great weather
Move me,
Have carried me away
And move my inward parts of joy.

  Uvavnuk   Mysticism   Canada (Inuit)   1900

above—below

My eyes in the sun-swimming clouds,
I soar toward heights I can never reach,
Nor see that I am crushing loveliness
Beneath my wingless feet.

Gloria Goddard   Aestheticism   United States   1910

from a lunar perspective

You develop an instant global consciousness, a people orientation, an intense dissatisfaction with the state of the world, and a compulsion to do something about it. From out there on the moon, international politics look so petty. You want to grab a politician by the scruff of the neck and drag him a quarter of a million miles out and say, "Look at that!"

Edgar Mitchell   Astronautics   United States   1974

with the Earth   from space

BUT UP THERE you go around every hour and a half, time after time after time. You wake up usually in the mornings, over the Middle East and over North Africa. As you eat breakfast you look out the window and there's the Mediterranean area, Greece and Rome and North Africa and the Sinai, that whole area. And you realize that in one glance what you're seeing is what was the whole history of humankind for years - the cradle of civilization. And you go down across North Africa and out over the Indian Ocean and you look up at that great subcontinent of India pointed down toward you as you go past it, Ceylon off to the side, then Burma, Southeast Asia, out over the Philippines and up across that monstrous Pacific Ocean, that vast body of water — you've never realized how big that is before. And you finally come up across the coast of California, and you look for those friendly things, Los Angeles and Phoenix, and on across to El Paso. And there's Houston, there's home, you know, and you look out, and you identify with it. . . . And you go out across the Atlantic Ocean and back across Africa, and you do it again and again and again. . . . And it all becomes friendly to you.

And you identify with Houston and then you identify with Los Angeles and Phoenix and New Orleans. And the next thing you recognize in yourself is that you're identifying with North Africa. You look forward to it, you anticipate it, and there it is. And that whole process of what it is you identify with begins to shift. When you go around the Earth in an hour and half, you begin to recognize that your identity is with the whole thing. And that makes a change.

You look down there and you can't imagine how many borders and boundaries you cross, again and again and again, and you don't even see them. There you are - hundreds of people in the Middle East killing each other over some imaginary line that you're not even aware of, that you can't see. And from where you see it, the thing is a whole, the earth is a whole, and it's so beautiful. You wish you could take a person in each hand, one from each side in the various conflicts, and say, "Look. Look at it from this perspective. Look at that. What's important?"

And a little later on, your friend goes out to the moon. And now he looks back and he sees the Earth not as something big, where he can see the beautiful details, but now he sees the Earth as a small thing out there. And the contrast between that bright blue and white Christmas tree ornament and the black sky, that infinite universe, really comes through, and the size of it, the significance of it. It is so small and so fragile and such a precious little spot in the universe that you can block it out with your thumb. And you realize that on that small spot, that little blue and white thing, is everything that means anything to you - all love, tears, joy, games, all of it on that little spot out there that you can cover with your thumb. And you realize from that perspective that you've changed, that there's something new there, that the relationship is no longer what it was. . . .

And you think about what you're experiencing and why. Do you deserve this? Have you earned this in some way? Are you separated out to be touched by God, to have some special experience that others cannot have? And you know the answer to that is no. There's nothing you've done that deserves this experience, that earned it. It's not a special thing just for you. And you know very well at that moment, for it comes through to you so powerfully, that you are the sensing element for all of humanity, you as an individual are experiencing this for everyone. You look down and see the surface of that globe you've lived on all this time, and you know all those people down there and they are like you, they are you - and somehow you represent them. You are up there as the sensing element, that point out on the end, and that's a humbling feeling. It's a feeling that says you have a responsibility. It's not for yourself. The eye that doesn't see doesn't do justice to the body. That's why it's there. That's why you are out there. And somehow you recognize that you're a piece of this total life. And you're out there on that forefront and you have to bring that back somehow. And that becomes a rather special responsibility and it tells you something about your relationship with this thing we call life. And that's a change. That's something new. And when you come back there's a difference in that world now. There's a difference in that relationship between you and that planet, and you and all those other forms of life on that planet, because you've had that kind of experience. It's a difference and it's so precious.

And all through this I've used the work "you" because it's not me. It's not Dace Scott, it's not Dick Gordon, Pete Conrad, John Glenn — it's you, it's we. It's life that's had that experience.

Russell Schweickart   Astronautics   United States   1977

of nations

To the Nations - Remain in your own line, but move upward toward greater consciousness and greater love. At the summit you will find yourselves united with all those who from every direction have made the same ascent. For everything that rises must converge. . . . The age of Nations is past. The task before us now, if we would not perish, is to build the Earth.

Pierre Teilhard de Chardin   Christianity   France   1955

humanity—Earth   with nature

What . . . is the body made of? At any given moment it is made of the world, for there is no fixed borderline between you and your surroundings yet reflecting on it at length and in the full context of time, the body progressively becomes as abstract as a melody — a melody one may with reason call the melody of life. . . . I tried to define the physical boundaries of the body and began to realize they are virtually indefinable, for the air around any air-breathing creature from a weed to a whale is obviously a vital part of it even while it is also part of other creatures. The atmosphere in fact binds together all life on earth, including life in the deep sea, which "breathes" oxygen (and some air) constantly. And the water of the sea is another of life's common denominators noticeable in the salty flavor of our blood, sweat and tears, as are the solid Earth and its molecules present in our protoplasm compounded of carbon, hydrogen, oxygen, nitrogen and a dozen lesser elements.

Yes, life as a whole breathes and owns the common sky and drinks the mutual rain and we are all embodied in the sea and the clouds and in fire and forest and earth alike.

Guy Murchie   Bahá'í   United States   1978

sins and nature

[From a confessional]
The voice of Father Mat's absolving
Rises and falls like a briar in the breeze.
As the sins pour in the old priest is thinking
His fields of fresh grass, his horses, his cows,
His earth into the fires of Purgatory.
It cools his mind.
"They confess to the fields," he mused,
"They confess to the fields and the air and the sky,"
And forgiveness was the soft grass of his meadow by the river;
His thoughts were walking through it now.

Patrick Kavanagh   Poetry   Ireland   1947

in work

No task, rightly done, is truly private. It is part of the world's work.

Woodrow Wilson   Politics   United States   1902

in the godhead

For thou surveyest this boundless ether all,
And every part of this terrestrial fall
Abundant, blessed; and thy piercing sight
Extends beneath the gloomy, silent night;
The world's wide bounds, all-flourishing, are thine,
Thyself of all the source and end divine.

Orpheus   Mysticism   Greece   600 BCE

of disparate things   above–below

. . . nothing's small!
No lily-muffled hum of a summer-bee,
But finds some coupling with the spinning stars;
No pebble at your foot, but proves a sphere;
No chaffinch, but implies the cherubim:
And,–glancing on my own thin, veined wrist,–
In such a little tremour of the blood
The whole strong clamour of a vehement soul
Doth utter itself distinct. Earth's crammed with heaven,
And every common bush afire with God:
But only he who sees, takes off his shoes,
The rest sit round it, and pluck blackberries,
And daub their natural faces unaware
More and more, from the first similitude.

Elizabeth Barrett Browning   Poetry   United Kingdom   1856

micro–macro

To see the World in a Grain of Sand
And a Heaven in a Wild Flower
Hold Infinity in the palm of your hand
And Eternity in an hour

William Blake   Mysticism   United Kingdom   1803

with the godhead   with God

What thou hast to see, this thy human eye cannot grasp; but there is a divine eye (an inmost seeing) and that eye I now give to thee. Behold Me in My divine Yoga. . . .

Having thus spoken, O King, the Master of the great Yoga. Hari [Krishna], showed to Partha [Arjuna] His supreme Form. It is that of the infinite Godhead whose faces are everywhere and in whom are all the wonders of existence, who multiplies unendingly all the many marvellous revelations of His being, a world-wide Divinity seeing with innumerable eyes, speaking from innumerable mouths, armed for battle with numberless divine uplifted weapons, glorious with divine ornaments of beauty, robed in heavenly raiment of deity, lovely with garlands of divine flowers, fragrant with divine perfumes. Such is the light of this body of God as if a thousand suns had risen at once in heaven. The whole world multitudinously divided and yet unified is visible in the body of the God of Gods. Arjuna sees him (God magnificent and beautiful and terrible, the Lord of souls who has manifested in the glory and greatness of his spirit this wild and monstrous and orderly and wonderful and sweet and terrible world) and overcome with marvel and joy and fear he bows down and adores with words of awe and with clasped hands the tremendous vision.

The Bhagavad Gita   Hinduism   India   600 BCE

in the sea

Sea full of food, the nourisher of kinds,
Purger of earth, and medicine of men;
Creating a sweet climate by my breath,
Washing out harms and griefs from memory,
And, in my mathematic ebb and flow
Giving a hint of that which changes not.

Ralph Waldo Emerson   Transcendentalism   United States   1882

person—world

Everywhere
your hands
meet mine. . . .
Yes,
when your hands
touch me, oh then
a thousand years become one moment. . . .
Between the field furrows in Kyongju,
you become a huge lightening flash
which burns up darkness;
become an immortal element of the sky's blue;
an ever-flowing rich river,
holding and embracing countless deaths;
something hot that runs over your eyes,
dewdrops engraved with ten, a hundred, a thousand suns, and
  yourself falling down to your all souls and bodies, waiting
  for such as you.

   Chŏn Ponggŏn   Poetry   Korea   1959

by art   in contradiction

There is no better deliverance from the world than through art; and a man can form
no surer bond with it than through art.

   Johann Wolfgang von Goethe   Literature   Germany   1809

in humanity

Man is not only a contributory creature, but a total creature; he does not only make
one, but he is all; he is not a piece of the world, but the world itself; and next to the
glory of God, the reason why there is a world.

   John Donne   Christianity   United Kingdom   1630

in the body

The world is a great volume, and man the index of that book; even in the body of man, you may turn to the whole world.

John Donne   Christianity   United Kingdom   1630

God—world

What is a ripple?

The wind's small hand has written on the water.

What is a ripple?

The chilled creek shrank back when the wind went through
With terrifying whistling in the grasses.
The child of cramp and of the dusk are you,
The chain-mail of the lake as daylight passes.

What is a ripple?

And suddenly I came to understand:
With giant-like fingerprints the water's sealed.
And this, Lord, is the doing of Your hand:
You made this world, and here You stand revealed.

Ivan Elagin   Poetry   Russia   1947

in nature

Downward we hurried fast,
And, with the half-shaped road which we had missed,
Entered a narrow chasm. The brook and road
Were fellow-travelers in this gloomy strait,
And with them did we journey several hours
At a slow pace. The immeasurable height
of woods decaying, never to be decayed,
The stationary blasts of waterfalls,
And in the narrow rent at every turn
Winds thwarting winds, bewildered and forlorn,
The torrents shooting from the clear blue sky,
The rocks that muttered close upon our ears,
Black drizzling crags that spake by the way-side
As if a voice were in them, the sick sight
And giddy prospect of the roving stream
The unfettered clouds and region of the Heavens,
Tumult and peace, the darkness and the light —
Were all like workings of one mind, the features
Of the same face, blossoms upon one tree;
Characters of the great apocalypse,
The types and symbols of Eternity,
Of first, and last, and midst, and without end.

    William Wordsworth   Mysticism   United Kingdom   1850

with nature

By the western cliff an old fisherman sleeps
    through the night.
At dawn he draws water from the Hsiang River
    and makes a bamboo fire.
Mists melt away, the sun rises, no man has yet appeared.
The oar rasps; suddenly the mountain and
    the river are green.
Sailing in the middle of the stream, he gazes back toward
    the infinite sky.
From the cliffs the clouds follow him without intention.

    Liu Chung-yuan   Taoism   China   819

with nature

Over the great clear pool
Rocks ranged in steep files:
Water, transparent and cool,
Reflected their black faces.

Over the great clear pool
Black clouds chased for miles:
Water, transparent and cool,
Reflected their dwindling traces.

Over the great clear pool
Lightning burst, thunder spread.
Water, transparent and cool,
Reflected the light:
the sound fled.
Clear as before, the pool
Lay transparent and cool.

This pool surrounds me and
I reflect what's to see
Whether the rocks still stand
or lightning flashes free.

Black rocks forebode me ill.
The clouds have rain to spill.
Loud lightning has to glow.
I have to flow, to flow.

    Adam Mickiewicz   Romanticism   Poland (Belarus)   1840

with nature

I go to sleep as spontaneously as the birds go back to the forest.
During the day my mind is as carefree as that of the begging monk.
My life is like the crane's who cries a few times under the pine tree.
And like the silent light from the lamp in the bamboo grove.
In the middle of the night I sit with legs crossed.
I do not even answer the call from my daughter or my wife.

    Po Chü-I   Taoism   China   846

with nature with creatures

Men and creatures were more alike then than now. Our fathers were black, like the caves they came from; their skins were cold and scaly like those of mud creatures; their eyes were goggled like an owl's; their ears were like those of cave bats; their feet were webbed like those of walkers in wet and soft places; they had tails, long or short, as they were old or young. Men crouched when they walked, or crawled along the ground like lizards. They feared to walk straight, but crouched as before time they had in their cave worlds, that they might not stumble and fall in the uncertain light.

When the morning star rose, they blinked excessively when they beheld its brightness and cried out that now surely the Father was coming. But it was only the elder of the Bright Ones, heralding with his shield of flame the approach of the Sun-father. And when, low down in the east, the Sun-father himself appeared, though shrouded in the mist of the world-waters they were blinded and heated by his light and glory. They fell down wallowing and covered their eyes with their hands and arms, yet ever as they looked toward the light, they struggled toward the sun as moths and other night creatures seek the light of a campfire.

Raymon Van Over   Native America   America (Zuni)   Traditional

in division

Slowly, slowly as the kauri tree did Tane [their son] rise between the Earth and Sky [his parents]. At first he strove with his arms to move them, but with no success. And so he paused, and the pause was an immense period of time. Then he placed his shoulders against the Earth his mother, and his feet against the Sky. Soon, and yet not soon, for the time was vast, the Sky and Earth began to yield. The sinews that bound them stretched and ripped. With heavy groans and shrieks of pain, the parents of the sons cried out and asked them why they did this crime, why did they wish to slay their parents' love? Great Tane thrust with all his strength, which was the strength of growth. Far beneath him he pressed the Earth. Far above he thrust the Sky, and held him there. As soon as Tane's work was finished the multitude of creatures were uncovered whom Rangi [the Sky] and Papa [the Earth] had begotten and who had never known the light.

Unknown   Maori Mythology   New Zealand (Maori)   Traditional *at the center   in timelessness*

Above the broad, unmoving depths, beneath the nine spheres and the seven floors of heaven, at the central point, the World Navel, the quietest place of the earth, where the moon does not wane, nor the sun go down, where eternal summer rules and the cuckoo everlasting calls, there the White Youth came to consciousness.

Unknown   Mythology   Russia (Yakuta)   Traditional

godhead—world

I the ritual action; I the sacrifice, I the food-oblation, I the fire-giving herb, the mantra I, I also the butter, I the flame, the offering I.

I the Father of this world, the Mother, the Ordainer, the first Creator, the object of knowledge, the sacred syllable OM and also the . . . [the Vedas].

I the path and goal, the upholder, the master, the witness, the house and country, the refuge, the benignant friend; I the birth and status and destruction of apparent existence; I the imperishable seed of all and their eternal resting-place.

Unknown   Hinduism   India   600 BCE

with environment

The fox realizes that
in this desolate sunbright field
there is only him alone.
That because of this he himself is a part of the field,
that he is the whole of it.
To turn into the wind too, to turn into the dried grasses too,
and even to turn into a streak of light too
inside the fox-colored desolate field,
almost like existing or not existing,
is being like a shadow, that he too realizes.
He realizes how to run almost like the wind, too,
  to run even quicker than light too.
Because of this he believes that his figure is invisible to
  anybody.
A thing that is invisible is running while thinking.
A thought alone is running.
Without anyone being aware of it the midday moon has risen above
  the desolate field.

Shinjiro Kurashara   Poetry   Japan   1965

in art   in scale

If you study Japanese art, you see a man who is undoubtedly wise, philosophic and intelligent, who spends his time how? In studying the distance between the earth and the moon? No. In studying the policy of Bismarck? No. He studies a single blade of grass. But this blade of grass leads him to draw every plant and then the seasons, the wide aspects of the countryside, then animals, then the human figure.

    Vincent Van Gogh   Art   The Netherlands   1888

above—below   in nature

Let's take
the duckweed way
to clouds.

    Kobayashi Issa   Zen Buddhism   Japan   1827

in duality   with other realities

I was thinking the day most splendid till I saw what the not-day
   exhibited,
I was thinking this globe enough till there sprang out so noiselessly
   around me myriads of other globes.

Now while the great thoughts of space and eternity fill me I will
   measure myself by them,
And now touch'd with the lives of other globes arrived as far along
   as those of earth . . .

O I see that life cannot exhibit all to me, as the day cannot,
I see that I am to wait for what will be exhibited by death.

    Walt Whitman   Mysticism   United States   1855

Cosmos

with the cosmos

Why should I feel lonely? Is not our planet in the Milky Way?

Henry David Thoreau   Transcendentalism   United States   1854

in language

Take a few moments to study the word "universe," the term that we use to describe this immense world of form in which we find ourselves thinking and breathing, day in and day out. Breaking the word down, we have "uni," meaning "one," and "verse," a "song." One song! That is our universe, my friends. Just one song. No matter how we separate into little notes, we are all still involved in the onesong.

Wayne W. Dyer   Psychology   United States   1989

individuation to achieve oneness

The One extended in universality exists in each being and affirms himself in this individuality of himself. In the individual he discloses his total existence by oneness with all in the universality. In the individual he discloses too his transcendence as the Eternal in whom all the universal unity is founded. This trinity of self-manifestation, this prodigious Lila of the manifold Identity, this magic of Maya or protean miracle of the conscious truth of being of the Infinite, is the luminous revelation which emerges by a slow evolution from the original Inconscience.

Sri Aurobindo   Yoga   India   1940

in imperfection

If the world were perfect, it wouldn't be.

Yogi Berra   Baseball   United States   1998

with humanity   in exploration

That's one small step for man, one giant leap for mankind.

Neil Armstrong   Astronautics   United States   1969

in work   in exploration

I am Earthman Gagarin

I am Gagarin
I was the first to fly up,
          but now you have flown
          after me.
I am an offspring
for keeps, a child of mankind —
               I land in heaven. . . .

Now blazing like a bonfire
the fearless wings flew along
and around you, boys of your time,
Aldrich, Collins, Armstrong.

And all filled with hope
that you're one big family, people,
among the crew of Apollo
I myself turned invisible.

We took our meals out of tubes,
wished for a drink on the way.
And as we embraced Elbe,
we embraced in the Milky Way.

On went work, not a start wrong.
Life itself played the pawn,
and with the boot of Armstrong
I set foot on the moon!

Yevgeni Yevtushenko   Poetry   Russia   1969

micro—macro

After all, after all we endured, who has grown wise?
We take our mortal momentary hour
With too much gesture, the derisive skies
Twinkle against our wrongs, our rights, our power.
Look up the night, starlight's a steadying draught
For nerves at angry tension.

Robinson Jeffers   Poetry   United States   1918

in balance with all

Our message can be summed up in the phrase, "Walk in Balance on the Earth Mother."
This reflects all the attitudes of my people, a people who felt that their lives had to
blend with all the things around and within them. They felt, as we do, that we have to
come to a point where we truly feel the oneness, the unity, that connects us to all of the
universe, and that we have to reflect that unity in all aspects of our lives.

Sun Bear and Wabun   Native America   America (Chippewa)   1980

with children

And every time I hear a youngster cry
I fancy that the Universe is weeping.

Kaisyn Kuliev   Poetry   Russia   1966

in education   in things

The essential business of the school is not so much to teach and communicate a variety
and multiplicity of things as to give prominence to that living unity that is in all things.

Friedrich Wilhelm Froebel   Education   Germany   1800

with the cosmos   change—world

The world cannot be transformed by changing the economic structure, or the social structure, or the religious structure. The only real change will come by spiritual commitment of the individual. When each individual shifts the center of reference from his ego to his deeper self, it will happen. Once I accept my responsibility to the world, once I realize that my true allegiance is not only to the country of my birth but to the universe, only then will true freedom thrive.

M.P. Pandit   Yoga   India   1980

micro—macro   in the Medicine Wheel

In many ways this Circle, this Medicine Wheel, can best be understood if you think of it as a mirror in which everything is reflected. "The Universe is the Mirror of the People," the old Teachers tell us, "and each person is a Mirror to every other person."

Any idea, person or object can be a Medicine Wheel, a Mirror, for man. The tiniest flower can be such a Mirror, as can a wolf, a story, a touch, a religion or a mountain top. For example, one person alone on a mountain top at night might feel fear. Another might feel calm and peaceful. . . . In each case the mountain would be the same, but it would be perceived differently as it reflected the feelings of the different people who experienced it. . . .

Each one of these tiny stones within the Medicine Wheel represents one of the many things in the Universe. One of them represents you, and another represents me. Others within them our mothers, fathers, sisters, brothers, and our friends. Still others symbolize hawks, buffalo, elks and worlds. There are also some which represent religions, governments, philosophies, and even entire nations. All things are contained within the Medicine Wheel, and all things are equal within it. The Medicine Wheel is the Total Universe. . . .

Within every man there is the Reflection of a Woman, and within every woman there is also the Reflection of a Man. Within every man and woman there is also the Reflection of an Old Man, an Old Woman, a Little Boy, and a Little Girl. . . .

The Medicine Wheel Circle is the Universe. It is change, life, death, birth and learning. This Great Circle is the lodge of our bodies, our minds, and our hearts. It is the cycle of all things that exist. The Circle is our Way of Touching, and of experiencing Harmony with every other thing around us.

Hyemeyohsts Storm   Native America   America (Cheyenne)   1972

circles–cycles   geometry–culture

The native people knew about this magic circle. They respected it and used it often in their everyday lives so they would always remember all of the things that they had learned. When they built their homes, most often these were circles, whether they were tipis, wigwams, or hogans. When they went to purify their bodies and their minds, they did so in the circle of the sweat bath, a cleansing lodge which represented the womb of the human mother from whom they came, and the womb of the Earth Mother, who sustained them throughout their lives. When they came together in council, they sat in a circle, so that everyone was included, as an equal, with an equal voice.

When they made music, they made it upon a round drum. They danced in a circle. The beat of the drum represented the beat of their hearts and the beat of the Earth Mother. They raised their arms and legs toward the heavens, they then placed them upon the earth, creating a circle that extended from the earth to the sky and back to the earth, with their bodies as the transmitters.

They saw life as a circle, from birth to death to rebirth. They know how to acknowledge and celebrate the circles of their own lives so that they were able to flow and change with the changing energies that came with different ages. They knew that they, like the seasons, passed through several phases as the circle of life and time passed around them. They knew that to fall out of this circle was to fall out of rhythm with life and to cease to grow.

The circle was so important to them, so essential to life continuing in the ways that it should, that they immortalized this figure in their ceremonies and structures. The mounds of the mound-building culture were round. The calendars of the Aztecs were round and the medicine wheels of stone were round. In everything they reminded themselves that the earth and everything on her were part of the magic circle of life.

Sun Bear and Wabun   Native America   America (Chippewa)   1980

with the godhead

He who sees Me everywhere and sees all in Me, to him I do not get lost, nor does he get lost to Me.

The Bhagavad Gita   Yoga   India   600 BCE

in knowledge by identity

The cosmic consciousness of things is founded upon knowledge by identity; for the universal Spirit knows itself as the Self of all, knows all as itself and in itself, knows all nature as part of its nature. It is one with all that it contains and knows it by that identity and by a containing nearness; for there is at the same time an identity and an exceeding, and, while from the point of view of the identification there is a oneness and complete knowledge, so from the point of view of the exceeding there is an inclusion and a penetration, an enveloping cognition of each thing and all things, a penetrating sense and vision of each thing and all things. For the cosmic Spirit inhabits each and all, but is more than all; there is therefore in its self-view and world-view a separative power which prevents the cosmic consciousness from being imprisoned in the objects and beings in which it dwells: it dwells within them as an all-pervading spirit and power; whatever individualisation takes place is proper to the person or object, but is not binding on the cosmic Being. It becomes each thing without ceasing from its own larger all-containing existence. . . .

But when the subject draws a little back from itself as object, then certain tertiary powers of spiritual knowledge, of knowledge by identity, take their first origin, which are the sources of our own normal modes of knowledge. There is a spiritual intimate vision, a spiritual pervasive entry and penetration, a spiritual feeling in which one sees all as oneself, feels all as oneself, contacts all as oneself. There is a power of spiritual perception of the object and all that it contains or is, perceived in an enveloping and pervading identity, the identity itself constituting the perception. There is a spiritual conception that is the original substance of thought, not the thought that discovers the unknown, but that which brings out the intrinsically known from oneself and places it in self-space, in an extended being of self-awareness, as an object of conceptual self-knowledge. There is a spiritual emotion, a spiritual sense, there is an intermingling of oneness with oneness, of being with being, of consciousness with consciousness, of delight of being with delight of being. There is a joy of intimate separateness in identity, of relations of love joined with love in a supreme unity, a delight of the many powers, truths, beings of the eternal oneness, of the forms of the Formless; all the play of the becoming in the being founds its self-expression upon these powers of the consciousness of the Spirit. But in their spiritual origin all these powers are essential, not instrumental, not organised, devised or created; they are the luminous self-aware substance of the spiritual Identical made active on itself and in itself, spirit made sight, spirit vibrant as feeling, spirit self-luminous as perception and conception. All is in fact the knowledge by identity, self-powered, self-moving in its multitudinous selfhood of one-awareness. The Spirit's infinite self-experience moves between sheer identity and a multiple identity, a delight of intimately differentiated oneness and an absorbed self-rapture.

Sri Aurobindo   Yoga   India   1940

self–creations

In other words, when all are realized as one, who is there to quarrel with? The true vision, therefore, consists in seeing everything in oneself and oneself in everything.

Swami Nirmalananda   Hinduism   India   1975

God–life

There is but One Life, the Life of God, within everything in His universe.

Annie Besant   Theosophy   United Kingdom   1899

in God

His hands and feet are on every side of us, his heads and eyes and faces are those innumerable visages which we see wherever we turn, his ear is everywhere, he immeasurably fills and surrounds all this world with himself, he is the universal Being in whose embrace we live.

The Bhagavad Gita   Yoga   India   600 BCE

itself

Behold but One in all things; it is the second that leads you astray.

Kabir   Mysticism   India   1449

in vastitude

The whole world says that my way is vast and resembles nothing. It is because it is vast that it resembles nothing. If it resembled anything, it would, long before now, have become small.

Lao Tzu   Taoism   China   500 BCE

by mind   mind–universe   wisdom–compassion–action

The third and last illusion is self. Only when self is anlaysed, and the student finds for himself that none of its parts is permanent, will this chattering monkey be quietened and in the end dissolved. Then the mind, in increasing harmony with All-Mind — and the nature of this is a matter of experience — knows itself as one with the universe, and an instrument in the evolution of the Whole. Wisdom-Compassion are found to be twin forces for the using, not for possession, and as room is made for them in place of self, the size and strength of these forces in the mind increase accordingly.

Christmas Humphreys   Buddhism   United Kingdom   1974

in self   between individuals   between nations

[Black Elk Speaking of the Making of Relatives ceremony in the Sacred Pipe]

Through the rites a three-fold peace is established. The first peace, which is the most important, is that which comes within the souls of men when they realize their relationship, their oneness, with the universe and all its Powers, and when they realize that at the center of the universe dwells Wakun-Tanka, and that this center is really everywhere, it is within each of us. This is the real Peace, and the others are but reflections of this. The second peace is that which is made between two individuals, and the third is that which is made between two nations. But above all you should understand that there can never be peace until there is first known that true peace which, as I have often said, is within the souls of men.

Black Elk   Native America   America (Sioux)   1930

solitariness–solidarity   universe–humanity   with stars

Have you looked out up the night sky
At the moon eclipsed
In Africa, away from city lights,
And felt alone
Yet expanded in bright company
Holding in your very being
Stars, milky ways Universes
In a sky you form
With other beings of your kind?

A. Karpper Mensah   Nationalism   Ghana   1940

nature–life with stars

My cluster of stars growing into the ocean
Their light like tendrils swaying with water
The moon comes closer to observe our dancing
Her loneliness draws pity from our lips
We invite her into the white sand to sit and listen
To listen to our song and clap her long thin hands
We send our youngest sister of the star
To carry the flower, to carry a drop of the red flower
Soon we see them from our distance
We see them begin to dance, we see them embrace
Eyes of a thousand stars laugh with them, with us in the night.

Mazisi Kunene   Poetry   South Africa (Zulu)   1950

problems–solutions   in principles of universal comprehension

Dare to be naive. . . .

It is one of our most exciting discoveries that local discovery leads to a complex of further discoveries. Corollary to this we find that we no sooner get a problem solved than we are overwhelmed with a multiplicity of additional problems in a most beautiful payoff of heretofore unknown, previously unrecognized, and as-yet unsolved problems.

A complex of further discoverabilities is inherent in eternally regenerative Universe and its omni-interaccommodative complex of unique and eternal generalized principles. It is inherently potential in the integrity of eternal regeneration and the inherent complexity of unity that god is the unknowable totality of generalized principles which are only surprisingly unveiled, thereby synergetically inaugurating entirely new, heretofore unpredicted — because unpredictable — ages.

Each age is characterized by its own astronomical myriads of new, special-case experiences and problems to be stored in freshly born optimum capacity human brains — which storages in turn may disclose to human minds the presence of heretofore undiscovered, unsuspectedly existent eternal generalized principles.

Buckminster Fuller   Geometry   United States   1975

from cosmic perspective

When I pause and reflect on our expanding universe, with its galaxies hurtling away from one another, embedded within the ever-stretching, four-dimensional fabric of space and time, sometimes I forget that uncounted people walk this Earth without food or shelter, and that children are disproportionately represented among them. . . . Sometimes I forget that every day — every twenty-four-hour rotation of the Earth — people kill and get killed in the name of someone else's conception of God . . . [or] in the name of their nation's needs and wants. . . .

Now imagine a world in which everyone, but especially people with power and influence, holds an expanded view of our place in the cosmos. With that perspective, our problems would shrink — or never arise at all and we could celebrate our earthly differences while shunning the behavior of our predecessors who slaughtered each other because of them.

Neil deGrasse Tyson   Physics   United States   2012

holism

The snow on the high mountains is melting fast, and the streams are singing bankfull, swaying softly through the level meadows and bogs, quivering with sun-spangles, swirling in pot-holes, resting in deep pools, leaping, shouting in wild, exulting energy over rough boulder dams, joyful, beautiful in all their forms. No Sierra landscape that I have seen holds anything truly dead or dull, or any trace of what in manufactories is called rubbish or waste; everything is perfectly clean and pure and full of divine lessons. This quick, inevitable interest attaching to everything seems marvelous until the hand of God becomes visible; then it seems reasonable that what interests Him may well interest us. When we try to pick out anything by itself, we find it hitched to everything else in the universe. One fancies a heart like our own must be beating in every crystal and cell, and we feel like stopping to speak to the plants and animals as friendly fellow-mountaineers. Nature as a poet, an enthusiastic workingman, becomes more and more visible the farther and higher we go; for the mountains are fountains — beginning places, however related to sources beyond mortal ken.

John Muir   Ecology   United States   1911

in cosmos

When to the new eyes of thee
All things by immortal power,
Near or far,
Hiddenly
To each other linked are,
That thou canst not stir a flower
Without troubling of a star; . . .
Seek no more,
O seek no more!

Francis Thompson   Poetry   United Kingdom   1893

in the godhead with all

Speaking of Jesus, St. Thomas described as saying: 'I am the Light that is above them all, I am the All, the All came forth from me and the All attained to me. Cleave wood, I am there; lift up the stone and you will find me there.'

Saint Thomas   Christianity   Palestine (Judea)   50

space–time–universe

Before 1915, space and time were thought of as a fixed arena in which events took place, but which was not affected by what happened in it. This was true even of the special theory of relativity. Bodies moved, forces attracted then repelled, but time and space simply continued, unaffected. It was natural to think that space and time went on forever.

The situation, however, is quite different in the general theory of relativity. Space and time are now dynamic quantities: when a body moves, or force acts, it affects the curvature of space and time — and the structure of the space-time affects the way in which bodies move and forces act. Space and time not only affect but also are affected by everything that happens in the universe. Just as one cannot talk about events in the universe without the notions of space and time, so in general relativity it became meaningless to talk about space and time outside the limits of the universe.

Stephen Hawking   Physics   United Kingdom   1988

in infinity

Ringed
Wide with the last oblivion of self
  The vague fantastic cloudscape slowly dies
Melting to grey monotony of dream,
Changing to windless empery of skies
Where nothing is immured or isolate.
  But oneness evens all —
  So mighty or so small
Be they soever, yet must equalize,
Ringed by the overshadowing Infinities.

  Arjava [J.A. Chadwick]   Yoga   United Kingdom   1936

infinite—finite

One day I was filled with longing
To behold in human form the splendours of 'the Friend',
To witness the Ocean gathered up into a drop,
The Sun compressed into a single atom;

  Jalal ad-Din Rumi   Sufism   Tajikistan, Turkey (Persia)   1230

person—cosmos

When Unity is established within yourself, everything is related, the whole universe becomes one vast tree of life; once we enter the life of that tree we can proceed to any point on its branches.

  N. Sri Ram   Theosophy   India   1973

person—cosmos

It is thus part of human destiny to be the necessary agent of the Cosmos in understanding more of itself.

  Julian Huxley   Biology   United Kingdom   1950

person—cosmos

Underneath all, individuals,
I swear nothing is good to me now that ignores individuals,
The American compact is altogether with individuals,
The only government is that which makes minute of individuals,
The whole theory of the universe is directed unerringly to one single
  Individual — namely to You.

Walt Whitman   Mysticism   United States   1855

with all

The great Mahāyāna Bodhisattva Avalokiteśhvara is a personification of the highest
ideal of the Mahāyāna Buddhist career. His legend recounts that when, following a
series of eminently virtuous incarnations, he was about to enter into the surcease of
nirvana, an uproar, like the sound of a general thunder, rose in all the worlds. The
great being knew that this was a wail of lament uttered by all created things — the
rocks and stones as well as the trees, insects, gods, animals, demons, and human
beings of all the spheres of the universe — at the prospect of his imminent departure
from the realms of birth. And so, in his compassion, he renounced for himself the
boon of nirvana until all beings without exception should be prepared to enter in
before him — like the good shepherd who permits his flock to pass first through the
gate and then goes through himself, closing it behind him.

Heinrich Zimmer   Buddhism   Germany   1953

in the body

Verily that body, so desecrated by Materialism and man himself, is the temple of the
Holy Grail, the Adytum of the grandest, nay, of all, the mysteries of nature in our solar
universe.

Helena Petrovna Blavatsky   Theosophy   Russia   1891

with all

A man is born but six feet tall. . . . However insignificant his body may be it takes a
whole universe to support it.

Kuo Hsiang   Taoism   China   312

in cosmic consciousness   with all

[Written in the third person by Richard Bucke]

It was in the early spring, at the beginning of his thirty-sixth year. He and two friends had spent the evening reading Wordsworth, Shelley, Keats, Browning, and especially Whitman. They parted at midnight, and he had a long drive in a hansom (it was in an English city). His mind, deeply under the influence of the ideas, images and emotions called up by the reading and talk of the evening, was calm and peaceful. He was in a state of quiet, almost passive enjoyment. All at once, without warning of any kind, he found himself wrapped around as it were by the flame-colored cloud. For an instant he thought of fire, some sudden conflagration in the great city; the next, he knew that the light was within himself. Directly afterwards came upon him a sense of exultation, of immense joyousness accompanied or immediately followed by an intellectual illumination quite impossible to describe. Into his brain streamed one momentary lightning-flash of the Brahmic Splendor which has ever since lightened his life; upon his life fell one drop of Brahmic Bliss, leaving thence-forward for always an aftertaste of heaven. Among other things he did come to believe, he saw and knew that the Cosmos is not dead matter but a living Presence, that the soul of man is immortal, that the universe is so built and ordered that without any peradventure all things work together for the good of each and all, that the foundation principle of the world is what we call love and that the happiness of every one is in the long run absolutely certain. He claims that he learned more within the few seconds during which the illumination lasted than in previous months or even years of study, and that he learned much that no study could ever have taught.

  Richard Bucke   Psychiatry   Canada   1899

with all

He, the door of whose breast has been opened,
Sees the sun reflected in every atom.

  Jalal ad-Din Rumi   Sufism   Tajikistan, Turkey (Persia)   1230

in things in nature

Certain kinds of bacteria in the oceans consume molecules of dissolved iron, concentrating them in their bodies over millions of years until they eventually settle into vast beds of iron deposit on the ocean floor that during a hundred million more years may be slowly pushed upward into mountains for men to dig into. And in the working of such mines a significant portion of the iron molecules inevitably diffuses into the air so that we unwittingly breathe and eat iron invisible dust and our marrow forms it into the iron-hungry nuclei of hemoglobin for our red blood cells. Thus, when you walk down the avenue and see a woman blush, you can be certain the red of her cheeks is closely related to the steel girders that are the bones of the city around her. Or when you glimpse the planet Mars shining red in the night sky, you can be assured it is akin to that blush because the deserts of Mars are made of iron-bearing sands. And, even more basic, the red light of the planet, like the red light of Betelgeuse, Archros, Antares and other red stars, is essentially an abstract frequency, a low pitch of colored light (about 5000 angstroms in wavelength), a kind of visual music of the Spheres that can exist anywhere in the material universe — and that, like iron, rust, blood, moon, planet, star and galaxy, it is just one small part of all the things that are involved in all things.

Guy Murchie   Bahá'í   United States   1978

in cosmic design

I hold (without appeal to revelation) that when we take a view of the universe, in all its parts, general or particular, it is impossible for the human mind not to perceive and feel a conviction of design, consummate skill, and indefinite power in every atom of its composition. The movements of the heavenly bodies, so exactly held the course by the balance of centrifugal and centripetal forces; the structure of our earth itself, with its distribution of lands, waters, and atmosphere; animal and vegetable bodies, examined in all their minutest particles; insects, mere atoms of life, yet as perfectly organized as man or mammoth; the mineral substances, their generation and uses; it is impossible, I say, for the human mind not to believe, there is in all this, design, cause, and effect, up to an ultimate cause, a fabricator of all things from matter and motion, their preserver and regulator while permitted to exist in their present forms, and their regeneration into new and other forms.

Thomas Jefferson   Government   United States   1823

humanity—universe   micro—macro

Present-day developments in cosmology are coming to suggest rather insistently that everyday conditions could not persist but for the distant parts of the Universe, that all our ideas of space and geometry would become entirely invalid if the distant parts of the Universe were taken away. Our everyday experience even down to the smallest details seems to be so closely integrated to the grand scale features of the Universe that it is well-nigh impossible to contemplate the two being separated.

Sir Fred Hoyle   Astronomy   United Kingdom   1955

in the godhead   in the individual

God's life . . . sees the one plan fulfilled through all the manifold lives, the single consciousness winning its purpose by virtue of all the ideas, of all the individual selves, and of all the lives. No finite view is wholly illusory. Every finite intent taken precisely in its wholeness is fulfilled in the Absolute. The least life is not neglected, the most fleeting act is a recognized part of the world's meaning. You are for the divine view all that you now know yourself at this instant to be. But you are also infinitely more. The preciousness of your present purposes to yourself is only a hint of that preciousness which in the end links their meaning to the entire realm of Being.

And despite the vastness, the variety, the thrilling complexity of the life of the finite world, the ultimate unity is not far from any one of us. All variety of idea and object is subject, as we have seen, to the unity of the purpose wherein we alone live. Even at this moment, yes, even if we transiently forget the fact, we mean the Absolute. We win the presence of God when most we flee. We have no other dwelling place but the single unity of the divine consciousness. In the light of the eternal we are manifest, and even this very passing instant pulsates with a life that all the worlds are needed to express.

Josiah Royce   Idealism   United States   1901

in wisdom

When is a man in mere understanding? I answer, "When a man sees one thing separated from another." And when is a man above mere understanding? That I can tell you: "When a man sees All in all, then a man stands beyond mere understanding."

Meister Eckhart   Mysticism   Germany   1320

in day and night   of opposites

We actually see with different parts of our retinas in daylight and in darkness and the night-time vision is not nearly so precise or clear. In fact if you look straight at a small object it tends to disappear. Daylight vision is infinitely superior, more exact and precise. But it has one limitation.

  Had the human race grown up in a world continually illuminated by the sun it would have considered the earth, the sun and the moon to be the whole universe. Whereas in fact we know that we live only in a tiny corner of that incredible system of matter and energy. It was only the dim night-time vision that made this knowledge possible in the first instance.

A.D. Hope   Poetry   Australia   1975

with all

Center yourself and then reach out. As your mind releases all things of daily life, you become free. There is nothing else in the world. No place else but where you are. And now you open up. Your mind energy surges out. You ride on the wind to the most distant places. You are free to search. You can feel and blend your energy with the natural forces. All of life becomes a song. You are part of the song of life. You become one with a hawk, an eagle, a bear, a rock. You are now a hawk dreaming of a person. Wherever your spirit will take you, you follow it. You are free to seek out the outermost or innermost parts of the universe.

Sun Bear and Wabun   Native America   America (Chippewa)   1980

with all

To see things through the light is not only to blend opposites into one but it is to enter into the unity of all things.

Chang Chung-yuan   Taoism   China   1963

in movement

Motion is eternal per se, and in the manifested Kosmos it is the Alpha and Omega of that which is called electricity, galvanism, magnetism, sensation — moral and physical — thought, and even life, on this plane.

Helena Petrovna Blavatsky   Theosophy   Russia   1891

micro—macro   in movement

The universe itself illustrates the actuality of perpetual motion; and the atomic theory, which has proved such a balm to the exhausted minds of our cosmic explorers, is based upon it. The telescope searching through space, and the microscope probing the mysteries of the little world in a drop of water, reveal the same law in operation.

     Helena Petrovna Blavatsky   Theosophy   Russia   1877

in diversity

Occultism, . . . maintains that every atom of matter, when once differentiated, becomes endowed with its own kind of Consciousness. Every cell in the human body (as in every animal) is endowed with its own peculiar discrimination, instinct, and, speaking relatively, with intelligence.

     Helena Petrovna Blavatsky   Theosophy   Russia   1891

bringing truth   eschewing falsehood

Where there is oneness and complete mutuality of consciousness-force even in multiplicity and diversity, there truth of self-knowledge and mutual knowledge is automatic and error of self-ignorance and mutual ignorance is impossible. So too where truth exists as a whole on a basis of self-aware oneness, falsehood cannot enter and evil is shut out by the exclusion of wrong consciousness and wrong will and their dynamisation of falsehood and error.

     Sri Aurobindo   Yoga   India   1940

through negation or affirmation   the supramental perception

The Absolute is in itself indefinable by reason, ineffable to the speech; it has to be approached through experience. It can be approached through an absolute negation of existence, as if it were itself a supreme Non-Existence, a mysterious infinite Nihil. It can be approached through an absolute affirmation of all the fundamentals of our own existence, through an absolute of Light and Knowledge, through an absolute of Love or Beauty, through an absolute of Force, through an absolute of peace or silence. It can be approached through an inexpressible absolute of being or of consciousness, or of power of being, or of delight of being, or through a supreme experience in which these things become inexpressibly one; for we can enter into such an ineffable state and, plunged into it as if into a luminous abyss of existence, we can reach a superconscience which may be described as the gate of the Absolute. It is supposed that it is only through a negation of individual and cosmos that we can enter into the Absolute. But in fact the individual need only deny his own small separate ego-existence; he can approach the Absolute through a sublimation of his spiritual individuality taking up the cosmos into himself and transcending it; or he may negate himself altogether, but even so it is still the individual who by self-exceeding enters into the Absolute. He may enter also by a sublimation of his being into a supreme existence or super-existence, by a sublimation of his consciousness into a supreme consciousness or superconscience, by a sublimation of his and all delight of being into a super-delight or supreme ecstasy. He can make the approach through an ascension in which he enters into cosmic consciousness, assumes it into himself and raises himself and it into a state of being in which oneness and multiplicity are in perfect harmony and unison in a supreme status of manifestation where all are in each and each in all and all in the one without any determining individuation — for the dynamic identity and mutuality have become complete; on the path of affirmation it is this status of the manifestation that is nearest to the Absolute. This paradox of an Absolute which can be realised through an absolute negation and through an absolute affirmation, in many ways, can only be accounted for to the reason if it is a supreme Existence which is so far above our notion and experience of existence that it can correspond to our negation of it, to our notion and experience of nonexistence; but also, since all that exists is That, whatever its degree of manifestation, it is itself the supreme of all things and can be approached through supreme affirmations as through supreme negations. The Absolute is the ineffable x overtopping and underlying and immanent and essential in all that we can call existence or non-existence.

Sri Aurobindo   Yoga   India   1940

through chanting   person—universe

The use of . . . a sand painting in connection with a curing ceremonial (a two-day, five-day, or occasionally nine-day chant) has the effect of harmonizing a disordered spirit, returning the patient to the "Pollen Path of Beauty" by setting him in accord again with the powers of the universe, which are the same, finally, as his own.

   Joseph Campbell   Mythology   America (Navaho)   Traditional

in painting   with the cosmos

People in the world know that I am good at painting and they all want to have an example of my work. However, few of them understand why I paint. . . . When we reach maturity in painting we are not attached to the mundane world whose affairs are nothing more than a single hair in the ocean. Whenever in the quiet of my room with my legs crossed I sit silently then I feel that I float up and down with the blue sky, vast and silent.

   Mi Yu-jen   Art   China   1153

in calligraphy   with the universe

There is a difference between K'ai Shu and Tsao Shu, "formal script" and "grass script." Whenever the calligraphist expresses an idea in the formal script such idea comes to an end with the completion of his writing, but when he completes his writing in the grass script, the movement seems to go on. Sometimes this script seems like the condensation and dispersion of mists and clouds, and sometimes it seems like the stroke of lightning or the floating stream of stars. It has the spiritual bones for its substance; it is in a permanent state of transformation. . . . No matter how noble the critics be, they cannot esteem it highly enough, no matter how well trained in mathematics, they cannot measure its strength. When we apply the non-action our brush work will be comparable to the works of Nature; when we identify our writing with the true nature of things we follow the fundamental principle of creativity. No one knows how this is done. It must be comprehended by our heart; it cannot be expressed in words.

   Chang Huai kuan   Taoism   China   Unknown

in architecture   in mathematics

The ziggurats of Babylon and the temple towers of both India and Mexico were models of a spatial-temporal universe, ordered mathematically to coincide with the laws of a cosmic harmony that are equally of man's moral nature. And yet, too, there is to be sensed about all such buildings the knowledge of a ground or meaning transcending such laws, made present architecturally not in the forms of majestic stone, but in the great silence surrounding and inhabiting those forms. Just as in the legend of Christ and the Virgin to whose mystery the cathedrals arose, so also in the legends to which the temple gongs are resounding, there is signified the knowledge of a seed or part within ourselves and all things that is antecedent to time and space, part and parcel of eternity, and which, like the everlasting light that in the sun, the moon, and the morning star seems to rise and set according to laws, never dies but is ever renewed. Begotten as it were of fire and wind, born as it were of water and earth, it is what lives in all lives, but also antecedes and survives them.

Joseph Campbell   Mythology   United States   1974

in synergy   part—whole   in chemistry   in metallurgy

Synergy means behavior of whole systems unpredicted by the behavior of their parts taken separately.

Synergy means behavior of integral, aggregate, whole systems unpredicted by behaviors of any of their components of subassemblies of their components taken separately from the whole. . . .

Chemists discovered that they had to recognize synergy because they found that every time they tried to isolate one element out of a complex or to separate atoms out, or molecules out of compounds, the isolated parts and their separate behaviors never explained the associated behaviors at all. It always failed to do so. They had to deal with the wholes in order to be able to discover the group proclivities as well as integral characteristics of parts. The chemist found the Universe already in complex association and working very well. . . .

Synergy alone explains metals increasing their strengths. All alloys are synergetic. Chrome-nickel-steel has an extraordinary total behavior. In fact, it is the high cohesive strength and structural stability of chrome-nickel-steel at enormous temperatures that has made possible the jet engine. The principle of the jet was invented by the squid and the jellyfish long ago. What made possible man's use of the jet principle was his ability to concentrate enough energy and to release it suddenly enough to give him tremendous thrust. The kinds of heat that accompany the amount of energies necessary for a jet to fly would have melted all engines of yesterday. Not until you had chrome-nickel-steel was it possible to make a successful jet engine, stable at the heats involved. The jet engine has changed the whole relationship of man to the Earth. And it is a change in the behavior of the whole of man and in the behavior of whole economics, brought about by synergy. . . .

There are progressive degrees of synergy, called synergy-of synergies, which are complexes of behavior aggregates holistically unpredicted by the separate behaviors of any of their subcomplex components. Any subcomplex aggregate is only a component aggregation of an even greater event aggregation whose comprehensive behaviors are never predicted by the component aggregation alone. There is a synergetic progression in Universe — a hierarchy of total complex behaviors entirely unpredicted by their successive subcomplexes' behaviors. It is manifest that Universe is the maximum synergy-of-synergies, being utterly unpredicted by any of its parts.

It is readily understandable why humans, born utterly helpless, utterly ignorant, have been prone to cope in an elementary way with successive experiences or "parts." They are so overwhelmed by the synergetic mystery of the whole as to have eschewed educational strategies commencing with Universe and the identification of the separate experiences within the cosmic totality.

Synergetics is the exploratory strategy of starting with the whole and the known behavior of some of its parts and the progressive discovery of the integral unknowns and their progressive comprehension of the hierarchy of generalized principles.

Universe apparently is omnisynergetic. No single part of experience will ever be able to explain the behavior of the whole. The more experience one has, the more opportunity there is to discover the synergetic effects, such as to be able to discern a generalized principle, for instance. Then discovery of a plurality of generalized principles permits the discovery of the synergetic effects of their complex interactions. The synergetic metaphysical effect produced by the interaction of the known family of generalized principles is probably what is spoken of as wisdom.

Buckminster Fuller   Geometry   United States   1975

in symbols   micro—macro

It sometimes seems as if the objects which surround us in this world of forms are a kind of miniature and concrete representation of some large and — to our human eyes — abstract truth: as if the whole of some great cosmic unity had to be re-made in a size perceptible to man's senses. Objects, then, become symbols of a bigger whole in which they are contained; and through a symbol a man is able to perceive what would otherwise be too blinding and big. Symbols are not invented: they are discovered by men with this special poetic capacity.

Irene Nicholson   Anthropology   United States   1959

in vision

I stretch my hand —
everything disappears.

I saw in the snake-head
my dead mother's face,

in ragged clouds
grief of my father.

Snap my fingers —
time's no more.

My hand's the universe,
it can do anything.

     Shinkichi Takahashi   Zen Buddhism   Japan   1960

in dream   micro—macro   dreams—mythology

The Indo-European verbal root div, from which the Latin divus and deus, Greek Zeús, and Old Irish dia as well as Sanskrit /deva/ (all meaning "deity") derive, signifies "to shine"; for the gods, like the figures of dream, shine of themselves. They are the macrocosmic counterparts of the images of dream, personifications of the same powers of nature that are manifest in dreams; so that on this plane the two worlds of the microcosm and macrocosm, interior and exterior, individual and collective, particular and general, are one. The individual dream opens to the universal myth, and gods in vision descend to the dreamer as returning aspects of himself.

  Mythologies are in fact the public dreams that move and shape societies; and conversely, one's own dreams are the little myths of the private gods, antigods, and guardian powers that are moving and shaping oneself: revelations of the actual fears, desires, aims, and values by which one's life is subliminally ordered. On the level, therefore, of Dream Consciousness one is at the quick, the immediate initiating creative now of one's life, experiencing those activating forces that in due time will bring to pass unpredicted events on the plane of Waking Consciousness and be there observed and experienced as "facts."

    Joseph Campbell   Mythology   United States   1974

in contrast   micro—macro

Meek in the Presence, with conceit we're drunk,
Seas of the unity, in sin we're sunk;
With treasure in our sleeves, with empty purse,
We, though road-dust, reflect the universe.

Hafez   Sufism   Iran (Persia)   1340

in revelation

When you eventually see through the veils to how things really are you keep saying
again and again this is certainly not like I thought it was.

Jalal ad-Din Rumi   Sufism   Tajikistan, Turkey (Persia)   1230

the supracosmic existence—the cosmic spirit—the individual Self

The Being is one, but this oneness is infinite and contains in itself an infinite plurality
or multiplicity of itself: the One is the All; it is not only an essential Existence, but an
All-Existence. The infinite multiplicity of the One and the eternal unity of the Many are
the two realities or aspects of one reality on which the manifestation is founded. By
reason of this fundamental verity of the manifestation the Being presents itself to our
cosmic experience in three poises, — the supracosmic Existence, the cosmic Spirit and
the individual Self in the Many. But the multiplicity permits of a phenomenal division
of consciousness, an effectual Ignorance in which the Many, the individuals, cease to
become aware of the eternal self-existent Oneness and are oblivious of the oneness of
the cosmic Self in which and by which they live, move and have their being. But, by
force of the secret Unity, the soul in becoming is urged by its own unseen reality and by
the occult pressure of evolutionary Nature to come out of this state of Ignorance and
recover eventually the knowledge of the one Divine Being and its oneness with it and at
the same time to recover its spiritual unity with all individual beings and the whole
universe. It has to become aware not only of itself in the universe but of the universe in
itself and of the Being of cosmos as its greater self; the individual has to universalise
himself and in the same movement to become aware of his supracosmic transcendence.
This triple aspect of the reality must be included in the total truth of the soul and of
the cosmic manifestation, and this necessity must determine the ultimate trend of the
process of evolutionary Nature.

Sri Aurobindo   Yoga   India   1940

with the cosmos

The Ch'annist, . . . lifting his finger, perceives the universe to move with it.

Chang Chung-yuan   Taoism   China   1963

nothing–all

We live in illusion and the appearance of things. There is a Reality. You are that Reality. Seeing this, you know that you are everything. And being everything, you are no-thing. That is all.

Kalu Rinpoche   Tibetan Buddhism   Tibet   1989

of the individual and the cosmic in the Divine

In what we may call the waking union of the individual with the Divine, as opposed to a falling asleep or a concentration of the individual consciousness in an absorbed identity, there is certainly and must be a differentiation of experience. . . . The action of the Divine in himself is that with which he is particularly and directly concerned; the action of the Divine in his other selves is that with which he is universally concerned, not directly, but through and by his union with them and with the Divine. The individual therefore exists though he exceeds the little separative ego; the universal exists and is embraced by him but it does not absorb and abolish all individual differentiation, even though by his universalizing himself the limitation which we call the ego is overcome.

  Now we may get rid of this differentiation by plunging into the absorption of an exclusive unity, but to what end? For perfect union? But we do not forfeit that by accepting the differentiation any more than the Divine forfeits His oneness by accepting it. We have the perfect union in His being and can absorb ourselves in it at any time, but we have also this other differentiated unity and can emerge into it and act freely in it at any time without losing oneness: for we have merged the ego and are absolved from the exclusive stresses of our mentality. Then for peace and rest? But we have the peace and rest by virtue of our unity with Him, even as the Divine possesses for ever His eternal calm in the midst of His eternal action. Then for the mere joy of getting rid of all differentiation? But that differentiation has its divine purpose: it is a means of greater unity, not as in the egoistic life a means of division; for we enjoy by it our unity with our other selves and with God in all, which we exclude by our rejection of His multiple being. In either experience it is the Divine in the individual possessing and enjoying in one case the Divine in His pure unity or in the other the Divine in that and in the unity of the cosmos; it is not the absolute Divine recovering after having lost

His unity. Certainly, we may prefer the absorption in a pure exclusive unity or a departure into a supracosmic transcendence, but there is in the spiritual truth of the Divine Existence no compelling reason why we should not participate in this large possession and bliss of His universal being which is the fulfilment of our individuality.

But we see farther that it is not solely and ultimately the cosmic being into which our individual being enters but something in which both are unified. As our individualisation in the world is a becoming of that Self, so is the world too a becoming of that Self. The world-being includes always the individual being; therefore these two becomings, the cosmic and the individual, are always related to each other and in their practical relation mutually dependent. But we find that the individual being also comes in the end to include the world in its consciousness, and since this is not by an abolition of the spiritual individual, but by his coming to his full, large and perfect self-consciousness, we must suppose that the individual always included the cosmos, and it is only the surface consciousness which by ignorance failed to possess that inclusion because of its self-limitation in ego. But when we speak of the mutual inclusion of the cosmic and the individual, the world in me, I in the world, all in me, I in all, — for that is the liberated self-experience, — we are evidently travelling beyond the language of the normal reason. That is because the words we have to use were minted by mind and given their values by an intellect bound to the conceptions of physical Space and circumstance and using for the language of a higher psychological experience figures drawn from the physical life and the experience of the senses. But the plane of consciousness to which the liberated human being arises is not dependent upon the physical world, and the cosmos which we thus include and are included in is not the physical cosmos, but the harmonically manifest being of God in certain great rhythms of His conscious force and self-delight. Therefore this mutual inclusion is spiritual and psychological; it is a translation of the two forms of the Many, all and individual, into a unifying spiritual experience, — a translation of the eternal unity of the One and the Many; for the One is the eternal unity of the Many differentiating and undifferentiating itself in the cosmos. This means that cosmos and individual are manifestations of a transcendent Self who is indivisible being although he seems to be divided or distributed; but he is not really divided or distributed but indivisibly present everywhere. Therefore all is in each and each is in all and all is in God and God in all; and when the liberated soul comes into union with this Transcendent, it has this self-experience of itself and cosmos which is translated psychologically into a mutual inclusion and a persistent existence of both in a divine union which is at once a oneness and a fusion and an embrace.

Sri Aurobindo   Yoga   India   1940

in action   in effort

The minute one stops going forward, one falls back. The moment one is satisfied and no longer aspires, one begins to die. Life is movement, it is effort, it is a march forward, the scaling of a mountain, the climb towards new revelations, towards future realizations. Nothing is more dangerous than wanting to rest. It is in action, in effort, in the march forward that repose must be found, the true repose of complete trust in the divine Grace, of the absence of desires, of victory over egoism.

True repose comes from the widening, the universalization of the consciousness. Become as vast as the world and you will always be at rest. In the thick of action, in the very midst of the battle, the effort, you will know the repose of infinity and eternity.

The Mother   Yoga   France   1957

with the universe

Alone he moved watched by the infinity
Around him and the Unknowable above.
All could be seen that shuns the mortal eye,
All could be known the mind has never grasped;
All could be done no mortal will can dare.
A limitless movement filled a limitless peace.
In a profound existence beyond earth's
Parent or kin to our ideas and dreams
Where Space is a vast experiment of the soul,
In an immaterial substance linked to ours
In a deep oneness of all things that are,
The universe of the Unknown arose.
A self-creation without end or pause
Revealed the grandeurs of the Infinite:
It flung into the hazards of its play
A million moods, a myriad energies,
The world-shapes that are fancies of its Truth
And the formulas of the freedom of its Force.
It poured into the Ever-stable's flux
A bacchic rapture and revel of Ideas,
A passion and motion of everlastingness.
. . .
Here all experience was a single plan,
The thousandfold expression of the One.
. . .

All thought can know or widest sight perceive
And all that thought and sight can never know,
All things occult and rare, remote and strange
Were near to heart's contact, felt by spirit-sense.
Asking for entry at his nature's gates
They crowded the widened spaces of his mind,
His self-discovery's flaming witnesses,
Offering their marvel and their multitude.
These now became new portions of himself,
The figures of his spirit's greater life,
The moving scenery of his large time-walk
Or the embroidered tissue of his sense:
These took the place of intimate human things
And moved as close companions of his thoughts,
Or were his soul's natural environment.
Tireless the heart's adventure of delight,
Endless the kingdoms of the Spirit's bliss,
Unnumbered tones struck from one harmony's strings;
Each to its wide-winged universal poise,
Its fathomless feeling of the All in one,
Brought notes of some perfection yet unseen,
Its single retreat into Truth's secrecies,
Its happy sidelight on the Infinite.
All was found there the Unique has dreamed and made
Tinging with ceaseless rapture and surprise
And an opulent beauty of passionate difference
The recurring beat that moments God in Time.
Only was missing the sole timeless Word
That carries eternity in its lonely sound,
The Idea self-luminous key to all ideas,
The integer of the Spirit's perfect sum
That equates the unequal All to the equal One,
The single sign interpreting every sign,
The absolute index to the Absolute.

Sri Aurobindo   Yoga   India   1950

Release

the godhead—the universe

Of the Absolute, the Infinite, the All-embracing, we can at our present stage know nothing, except that It is; we can say nothing that is not a limitation, and therefore inaccurate.

In it are innumerable universes; in each universe countless solar systems. Each solar system is the expression of a mighty Being, whom we call the Logos, the Word of God, the Solar Deity. He is to it all that men mean by God. He permeates it; there is nothing in it which is not He; it is the manifestation of Him in such a matter as we can see. Yet He exists above it and outside it, living a stupendous life of His own among His Peers. As is said in an Eastern Scripture: "Having permeated this whole universe with one fragment of Myself I remain."

C.W. Leadbeater   Theosophy   United Kingdom   1912

of source   of soul

Know ye not why We created you all from the same dust? That no one should exalt himself over the other. Ponder at all times in your hearts how ye were created. Since We have created you all from one same substance it is incumbent on you to be even as one soul, to walk with the same feet, eat with the same mouth and dwell in the same land, that from your inmost being, by your deeds and actions, the signs of oneness and the essence of detachment may be made manifest.

Bahá'u'lláh   Bahá'í   Iran (Persia)   1863

in God   God—universe

Listen, my child: there is only one eternal being — only one God. In everything alive there lives this one single being, there lives this one single God. God is the indivisible unity, he is present everywhere, he fills the entire universe. The whole universe lives because God animates it with his own eternal being!

Elisabeth Haich   Yoga   Hungary   1960

in geometry   in animals

For reasons known
only to itself
(maybe to Konrad Lorenz)
my cat has described a perfect circle
and is sleeping within it
like an animal scone
like half an orange 11 inches in diameter
like the knitted top of a head

usually when it's sleeping it twitches
stalking birds
down the long slanting
lawns of a dream
or its ears listen to what I say

not today
it's beyond us now
it's animal geometry
a feline planet
it can be anything or nothing
not even its name washes ashore
if I touch it
it makes a noise like the sea

Andrew Taylor   Poetry   Australia   1975

in space   beyond vision

To be keen-eyed is to see, not the mountain, but what lies behind it.

Unknown   Proverb   Russia   Traditional

the physical—the sensible

There are two worlds; the world that we can measure with line and rule, and the world that we feel with our hearts and imaginations. To be sensible of the truth of only one of these, is to know truth but by halves.

James Henry Leigh Hunt   Criticism   United Kingdom   1847

truth–all

All truths wait in all things,
They neither hasten their own delivery nor resist it,
They do not need the obstetric forceps of the surgeon,
The insignificant is as big to me as any,
(What is less or more than a touch?)

Walt Whitman   Mysticism   United States   1855

spirit–body

What is significant in psychic life is always below the horizon of consciousness, and
when we speak of the spiritual problem of modern man we are dealing with things that
are barely visible — with the most intimate and fragile things — with flowers that open
only in the night . . . the ideal of humanism is made to embrace the body also. . . . The
attractive power of the psyche brings about a new self-estimation — a re-estimation of
basic facts of human nature. We can hardly be surprised if this leads to the rediscovery
of the body after its long depreciation in the name of spirit. . . . If we are still caught by
the old idea of an antithesis between mind and matter, the present state of affairs
means an unbearable contradiction; it may even divide us against ourselves. But if we
can reconcile ourselves with the mysterious truth that spirit is the living body seen
from within and the body the outer manifestation of the living spirit — the two being
really one — then we can understand why it is that the attempt to transcend the present
level of consciousness must give its due to the body.

Carl Jung   Psychology   Switzerland   1933

with the infinite

To those leaning on the sustaining infinite, today is big with blessings.

Mary Baker Eddy   Christian Science   United States   1840

beyond speech

What is the operation we call Providence? There lies the unspoken thing, present,
omnipresent. Every time we converse we translate it into speech.

Ralph Waldo Emerson   Transcendentalism   United States   1841

through language

The Holidays

These words we say, what do they mean? Only
a greeting? Season's greetings. But what season
absorbs the phrase? A season of holidays,
the holiday season. Is this a holy time?
For **holiday**, with an **i** for the **y**, was holy.
Appearances notwithstanding, we notice all

it does is organize the word for all
conventional uses, like greeting cards — only
the rites of social life. Not that holy
purpose haunting depths beyond the season
surfaces, but ordinating a time
of merchant heights gives the holidays

their business priesthood. So, the holidays
in that way are stuck. After all,
we can't expect fluency this time
of year, drummed with selling and shopping. Only
a fool, illusion's genius, sees the season —
bound by its bottom line — as happily holy.

But if not the mass of Christ, Christmas, what holy
agent in the life that's ours, what holiday
of the year exceeds itself, crowned by its season?
If we dis his birth, does Easter live at all?
Then after spring, the Fourth; but a nation only
borne on its birth loses July in time,

fades in its own shadow, dependent on time
and the pennants of history, missing its holy
truth, its destiny — the one and only
matter that matters, like holy in holidays.
So really, what is holy? The whole, the all.
We've just undone the **w**, in season

and out. The holy knows no exclusions, its season-
ing is piquant with every spice, its time
is not just past, tradition, but the all
of every now, the grand pulse, the holiness of every name, the holidays
of Allah, the Buddha, Confucius, Krishna, the Tao and Yahu, not only

our sweet Jesus and all those weeks, his season.
That root is an only alchemy of time,
the holy of our lives, our holidays.

Ronald Jorgensen   Poetry   United States   2011

in spirit   beyond religion

The religions of authority can only divide men and set them in conscientious array
against each other; the religion of the spirit will progressively draw men together and
cause them to become understandingly sympathetic with one another. The religions of
authority require of men uniformity in belief, but this is impossible of realization in
the present state of the world. The religion of the spirit requires only unity of
experience — uniformity of destiny — making full allowance for diversity of belief. The
religion of the spirit requires only uniformity of insight, not uniformity of viewpoint
and outlook. The religion of the spirit does not demand uniformity of intellectual
views, only unity of spirit feeling.

Urantia Foundation   Urantia   United States   1955

in *occultism   hidden—whole*

Occultism is the study of the hidden side of nature; or rather, it is the study of the
whole of nature, instead of only that small part of it which comes under the
investigation of modern science.

C.W. Leadbeater   Theosophy   United Kingdom   1913

with the world

The existing world is not a dream, and cannot with impunity be treated as a dream;
neither is it a disease; but it is the ground on which you stand, it is the mother of
whom you were born.

Ralph Waldo Emerson   Transcendentalism   United States   1849

in truth

Each new grain of truth
Is packed, like radium, with whole worlds of life.

Alfred Noyes   Poetry   United Kingdom   1922

in simplicity   man–world

This world of the uncarved block is a world of free interfusion among men and among men and all things. Between all multiplicities there existed no boundaries. Man could work with man and share spontaneously together. Each identified with the other and all lived together as one. Man lived an innocent and primitive life, and all conceit and selfishness were put aside. In this uncarved simplicity we see the free movement of the divine. Nature was seen in its marks of spirituality. This we cannot expect in a merely moral and intellectual world, full of distinctions and differentiations. Only in the world of absolutely free identity does the great sympathy exist: the universal force that holds together man and man and all things.

Chang Cheng-yuan   Taoism   China   1963

in clarity

There is a poignancy in all things clear,
In the stare of the deer, in the ring of a hammer in the morning.
Seeing a bucket of perfectly lucid water
We fall to imagining prodigious honesties.

Richard Wilbur   Poetry   United States   1950

in chemistry   psyche–body

The deeper "layers" of the psyche lose their individual uniqueness as they retreat farther and farther into darkness. "Lower down," that is to say as they approach the autonomous functional systems, they become increasingly collective until they are universalized and extinguished in the body's materiality, i.e., in chemical substances. The body's carbon is simply carbon. Hence, "at bottom" the psyche is simply "world."

Carl Jung   Psychology   Switzerland   1959

in all   in excrement

Tung Kuo Tzu asked Chuang Tzu: "Where is this which you call Tao?" "Everywhere," Chuang Tzu replied. "Where specifically? insisted Tung Kuo Tzu. "It is in the ant," Chuang Tzu answered. "How can it be so low?" "It is in the earthwaren tiles." "Still worse." "It is in the excrement." To this Tung Kuo Tzu did not answer. Chuang Tzu proceeded to explain himself, "Your questions did not go to the heart of Tao. You must not ask for the specification of particular things in which Tao exists. There is no single thing without Tao!"

Chuang Tzu   Taoism   China   286 BCE

in truth

It betrays the consciousness that truth is the property of no individual, but is the treasure of all men. And inasmuch as any writer has ascended to a just view of man's condition, he has adopted this tone. . . . Truth is always present: it only needs to lift the iron lids of the mind's eye to read its oracles.

Ralph Waldo Emerson   Transcendentalism   United States   1875

through unlocking cages

The small man builds cages for everyone he knows,
While the sage,
Who has to duck his head when the moon is low,
Keeps dropping keys all night long
For the beautiful, rowdy prisoners.

Hafez   Poetry   Iran (Persia)   1390

in source

Consciousness=Energy=Love=Awareness=Light=Wisdom=Beauty=Truth=Purity
  It's all the same trip. It's all the same.
  Any trip you want to take leads to the same place.

Ram Dass   Psychology   United States   1978

in mind   in thought

Thought transference shows that there is a continuity of the mind as yogis call it, the mind is universal. Your mind, my mind and all the little minds are fragments of that Universal mind.

Swami Vivekananda   Hinduism   India   1902

in thought

There is only one Wisdom; it is to understand the thought by which all things are steered through all things.

Heraclitus of Ephesus   Philosophy   Greece   475 BCE

inner—outer

In a word, to let the spiritual, unbidden and unconscious, grow up through the common: this is to be my symphony.

William Ellery Channing   Unitarianism   United States   1987

in diversity   in art

Thanks to art, instead of seeing one world, our own, we see it multiplied and as many original artists as there are, so many worlds are at our disposal.

Marcel Proust   Literature   France   1913

spirit—soul   above—below

We have come from a world where we have known incredible standards of excellence, and we dimly remember beauties which we have not seized again. . . . The public for which masterpieces are intended is not on this earth.

Thornton Wilder   Drama   United States   1927

in peace

Peace is indivisible.

Maxim Maximovich Litvinov   Communism   Russia   1919

of virtues

All virtues arise from one and the same state of being, which is ever undivided.

N. Sri Ram   Theosophy   India   1973

inner–outer

Somewhere within our life is a standard as invisible as the equator, as relentless as the seasons.

T.S. Eliot   Literature   United Kingdom   1948

God–soul   God–cosmos

When you once begin to find God in your soul, presently you will begin to discover him in other men's souls and eventually in all the creatures and creations of a mighty universe.

Urantia Foundation   Urantia   United States   1955

in beauty

When one's inner nature is so awake that he sees the hidden beauty in all things, then his love is universal.

N. Sri Ram   Theosophy   India   1973

in art   inner–outer

Art does not reproduce the visible; rather, it makes visible.

Paul Klee   Art   Switzerland   1959

spirit–matter   with all

O Hidden Life, vibrant in every atom,
O Hidden Light, shining in every creature,
O Hidden Love, embracing all in oneness;
May all who feel themselves as one with thee,
Know they are therefore one with every other.

Annie Besant   Theosophy   United Kingdom   1923

in religion

   The prodigal sects are beginning to come home, as they discover that the far country of their freedom is in some curious way short of food: food for their own nourishing, and food to give to the hungry. Both these motives are powerfully at work in the ecumenical movement: the discovery that Christians are making that the other sects, whom they thought they could do without, have sources of life that they begin to hunger for; and the discovery that a sect in isolation cannot meet the questions pressing in upon it from the non-Christian world.

Harold Loukes   Education   United Kingdom   1930

inner–outer

The Buddhist does not believe in an independent or separately existing external world, into whose dynamic forces he could insert himself. The external world and his inner world are for him only two sides of the same fabric, in which threads of all forces and of all events, of all forms of consciousness and of their objects, are woven into an inseparable net of endless, mutually conditioned relations.

Lama Anagarika Govinda   Tibetan Buddhism   Tibet   1974

in truth   beyond religion

Nothing wonderful will happen to the world if the entire mankind be converted to Hinduism, Christianity, Buddhism or Islam. Or to any other religion. But assuredly something marvelous will happen if a dozen men and women pierce through the thick walls of church, temple, synagogue, and realize the Truth.

     Swami Nikhilananda   Hinduism   India   1963

in truth of religion

The origin of all religions — Judaeo-Christianity included — is to be found in a few primeval truths, not one of which can be explained apart from all the others, as each is a complement of the rest in some one detail.

     Helena Petrovna Blavatsky   Theosophy   Russia   1900

of religions   in paradise   with flowers

There is only one meeting place for all religions, and it is paradise. How nice to be there and wander about looking at the flowers. Or being the flowers.

     Thomas Merton   Christianity   United States   1965

of spiritual paths   in the godhead

Pass over names and look to qualities,
So that qualities may lead thee to essence!
The differences of sects arise from His names;
When they pierce to His essence, they find His peace.

     Jalal ad-Din Rumi   Sufism   Tajikistan, Turkey (Persia)   1230

across religions

Sects are stoves, but fire keeps its old properties through them all.

     Ralph Waldo Emerson   Transcendentalism   United States   1861

in godhead   of avatars

The Avatára is always one and the same. Plunging into the ocean of life, He rises up in one place and is known as Krishna; diving again and rising elsewhere, He is known as Christ. On the tree of Sachchidánanda grow innumerable fruits such as Rama, Krishna, Christ and others.

Sri Ramakrishna   Hinduism   India   1886

beyond form

The fishing net is used to catch fish. Let us take the fish and forget the net. The snare is used to catch hares. Let us take the hare and forget the snare. The word is used to convey ideas. When ideas are apprehended, let us forget the words. How delightful to be able to talk with such a man, who has forgotten the words!

Chuang Tzu   Taoism   China   286 BCE

of religions

The Divine is the sea. All religions are rivers leading to the sea. Some rivers wind a great deal. Why not go to the sea directly?

Mother Meera   Mysticism   Germany   1991

with the universe

A human being is a part of the whole, called by us "Universe," a part limited in time and space. He experiences himself, his thoughts and feelings as something separate from the rest — a kind of optical delusion of his consciousness. The striving to free oneself from this delusion is the one issue of true religion. Not to nourish it but to try to overcome it is the way to reach the attainable measure of peace of mind.

Albert Einstein   Physics   Germany   1950

spirit—matter

Every form you see has its archetype in the placeless world,
If the form perished, no matter, since its original is everlasting,
Every fair shape you have seen, every deep saying you have heard,
Be not cast down that it perished, for that is not so.

Shams-i-Tabrizi   Sufism   Iran (Persia)   1246

in person

The universal does not attract us until it is housed in an individual.

Ralph Waldo Emerson   Transcendentalism   United States   1882

self—all

If you did not have a body with a precise form, if you were not a formed individuality, fully conscious and having its own qualities, you would all be fused into one another and be indistinguishable. Even if we go only a little inwards, into the most material vital being, there is such a mixture between the vibrations of different people that it is very difficult to distinguish any of you. And if you did not have a body, it would be a sort of inextricable pulp. Therefore, it is the form, this precise and apparently rigid form of the body which distinguishes you one from another. So this form serves as a mould.

The Mother   Yoga   France   1930

in God

See ye what I behold? Verily, the Lord hath become the One in all, the All in one!

Sri Ramakrishna   Hinduism   India   1886

micro—macro

Take thou the hundredth part of a point of hair, divide it into a hundred parts again; then as is a part of that hundredth, such shalt thou find this Spirit in man, if thou seek to separate Him; yet 'tis this in thee that availeth towards Infinity.

Not woman is He, nor man either, not yet sexless; but whatsoever body He take, that confineth and preserveth Him.

Shwetashwatara Upanishad   Hinduism   India   Traditional

surface—depths

The wide pond expands like a mirror,
The heavenly light and cloud shadows play upon it.
How does such clarity occur?
It is because it contains the living stream from the Fountain.

Chu His   Neo-Confucianism   China   1150

nature—God

O flower of gold and green, thou art
A gift from Life's eternal heart.
As deep into thine eyes I gaze,
My own behold God's mystic ways.

For mirrored in thy soul I see
The secret laws of harmony.
Thy lovely form, with beauty bright,
Rebears the wonderment of light.

Thy perfume-breathing petals lend
A presence like a noble friend.
A brilliant gleam to gild the lea,
A gift from Heaven thou art to me.

Jakobina Johnson   Poetry   Iceland   1939

beyond change in the ultimate

We study the Changes (I Ching) after the lines have been put together.
Why should we not set our minds on that which was before any line was drawn?
When we understand that Two Forms have originated from the Ultimate
We can safely say that we can cease to study the I Ching.

Chu His   Neo-Confucianism   China   1150

dreaming—waking

Waking is long and a dream is short; other than this there is no difference. Just as waking happenings seem real while awake, so do those in a dream while dreaming. In dream the mind takes on another body.

Ramana Maharshi   Hinduism   India   1931

in dream

The dream is a little hidden door in the innermost and most secret recesses of the soul, opening into that cosmic night which was psyche long before there was any ego-consciousness, and which will remain psyche no matter how far out our ego-consciousness may extend. For all ego-consciousness is isolated: because it separates and discriminates, knows only particulars, and it sees only those that can be related to the ego. Its essence is limitation, even though it reaches to the farthest nebulae among the stars. All consciousness separates; but in dreams we put on the likeness of that more universal, truer, more eternal man dwelling in the darkness of primordial night. There he is still the whole, and the whole is in him, indistinguishable from nature and bare of all egohood.

  It is from these all-uniting depths that the dream arises, be it ever so childish, grotesque, and immoral. So flower-like is it in its candor and veracity that it makes us blush for the deceitfulness of our lives.

Carl Jung   Psychology   Switzerland   1964

in the heart

By gentleness the hardest heart may be softened. But try to cut and polish it — 'twill glow like fire or freeze like ice. In the twinkling of an eye it will pass beyond the limits of the four seas. In repose, profoundly still; in motion far away in the sky. No bolt can bar, no bond can bind — such human heart.

Chuang Tzu   Taoism   China   286 BCE

in life and death

Great is life and real and mystical, wherever and whoever,
Great is death — sure as life holds all parts together, death holds all parts together;
Sure as the stars return again after they merge in the light, death is great as life.

Walt Whitman   Mysticism   United States   1856

with night

The face of the night, the heart of the dark, the tongue of the flame — I had known all things that lived or stirred or worked below her destiny. I was the child of night, a son among her mighty family, and I knew all that moved within the hearts of men who loved the night.

Thomas Wolfe   Literature   United States   1933

in the godhead

I am Yesterday, Today and Tomorrow, and I have the power to be born a second time. I am the divine hidden soul who creates the gods and who gives sepulchral meals to the denizens of the underworld, of the deep, and of heaven. I am the rudder of the east, the possessor of two divine faces wherein His beams are seen. I am the lord of the men who are raised up; the lord who comes forth out of darkness and whose forms of existence are of the house wherein are the dead. Hail, lord of the shrine that stands in the middle of the earth. He is I, and I am He.

Unknown   Folklore   Egypt   1550 BCE

in time

A day is a miniature eternity.

Ralph Waldo Emerson   Transcendentalism   United States   1882

in God

Shun asked Ch'eng, saying, "Can one get Tao so as to have it for oneself?"
    "Your very body," replied Ch'eng, "is not your own. How should Tao be?"
    "If my body," said Shun, "is not my own, pray whose is it?"
    "It is the delegated image of God," replied Ch'eng. "Your life is not your own. It is the delegated harmony of God. Your individuality is not your own. It is the delegated adaptability of God. Your posterity is not your own. It is the delegated exuviae of God. You move, but know not how. You are at rest, but know not why. You taste, but know not the cause. These are the operations of God's laws. How then should you get Tao so as to have it for your own?"

Chuang Tzu   Taoism   China   286 BCE

of thought

The lightning-spark of Thought, generated or say rather heaven-kindled, in the solitary mind, awakens its express likeness in another mind, in a thousand other minds, and all blaze up together in combined fire.

Thomas Carlyle   Philosophy   United Kingdom   1881

in explanations

As in Science, so in metaphysical thought, that general and ultimate solution is likely to be the best which includes and accounts for all so that each truth of experience takes its place in the whole: that knowledge is likely to be the highest knowledge which illumines, integralises, harmonises the significance of all knowledge and accounts for, finds the basic and, one might almost say, the justifying reason of our ignorance and illusion while it cures them; this is the supreme experience which gathers together all experience in the truth of a supreme and all-reconciling oneness.

Sri Aurobindo   Yoga   India   1940

of thought   with nature

Profound quietude delivered me to the transparent moonlight. After enlightenment one understands that the six classics contain not even a word.

Wang Yang-Ming   Neo-Confucianism   China   1529

in wholeness   in perception

Most men think one thought after another, even as they have to say one word after another — they can't say more than one word at the same time, you know, or else they stammer. Well, most people think like that, they think one thought after another, and so their whole consciousness has a linear movement. But one begins to perceive things only when one can see spherically, globally, think spherically, that is, have innumerable thoughts and perceptions simultaneously.

Naturally, up to now, if one wanted to describe things, one had to describe them one after another, for one can't say ten words at once, one says one word after another; and that is why all one says is practically quite incapable of expressing the truth, quite incapable. For we have to say one thing after another — the minute we say them one after another, they are no longer true. They must all be said at the same time, just as they can all be seen at the same time, and each one in its place.

So, when one begins to see like this — to see, to discuss, to feel, to think, to will like this — one draws near the Truth. But so long as one sees as one speaks, oh, what a lamentable poverty!

The Mother   Yoga   France   1956

in silence

I have been breaking silence these twenty-three years and have hardly made a rent in it. Silence has no end; speech is but the beginning of it.

Henry David Thoreau   Transcendentalism   United States   1906

in thought

The men who come on the stage at one period are all found to be related to each other. Certain ideas are in the air. . . . This explains the curious contemporaneousness of inventions and discoveries. The truth is in the air, and the most impressional brain will announce it first, but all will announce it a few minutes later.

Ralph Waldo Emerson   Transcendentalism   United States   1861

in spirit

Didst thou ever descry a glorious eternity in a winged moment of time? Didst thou ever see a bright infinite in the narrow point of an object? Then thou knowest what spirit means — the spire-top, whether all things ascend harmoniously, where they meet and sit contented in an unfathomed depth of life.

Peter Sterry   Christianity   United Kingdom   1645

in change   through vibration   through contagion

[Question: How can all the work you do on your body have an effect on the corporeal substance outside of you?]

Always in the same way because the vibration spreads. It is a question of contagion. Spiritual vibrations are contagious, it's quite obvious. Mental vibrations are contagious. Vital vibrations are also contagious (not always pleasantly, but it's obvious: a man's anger for instance spreads very easily). Similarly the quality of cellular vibrations must be contagious. For example, each time I have been able to overcome something (I mean find the true solution to what is called an illness or bad functioning — the true solution that is the vibration that removes the disorder and sets things straight), I always have found it very easy to cure those who had the same thing by sending out that vibration. It works that way because the entire substance is ONE. Everything is one, you know, that's what we keep forgetting! We live constantly with a sense of separation — but that's a complete falsehood! Because we rely on what our eyes see — that's really falsehood. It's like a fake picture plastered over something, you know. But it's true. Even for the most material form of matter, even in a stone, the moment you change your consciousness, that whole sense of separation, all that division, disappears totally. There are only . . . (what shall I say?) modes of concentration, or modes of vibration WITHIN THE SAME THING.

The Mother   Yoga   France   1961

with all

One Nature, perfect and pervading, circulates in all natures.
One Reality, all-comprehensive, contains within itself all realities.
The one moon reflects itself wherever there is a sheet of water,
And all the moons in the waters are embraced within the one moon.
The Absolute of all the Buddhas enters into my own being
And my own being is found in union with theirs.

Yung-chia Ta-shih   Buddhism   China   713

of all

The Tao has no opposite.

Chéng Hào   Neo-Confucianism   China   1085

in nature

The opposite of nature is impossible.

Buckminster Fuller   Architecture   United States   1965

matter–spirit

Zen is not an idealistic rejection of sense and matter in order to ascend to a supposedly invisible reality which alone is real. The Zen experience is a direct grasp of the unity of the invisible and the visible, the noumenal and the phenomenal, or, if you prefer, an experiential realization that any such division is found to be pure imagination.

Thomas Merton   Christianity   United States   1968

in contradiction

The wise student hears of the Tao and practices it diligently.
The average student hears of the Tao and gives it thought now and again.
The foolish student hears of the Tao and laughs aloud.
If there were no laughter, the Tao would not be what it is.

Hence it is said:
The bright path seems dim;
Going forward seems like retreat;
The easy way seems hard;
The highest Virtue seems empty;
Great purity seems sullied;
A wealth of Virtue seems inadequate;
The strength of Virtue seems frail;
Real Virtue seems unreal;
The perfect square has no corners;
Great talents ripen late;
The highest notes are hard to hear;
The greatest form has no shape.
The Tao is hidden and without name.
The Tao alone nourishes and brings everything to fulfillment.

Lao Tzu   Taoism   China   500 BCE

through time

Only that day dawns to which we are awake. There is more day to dawn. The sun is but a morning star.

Henry David Thoreau   Transcendentalism   United States   1854

motion—stillness

If you are desirous of the truly immovable, the immovable is in the moving.

Hui-neng   Zen Buddhism   China   713

micro—macro   time—space   ancient—modern

In nineteen sixty-four
Plumbing the world abyss,
I, Pythagoras, saw
The holy tetraktys
And knew by its witnesses
I had been here before.

Brookhaven was the place
Where, from our cyclotron
Probing the bottom of space,
The shield of Euphorbos shone.
What the world rests upon
Stared me once more in the face:

The mathematical ark
On which I first set forth
To chart the void, to mark
The eightfold way's true north.
My dove, for what it is worth,
Returned as a triple quark;

My pebbles were baryons now
And the charges they bore not mine
But the frame was enough to show
A craft of the same design;
And there for a seal and a sign
Shone Omega at the prow.

She was rigged by more subtle men;
They had probed far deeper than I;
Yet when I looked again
Something had gone awry;
Where was the harmony
Plucked from the sacred ten?

Deep in the atom's core
Number was still the frame
Of all things as before
But music no more than a name
And the rainbow never came
Down to that final floor.

Yet I who had scanned the night
Lit with its lamps above
And measured the boundless height
Knew, though I could not prove,
As the soul is tempered by love
Or darkness tempered by light,

That here at the bottom of things
The infinitesimally small
Was tuned like the phorminx strings
To the limitless and the all —
But Furies rise to appeal
And destroy the poet who sings;

And the dogs of song give chase
Loosed from their leash of rhyme;
And the dove on the water's face
Is drowned for Hippaso's crime
If she tells how the sphere called time
Joins there with the sphere called space.

I saw and was silent then;
There is peril in truths concealed
By Zeus from the minds of men
Shall this, too, be revealed?
Shall I look once more on the shield?
I must wait to be born again.

A.D. Hope   Science   Australia   1975

in time   micro—macro

In India, for example, where the first form to appear in the lotus of Vishnu's dream is seen as Brahma, it is held that when the cosmic dream dissolves, after 100 Brahma years, its Brahma too will disappear — to reappear, however, when the lotus again unfolds. Now one Brahma year is reckoned as 360 Brahma days and nights each night and each day consisting of 12,000,000 divine years. But each divine year, in turn, consists of 360 human years; so that one full day and night of Brahma, or 24,000,000 divine years, contains 24,000,000 times 360 or 8,640,000,000 human years, just as in our own system of reckoning the 24 hours of a day contain 86,400 seconds — each second corresponding to the length of time, furthermore, of one heartbeat of a human body in perfect physical condition. Thus it appears not only that the temporal order written on the faces of our clocks is the same as that of the Indian god Vishnu's dream, but also that there is built into this system the mythological concept of a correspondence between the organic rhythms of the human body as a microcosm and the cycling eons of the universe, the macrocosm.

Joseph Campbell   Mythology   United States   1974

at new year

All beings move to the lip of love
Opened wider now, this time of year,
As air carries the tincture of the white dove
Descended in our mass of doubt, and fear

Which in its peace are held, its light illumed
Until that center edges out in sounds
Of dawning radiance now costumed
In joy: the Old's fulfilled, the New abounds.

Ronald Jorgensen   Yoga   United States   1994

on the spiritual path

One can be amused by beautiful words.
One also tries to frequently please others
   by what he says.
Are we aware of what we say?
Much speech is not good.
Less speech is favorable.
Speechlessness is best.
Unite your energy
   to the mystery of the universe,
   and in the quiet depth within yourself
   meet the totality of universal truth.
Keep the three "mystics"
   — mouth, mind, and will —
firmly united in one.
Roaming, thinking, and myth-creating
   are wasteful.
Hold fast to the true origin of life;
   this is of real value to cultivation.
To follow many religious teachings is confusing;
   to follow their essence is useful.
But to follow some plain truth of nature
   is best.
The deepest mysteries
   are found without any teachings.
Only by being of the highest spirit
   can you be among Shien, the whole beings.
Too many methods bewilder;
   use only one path
   to the most subtle realms.

Ni Hua Ching   Taoism   China   1983

in goal   despite paths

It has been called by various names, each one has presented it in his own way. According to the angle of seeing, one's experience differs. All those who have found the Divine within themselves have found Him in a certain way, following a certain experience and from a certain angle, and this angle was self-evident to them. But then, if they are not well on their guard, they begin to say: "To find the Divine, one must do this and do that. And it is like that and it is that path one should follow", because for them that was the path of success. When one goes a little further, has a little more experience, one becomes aware that it is not necessarily like that, it can be done through millions of ways. . . . There is only one thing that is certain, it is that what is found is always the same. And that's remarkable, that whatever the path followed, whatever the form given to it, the result is always the same. Their experience and everyone's is the same. When they have touched the Thing, it is for all the same thing. And this is just the proof that they have touched That, because it is the same for all. If it is not the same thing, it means that they have not yet touched That. When they have touched That, it is the same thing. And That, you may give all the names you like, it makes no difference.

The Mother   Yoga   France   1953

in the godhead   in the body

The Formless and the Formed were joined in her:
Immensity was exceeded by a look,
A Face revealed the crowded Infinite.
Incarnating inexpressibly in her limbs
The boundless joy the blind world-forces seek,
Her body of beauty mooned the seas of bliss.

Sri Aurobindo   Yoga   India   1950

inner–outer   in art

Chang Seng-yu of the sixth century, famous for his dragon paintings, . . . is said to have left the eyes of the dragon untouched up to the last moment. The reason for this odd procedure was given by a later commentator who claimed that as soon as the eyes were painted the dragons would fly away!

Chang Chung-yuan   Taoism   China   500

inner–outer   in art

During the eighth century Wu Tao-tzu (died 792) completed his last masterpiece for the royal court. It was a landscape painted on a wall of the court. Wu Tao-tzu worked patiently on it in solitude and kept the work draped until it was completed and the Emperor arrived for its unveiling. Wu Tao-tzu drew aside the coverings and the Emperor gazed at the vast and awesome scene and its magnificent detail: woods, mountains, limitless expanses of sky, speckled with clouds and birds, and even men in the hills. "Look," said the artist pointing, "here dwells a spirit in a mountain cave." He clapped his hands and the gate of the cave immediately flew open. The artist stepped in, turned and said, "The inside is even more beautiful. It is beyond words. Let me lead the way!" But before the Emperor could follow or even bring himself to speak, the gate, the artist, the painting and all faded away. Before him remained only the blank wall with no trace of any brush marks.

Chang Chung-yuan   Taoism   China   792

in music   in architecture   in flowers

I am a singer, my fragrant songs, my flowers, fall like strewn petals in the presence of others.

Great are the stones as I carve them, massive the beams as I paint them: they are my song: for I shall be heard when I have departed. I leave my song-sign behind me on earth.

The Prince Flower (ultimate truth) breathes its aroma. Our flowers are one. My song is heard, it takes root. My transplanted word is sprouting. Our flowers stand up in the rain.

Nahua tradition   Folklore   Mexico (Aztec)   Traditional

in pure existence   beyond pain and pleasure

An infinite, indivisible existence all-*blissful* in its pure self-consciousness moves out of its fundamental purity into the varied play of Force that is consciousness, into the movement of Prakriti which is the play of Maya. The delight of its existence is at first self-gathered, absorbed, subconscious in the basis of the physical universe; then emergent in a great mass of neutral movement which is not yet what we call sensation; then further emergent with the growth of mind and ego in the triple vibration of pain, pleasure and indifference originating from the limitation of the force of consciousness in the form and from its exposure to shocks of the universal Force which it finds alien to it and out of harmony with its own measure and standard; finally, the conscious emergence of the full Sachchidananda in its creations by universality, by equality, by self-possession and conquest of Nature. This is the course and movement of the world.

If it then be asked why the One Existence should take delight in such a movement, the answer lies in the fact that all possibilities are inherent in Its infinity and that the delight of existence — in its mutable becoming, not in its immutable being, — lies precisely in the variable realisation of its possibilities. And the possibility worked out here in the universe of which we are a part, begins from the concealment of Sachchidananda in that which seems to be its own opposite and its self-finding even amid the terms of that opposite. Infinite being loses itself in the appearance of non-being and emerges in the appearance of a finite Soul; infinite consciousness loses itself in the appearance of a vast indeterminate inconscience and emerges in the appearance of a superficial limited consciousness; infinite self-sustaining Force loses itself in the appearance of a chaos of atoms and emerges in the appearance of the insecure balance of a world; infinite Delight loses itself in the appearance of an insensible Matter and emerges in the appearance of a discordant rhythm of varied pain, pleasure and neutral feeling, love, hatred and indifference; infinite unity loses itself in the appearance of a chaos of multiplicity and emerges in a discord of forces and beings which seek to recover unity by possessing, dissolving and devouring each other. In this creation the real Sachchidananda has to emerge. Man, the individual, has to become and to live as a universal being; his limited mental consciousness has to widen to the superconscient unity in which each embraces all; his narrow heart has to learn the infinite embrace and replace its lusts and discords by universal love and his restricted vital being to become equal to the whole shock of the universe upon it and capable of universal delight; his very physical being has to know itself as no separate entity but as one with and sustaining in itself the whole flow of the indivisible Force that is all things; his whole nature has to reproduce in the individual the unity, the harmony, the oneness-in-all of the supreme Existence-Consciousness-Bliss.

Through all this play the secret reality is always one and the same delight of existence, — the same in the delight of the subconscious sleep before the emergence of the individual, in the delight of the struggle and all the varieties, vicissitudes, perversions, conversions, reversions of the effort to find itself amid the mazes of the half-conscious dream of which the individual is the centre, and in the delight of the eternal superconscient self-possession into which the individual must wake and there become one with the indivisible Sachchidananda. This is the play of the One, the Lord, the All as it reveals itself to our liberated and enlightened knowledge from the conceptive standpoint of this material universe.

Sri Aurobindo   Yoga   India   1940

of the soul   in division

But, all the same, in each of the bodily parts there are present all the parts of soul, and the souls so present are homogeneous with one another and with the whole; this means that the several parts of the soul are indisseverable from one another, although the whole soul is divisible (in a sense, i.e., so as to preserve its homogeneity in even its smallest part).

Aristotle   Philosophy   Greece   350 BCE

of freedom and will

Freedom is absence of all limitation, and how can there be any more limitations to our will when it is the Will, besides which there is nothing and by which all is determined. Thus in the world of the Real determination and free will are one and the same thing.

J.J. van der Leeuw   Theosophy   United Kingdom   1947

with the godhead

[A past life] event exists with all its surrounding circumstances, "remembered" and "forgotten" alike, in but one state, the memory of the LOGOS, the Universal Memory. Anyone who is able to place himself in touch with that memory can recover the whole circumstance. . . . The events through which we have passed are not ours, but form part of the contents of His consciousness; and our sense of property in them is only due to the fact that we have previously vibrated to them, and therefore vibrate again to them more readily than if we contacted them for the first time.

Annie Besant   Theosophy   United Kingdom   1915

of opposites   freedom–service   love–unity   unity–freedom

[Pavitra]: What does this paragraph mean: "Freedom is the law of being in its illimitable unity, secret master of all Nature: servitude is the law of love in the being voluntarily giving itself to serve the play of its other selves in the multiplicity."

[The Mother]: At a superficial glance these two things appear absolutely contradictory and incompatible. Outwardly one cannot conceive how one can be at once in freedom and in servitude, but there is an attitude which reconciles the two and makes them one of the happiest states of material existence.

Freedom is a sort of instinctive need, a necessity for the integral development of the being. In its essence it is a perfect realization of the highest consciousness, it is the expression of Unity and of union with the Divine, it is the very sense of the Origin and the fulfillment. But because this Unity has manifested in the many — in the multiplicity — something had to serve as a link between the Origin and the manifestation, and the most perfect link one can conceive of is love. And what is the first gesture of love? To give oneself, to serve. What is its spontaneous, immediate, inevitable movement? To serve. To serve in a joyous, complete, total self-giving.

So, in their purity, in their truth, these two things — freedom and service — far from being contradictory, are complementary.

It is in perfect union with the supreme Reality that perfect freedom is found, for all ignorance, all unconsciousness is a bondage which makes you inefficient, limited, powerless. The least ignorance in oneself is a limitation, one is no longer free. As long as there is an element of unconsciousness in the being, it is a limitation, a bondage. Only in perfect union with the supreme Reality can perfect freedom exist. And how to realize this union if not through a spontaneous self-giving: the gift of love. And as I said, the first gesture, the first expression of love is service. . . .

Independence! . . . I remember having heard an old occultist and sage give a beautiful reply to someone who said, "I want to be independent! I am an independent being! I exist only when I am independent!" And the other answered him with a smile, "Then that means that nobody will love you, because if someone loves you, you immediately become dependent on this love."

It is a beautiful reply, for it is indeed love which leads to Unity and it is Unity which is the true expression of freedom. And so those who in the name of their right to freedom claim independence, turn their backs completely on this true freedom, for they deny love.

The Mother   Yoga   France   1957

in contradiction

Constancy in love is a perpetual inconstancy whereby we are successively enthralled by each of the qualities of our beloved, exalting now one, now another, until our constancy becomes inconstancy within fixed limits.

Francois de La Rochefoucauld   Literature   France   1665

in contradiction

Truth is that which most contradicts itself.

Lawrence Durrell   Literature   United Kingdom   1960

in truth

Deep truth is imageless.

Percy Bysshe Shelley   Romanticism   United Kingdom   1810

of truth

Truth is a river that is always splitting up into arms that reunite. Islanded between the arms the inhabitants argue for a lifetime as to which is the main river.

Cyril Connolly   Criticism   United Kingdom   1945

grieflessness

Whence shall he have grief, how shall he be deluded who sees everywhere the Oneness?

Isha Upanishad   Hinduism   India   1200 BCE

despite ignorance

[Question]: Sweet Mother, here it is written: "All are linked together by a secret Oneness." What is this secret Oneness?

[The Mother]: Sri Aurobindo says: the Oneness exists; whether you are aware of it or not, it exists, in reality it makes no difference; but it makes a difference to you: if you are conscious, you have the joy; if you are not conscious, you miss the joy. . . .

Whether you know it or not, whether you want it or not, you are all united by the divine Presence which, though it appears fragmented, is yet One. The Divine is One, He only appears fragmented in things and beings. And because this Unity is a fact, whether you are aware of it or not, doesn't alter the fact at all. And whether you want it or not, you are in spite of everything subject to this Unity.

This is what I have explained to you I don't know how many times: you think you are separate from one another, but it is the same single substance which is in you all, despite differences in appearance; and a vibration in one center automatically awakens a vibration in another.

The Mother   Yoga   France   1956

in time

Now in her spaceless self released from bounds
Unnumbered years seemed moments long drawn out,
The brilliant time-flakes of eternity.
Outwingings of a bird from its bright home,
Her earthly morns were radiant flights of joy.
Boundless she was, a form of infinity.
Absorbed no longer by the moment's beat
Her spirit the unending future felt
And lived with all the unbeginning past.
Her life was a dawn's victorious opening,
The past and unborn days had joined their dreams,
Old vanished eves and far arriving noons
Hinted to her a vision of prescient hours.

Sri Aurobindo   Yoga   India   1950

Transcendent

above—below

How all things weave themselves to one,
Working, living, each in other,
While up and down the angelic powers go,
Bearing the golden pitchers to and fro!
The splendor swings from hand to hand!
On wings of fragrance, on wings that bless
From heaven through all the world they press
Till all rings loud with their loveliness.

Johann Wolfgang von Goethe   Literature   Germany   1808

seeking—receiving   person—God

(A dervish was tempted by the devil to cease calling upon Allah, on the ground that
Allah never answered, "Here am I." The Prophet Khadir appeared to him in a vision
with a message from God).

Was it not I who summoned thee to my service?
Was it not I who made thee busy with my name?
Thy calling "Allah!" was my "Here am I."

Jalal ad-Din Rumi   Sufism   Tajikistan, Turkey (Persia)   1230

in vision

But higher still can climb the ascending light;
There are vasts of vision and eternal suns,
Oceans of an immortal luminousness,
Flame-hills assaulting heaven with their peaks,
There dwelling all becomes a blaze of sight;
A burning head of vision leads the mind,
Thought trails behind it its long comet tail;
The heart glows, an illuminate and seer,
And sense is kindled into identity.
A highest flight climbs to a deepest view:
In a wide opening of its native sky
Intuition's lightnings range in a bright pack
Hunting all hidden truths out of their lairs,
Its fiery edge of seeing absolute

Cleaves into locked unknown retreats of self,
Rummages the sky-recesses of the brain,
Lights up the occult chambers of the heart;
Its spear-point ictus of discovery
Pressed on the cover of name, the screen of form,
Strips bare the secret soul of all that is.
Thought there has revelation's sun-bright eyes;
The Word, a mighty and inspiring Voice,
Enters Truth's inmost cabin of privacy
And tears away the veil from God and life.
Then stretches the boundless finite's last expanse,
The cosmic empire of the Overmind,
Time's buffer state bordering Eternity,
Too vast for the experience of man's soul:
All here gathers beneath one golden sky:
The Powers that build the cosmos station take
In its house of infinite possibility;
Each god from there builds his own nature's world;
Ideas are phalanxed like a group of suns,
Each marshalling his company of rays.
Thought crowds in masses seized by one regard;
All Time is one body, Space a single look:
There is the Godhead's universal gaze
And there the boundaries of immortal Mind:
The line that parts and joins the hemispheres
Closes in on the labour of the Gods
Fencing eternity from the toil of Time.
In her glorious kingdom of eternal light
All-ruler, ruled by none, the Truth supreme,
Omnipotent, omniscient and alone,
In a golden country keeps her measureless house;
In its corridor she hears the tread that comes
Out of the Unmanifest never to return
Till the Unknown is known and seen by men.
Above the stretch and blaze of cosmic Sight,
Above the silence of the wordless Thought,
Formless creator of immortal forms,
Nameless, investitured with the name divine,
Transcending Time's hours, transcending Timelessness,
The Mighty Mother sits in lucent calm
And holds the eternal Child upon her knees

Attending the day when he shall speak to Fate.

There is the image of our future's hope;

There is the sun for which all darkness waits,

There is the imperishable harmony;

The world's contradictions climb to her and are one:

There is the Truth of which the world's truths are shreds,

The Light of which the world's ignorance is the shade

Till Truth draws back the shade that it has cast,

The Love our hearts call down to heal all strife,

The Bliss for which the world's derelict sorrows yearn:

Thence comes the glory sometimes seen on earth,

The visits of Godhead to the human soul,

The Beauty and the dream on Nature's face.

There the perfection born from eternity

Calls to it the perfection born in Time,

The truth of God surprising human life,

The image of God overtaking finite shapes.

There in a world of everlasting Light,

In the realms of the immortal Supermind

Truth who hides here her head in mystery,

Her riddle deemed by reason impossible

In the stark structure of material form,

Unenigmaed lives, unmasked her face and there

Is Nature and the common law of things.

There in a body made of spirit stuff,

The hearth-stone of the everliving Fire,

Action translates the movements of the soul,

Thought steps infallible and absolute

And life is a continual worship's rite,

A sacrifice of rapture to the One.

A cosmic vision, a spiritual sense

Feels all the Infinite lodged in finite form

And seen through a quivering ecstasy of light

Discovers the bright face of the Bodiless,

In the truth of a moment, in the moment's soul

Can sip the honey-wine of Eternity.

Sri Aurobindo   Yoga   India   1945

in vision   with all   in poetry

One day, late in the afternoon, I was pacing the terrace of our Jorasanko house. The glow of the sunset combined with the wan twilight in a way which seemed to give the approaching evening a specially wonderful attractiveness for me. Even the walls of the adjoining house seemed to grow beautiful. Is this uplifting of the cover of triviality from the everyday world, I wondered, due to some magic in the evening light? Never! I could see at once that it was the effect of the evening which had come within me; its shades had obliterated my self. While the self was rampant during the glare of day, everything I perceived was mingled with and hidden by it. Now, that the self was put into the background, I could see the world in its own true aspect. And that aspect has nothing of triviality in it, it is full of beauty and joy. . . .

Then I gained a further insight which has lasted all my life. The end of Sudder Street, and the trees on the Free School grounds opposite, were visible from our Sudder Street house. One morning I happened to be standing on the verandah looking that way. The sun was just rising through the leafy tops of those trees. As I continued to gaze, all of a sudden a covering seemed to fall away from my eyes, and I found the world bathed in a wonderful radiance, with waves of beauty and joy swelling on every side. This radiance pierced in a moment through the folds of sadness and despondency which had accumulated over my heart, and flooded it with this universal light.

That very day the poem, The Awakening of the Waterfall, gushed forth and coursed on like a veritable cascade. The poem came to an end, but the curtain did not fall upon the joy aspect of the Universe. And it came to be so that no person or thing in the world seemed to me trivial or unpleasing. A thing that happened the next day or the day following seemed specially astonishing.

There was a curious sort of person who came to me now and then, with a habit of asking all manner of silly questions. One day he had asked: "Have you, sir, seen God with your own eyes?" And on my having to admit that I had not, he averred that he had. "What was it you saw?" I asked. "He seethed and throbbed before my eyes!" was the reply. . . .

This time, when he came one afternoon, I actually felt glad to see him, and welcomed him cordially. The mantle of his oddity and foolishness seemed to have slipped off, and the person I so joyfully hailed was the real man whom I felt to be in nowise inferior to myself, and moreover closely related. Finding no trace of annoyance within me at sight of him, nor any sense of my time being wasted with him, I was filled with an immense gladness, and felt rid of some enveloping tissue of untruth which had been causing me so much needless and uncalled for discomfort and pain.

As I would stand on the balcony, the gait, the figure, the features of each one of the passers-by, whoever they might be, seemed to me all so extraordinarily wonderful, as they flowed past, — waves on the sea of the universe. From infancy I had seen only with my eyes, I now began to see with the whole of my consciousness. I could not look upon the sight of two smiling youths, nonchalantly going their way, the arm of one on the other's shoulder, as a matter of small moment; for, through it I could see the fathomless depths of the eternal spring of Joy from which numberless sprays of laughter leap up throughout the world.

I had never before marked the play of limbs and lineaments which always accompanies even the least of man's actions; now I was spell-bound by their variety, which I came across on all sides, at every moment. Yet I saw them not as being apart by themselves, but as parts of that amazingly beautiful greater dance which goes on at this very moment throughout the world of men, in each of their homes, in their multifarious wants and activities. Friend laughs with friend, the mother fondles her child, one cow sidles up to another and licks its body, and the immeasurability behind these comes direct to my mind with a shock which almost savours of pain.

When of this period I wrote:

I know not how of a sudden my heart flung open its doors,
And let the crowd of worlds rush in, greeting each other, —

it was no poetic exaggeration. Rather I had not the power to express all I felt.

For some time together I remained in this self-forgetful state of bliss. Then my brother thought of going to the Darjeeling hills. So much the better, thought I. On the vast Himalayan tops I shall be able to see more deeply into what has been revealed to me in Sudder Street; at any rate I shall see how the Himalayas display themselves to my new gift of vision.

But the victory was with that little house in Sudder Street. When, after ascending the mountains, I looked around, I was at once aware I had lost my new vision. My sin must have been in imagining that I could get still more of truth from the outside. However sky-piercing the king of mountains may be, he can have nothing in his gift for me; while He who is the Giver can vouchsafe a vision of the eternal universe in the dingiest of lanes, and in a moment of time.

Rabindranath Tagore   Poetry   India   1917

with God

Hear, O Israel, the Lord our God, the Lord is One.

Torah   Judaism   Israel   400 BCE

with sustenance

And as they were eating, Jesus took bread, and blessed it, and brake it, and gave it to the disciples, and said, "Take, eat; this is my body." And he took the cup, and gave thanks, and gave it to them, saying, "Drink ye all of it; For this is my blood of the new testament which is shed for many for the remission of sins."

Saint Matthew　　Christianity　　Israel (Galilee)　　50

in God　with all

And in the All is naught that is not God. Wherefore nor size, nor space, nor quality, nor form, nor time, surroundeth God; for He is All, and All surroundeth all, and permeateth all.

Hermes Trismegistus　　Hermetic Philosophy　　Egypt　　200

in the Transcendent

　All here where each thing seems its lonely self
Are figures of the sole transcendent One:
Only by him they are, his breath is their life;
An unseen Presence moulds the oblivious clay.

Sri Aurobindo　　Yoga　　India　　1950

spirit—matter

All are but parts of one stupendous whole,
Whose body Nature is, and God the soul.

Alexander Pope　　Poetry　　United Kingdom　　1733

subject–object

In the period just preceding the hour when success finally crowned a search that covered nearly a quarter of a century, certain features characteristic of the transcendent consciousness had become theoretically clear. I had attained an intellectual grasp of the vitally important fact that transcendent consciousness differs from the ordinary consciousness in the primary respect that it is a state of consciousness wherein the disjunction between the subject to consciousness and the object of consciousness is destroyed. It is a state wherein self-identity and the field of consciousness are blended in one indissoluble whole. This supplied the prime characteristic by which all our common consciousness could be differentiated from the transcendent. The former is all of the type that may be called subject-object or relative consciousness. . . . I also discovered the essential timelessness of the subject, or self, and that in its purity, unmixed with any objective element, it can never truly be an object of consciousness. I readily realized that if pure subjectivity, or the bare power to be aware, was a permanent or unchanging element and therefore must, as a consequence, stand outside of time and be unaffected by any history, then it must be, of necessity, immortal. I saw that this kind of immortality is wholly impersonal and does not, by itself, imply the unlimited persistence of the quality of individuality that distinguishes one man from another. But the finding of one immortal element affords a definite anchorage and security, grounded in certainty of an order far superior to that of any kind of faith. When I had reached this point in the unfoldment of my understanding, I really had achieved the positive value of decisive importance that, some years later, was to prove the effective entering wedge for opening the Way to the transcendent level of consciousness.

Franklin Merrell-Wolf   Philosophy   United States   1973

in the godhead

Everything in the Kingdom, every spiritual thing, refers to Christ and centres in him. His nature, his virtue, his presence, his power makes up all. Indeed he is all in all to a believer, only variously manifested and opened in the heart by the Spirit. He is the volume of the whole book, every leaf and line whereof speaks of him and writes of him in some or other of his sweet and beautiful lineaments. So that if I should speak further of other things . . . I should but speak further of his nature brought up, manifested and displaying itself in and through the creatures, by turning the wheel of life through his hearts. But my spirit hasteneth from words . . . (that it) may sink in spirit into the feeling of the life itself, and may learn what it is to enjoy it there and to be comprehended of it, and cease striving to know or comprehend concerning it.

Isaac Pennington   Quakerism   United Kingdom   1681

person—cosmos

A call was on him from intangible heights;
Indifferent to the little outpost Mind,
He dwelt in the wideness of the Eternal's reign.
His being now exceeded thinkable Space,
His boundless thought was neighbor to cosmic sight:
A universal light was in his eyes,
A golden influx flowed through heart and brain;
A force came down into his mortal limbs,
A current from eternal seas of Bliss;
He felt the invasion and the nameless joy.
Aware of his occult omnipotent Source,
Allured by the omniscient Ecstasy,
A living centre of the Illimitable
Widened to equate with the world's circumference,
He turned to his immense spiritual fate.

   Sri Aurobindo   Yoga   India   1950

with God

Three persons speak not privately together but He is their fourth; nor five but He is their sixth; nor fewer nor more, but wherever they be, He is with them.

   Mohammed   Islam   Saudi Arabia   662

with Christ

The sight of Christ is all there is to see. The song of Christ is all there is to hear. The hand of Christ is all there is to hold. There is no journey but to walk with him.

   Helen Schucman   Psychology   United States   1976

in aspects of Krishna

Among the Adityas, I am Vishnu; among lights and splendours, I am the radiant Sun . . . among the stars, the Moon am I. . . .

I am mind among the senses; in living beings, I am consciousness. . . .

Among the flowing waters, I am the ocean. . . .

I am the sacred syllable OM among words . . . among the mountain-ranges I am Himalaya.

Among men, the king of men. . . .

I am Time the head of all reckoning to those who reckon and measure; and among the beasts of the forest, I am the king of the beasts. . . .

I am the wind among purifiers . . . among the rivers, Ganges am I.

Of creation I am the beginning and the end and also the middle, O Arjuna. I am spiritual knowledge among the many philosophies, arts and sciences; I am the logic of those who debate.

I am the letter A among letters, the dual among compounds. I am imperishable Time; I am the Master and Ruler (of all existences), whose faces are everywhere.

I am all-snatching Death, and I am too the birth of all that shall come into being. Among feminine qualities, I am glory and beauty and speech and memory and intelligence and steadfastness and forgiveness. . . .

I am the mastery and power of all who rule and tame and vanquish and the policy of all who succeed and conquer; I am the silence of things secret and the knowledge of the knower.

And whatsoever is the seed of all existences, that am I, O Arjuna; nothing moving or unmoving, animate or inanimate in the world can be without me.

Whatever beautiful and glorious creature thou seest in the world, whatever being is mighty and forceful (among men and above man and below him), know to be a very splendour, light, and energy of Me and born of a potent portion and intense power of my existence.

But what need is there of a multitude of details for this knowledge, O Arjuna? Take it thus, that I am here in this world and everywhere. I support this entire universe with an infinitesimal portion of Myself.

The Bhagavad Gita   Hinduism   India   600 BCE

through love   in process

All our earth starts from mud and ends in sky,
And Love that was once an animal's desire,
Then a sweet madness in the rapturous heart,
An ardent comradeship in the happy mind,
Becomes a wide spiritual yearning's space.
A lonely soul passions for the Alone,
The heart that loved man thrills to the love of God,
A body is his chamber and his shrine.
Then is our being rescued from separateness;
All is itself, all is new-felt in God:
A Lover leaning from his cloister's door
Gathers the whole world into his single breast.
Then shall the business fail of Night and Death:
When unity is won, when strife is lost
And all is known and all is clasped by Love
Who would turn back to ignorance and pain?

Sri Aurobindo   Yoga   India   1950

in duality

He is Lord and Lady of duality.
He is Lord and Lady of our maintenance.
He is mother and father of the gods, the old god.
He is at the same time the god of fire, who dwells in the navel of fire.
He is the mirror of day and night.
He is the star which illuminates all things, and He is the Lady of the shining skirt of stars.
He is our mother, our father.
Above all, he is Ometéotl who dwells in the place of duality.

Unknown   Folklore   Mexico (Aztec)   500 BCE

all affirmations—all negations   the unmanifest—the manifest

The absolutist view of reality, consciousness and knowledge is founded on one side of the earliest Vedantic thought, but it is not the whole of that thinking. In the Upanishads, in the inspired scripture of the most ancient Vedanta, we find the affirmation of the Absolute, the experience-concept of the utter and ineffable Transcendence; but we find also, not in contradiction to it but as its corollary, an affirmation of the cosmic Divinity, an experience-concept of the cosmic Self and the becoming of Brahman in the universe. Equally, we find the affirmation of the Divine Reality in the individual: this too is an experience concept; it is seized upon not as an appearance, but as an actual becoming. In place of a sole supreme exclusive affirmation negating all else than the transcendent Absolute we find a comprehensive affirmation carried to its farthest conclusion: this concept of Reality and of Knowledge enveloping in one view the cosmic and the Absolute coincides fundamentally with our own; for it implies that the Ignorance too is a half-veiled part of the Knowledge and world-knowledge a part of self-knowledge. The Isha Upanishad insists on the unity and reality of all the manifestations of the Absolute; it refuses to confine truth to any one aspect. Brahman is the stable and the mobile, the internal and the external, all that is near and all that is far whether spiritually or in the extension of Time and Space; it is the Being and all becomings, the Pure and Silent who is without feature or action and the Seer and Thinker who organises the world and its objects; it is the One who becomes all that we are sensible of in the universe, the Immanent and that in which he takes up his dwelling. The Upanishad affirms the perfect and the liberating knowledge to be that which excludes neither the Self nor its creations: the liberated spirit sees all these as becomings of the Self-existent in an internal vision and by a consciousness which perceives the universe within itself instead of looking out on it, like the limited and egoistic mind, as a thing other than itself. To live in the cosmic Ignorance is a blindness, but to confine oneself in an exclusive absolutism of Knowledge is also a blindness: to know Brahman as at once and together the Knowledge and the Ignorance, to attain to the supreme status at once by the Becoming and the Non-Becoming, to relate together realisation of the transcendent and the cosmic self, to achieve foundation in the supra-mundane and a self-aware manifestation in the mundane, is the integral knowledge; that is the possession of Immortality. It is this whole consciousness with its complete knowledge that builds the foundation of the Life Divine and makes its attainment possible. It follows that the absolute reality of the Absolute must be, not a rigid indeterminable oneness, not an infinity vacant of all that is not a pure self-existence attainable only by the exclusion of the many and the finite, but something which is beyond these definitions, beyond indeed any description either positive or negative. All affirmations and negations are expressive of its aspects, and it is through both a supreme affirmation and a supreme negation that we can arrive at the Absolute.

Sri Aurobindo   Yoga   India   1940

in God   infinite–finite

The finite and the infinite are one in God.

Baruch de Spinoza   Rationalism   The Netherlands   1677

in God   in devotion   in existence

I (the Eternal Inhabitant) am equal in all existences, none is dear to Me, none hated; yet those who turn to Me with love and devotion, they are in Me and I also in them.

The Bhagavad Gita   Hinduism   India   600 BCE

with God   in death

[A speech the deceased must say:]

There is no member of my body which is not the member of a god. The god Thoth protecteth my body altogether, and I am Ra day by day.

Unknown   Egyptian Religion   Egypt   1240 BCE

with the universal

Let me stand in my age with all its waters flowing round me. If they sometimes subdue me, they must finally upbear me, for I seek the universal — and that must be the best.

Margaret Fuller   Journalism   United States   1844

with all

But now she sat by sleeping Satyavan,
Awake within, and the enormous Night
Surrounded her with the Unknowable's vast.
A voice began to speak from her own heart
That was not hers, yet mastered thought and sense.
As it spoke all changed within her and without;
All was, all lived; she felt all being one;
The world of unreality ceased to be:

There was no more a universe built by mind,
Convicted as a structure or a sign;
A spirit, a being saw created things
And cast itself into unnumbered forms
And was what it saw and made; all now became
An evidence of one stupendous truth,
A Truth in which negation had no place,
A being and a living consciousness,
A stark and absolute Reality.
There the unreal could not find a place,
The sense of unreality was slain:
There all was conscious, made of the Infinite,
All had a substance of Eternity.
Yet this was the same Indecipherable;
It seemed to cast from it universe like a dream
Vanishing for ever into an original Void.
But this was no more some vague ubiquitous point
Or a cipher of vastness in unreal Nought.
It was the same but now no more seemed far
To the living clasp of her recovered soul.
It was her self, it was the self of all,
It was the reality of existing things,
It was the consciousness of all that lived
And felt and saw; it was Timelessness and Time,
It was the Bliss of formlessness and form.
It was all Love and the one Beloved's arms,
It was sight and thought in one all-seeing Mind,
It was joy of Being on the peaks of God.
She passed beyond Time into eternity,
Slipped out of space and became the Infinite;
Her being rose into unreachable heights
And found no end of its journey in the Self.
It plunged into the unfathomable deeps
And found no end to the silent mystery
That held all world within one lonely breast,
Yet harboured all creation's multitudes.
She was all vastness and one measureless point,
She was a height beyond heights, a depth beyond depths,
She lived in the everlasting and was all
That harbours death and bears the wheeling hours.
All contraries were true in one huge spirit

Surpassing measure, change and circumstance.
An individual, one with cosmic self
In the heart of the Transcendent's miracle
And the secret of World-personality
Was the creator and the lord of all.
Mind was a single innumerable look
Upon himself and all that he became.
Life was his drama and the Vast a stage,
The universe was his body, God its soul.
All was one single immense reality,
All its innumerable phenomenon.
  Her spirit saw the world as living God;
It saw the One and knew that all was He.
She knew him as the Absolute's self-space,
One with her self and ground of all things here
In which the world wanders seeking for the Truth
Guarded behind its face of ignorance:
She followed him through the march of endless Time.
All Nature's happenings were events in her,
The heart-beats of the cosmos were her own,
All beings thought and felt and moved in her;
She inhabited the vastness of the world,
Its distances were her nature's boundaries,
Its closenesses her own life's intimacies.
Her mind became familiar with its mind,
Its body was her body's larger frame
In which she lived and knew herself in it
One, multitudinous in its multitudes.
She was a single being, yet all things;
The world was her spirit's wide circumference,
The thoughts of others were her intimates,
Their feelings close to her universal heart,
Their bodies her many bodies kin to her;
She was no more herself but all the world.
Out of the infinitudes all came to her,
Into the infinitudes sentient she spread,
Infinity was her own natural home.
Nowhere she dwelt, her spirit was everywhere,
The distant constellations wheeled round her;
Earth saw her born, all worlds were her colonies,
The greater worlds of life and mind were hers;

All Nature reproduced her in its lines,
Its movements were large copies of her own.
She was the single self of all these selves,
She was in them and they were all in her.
This first was an immense identity
In which her own identity was lost:
What seemed herself was an image of the Whole.
She was a subconscient life of tree and flower,
The outbreak of the honied buds of spring;
She burned in the passion and splendour of the rose,
She was the red heart of the passion-flower,
The dream-white of the lotus in its pool.
Out of subconscient life she climbed to mind,
She was thought and the passion of the world's heart,
She was the godhead hid in the heart of man,
She was the climbing of his soul to God.
The cosmos flowered in her, she was its bed.
She was Time and the dreams of God in Time;
She was Space and the wideness of his days.
From this she rose where Time and Space were not;
The superconscient was her native air,
Infinity was her movement's natural space;
Eternity looked out from her on Time.

Sri Aurobindo   Yoga   India   1950

in art

The only domain where the divine is visible is that of art, whatever name we choose to call it.

André Malraux   Literature   France   1957

in surrender

Accept His command and you will be able to execute it,
Seek union with him and you will find yourselves united.

Jalal ad-Din Rumi   Sufism   Tajikistan, Turkey (Persia)   1230

near–far

I have resolved . . . to run when I can, to go when I cannot run, and to creep where I cannot go. As to the main, I thank him who loves me, I am fixed; my way is before me, my mind is beyond the River that has no bridge.

John Bunyan   Christianity   United Kingdom   1678

in geography

The tension between the call to the desert and to the market place arises not from the greater presence of God in one or the other, but from our varying psychological needs to apprehend him in different ways.

Sheila Cassidy   Literature   United Kingdom   1962

in God

God Himself is existence, He liveth in all things, and liveth upon all things. He endureth without increase or diminution, He multiplieth Himself millions of times, and He possesseth multitudes of forms and multitudes of members.

Unknown   Egyptian Religion   Egypt   1240 BCE

with the God force

I have church with myself: I have church walking down the street. I believe in the God force that lives inside all of us, and once you tap into that, you can do anything.

Oprah Winfrey   Television   United States   1998

inner–outer

The more God is in all things, the more He is outside them. The more He is within, the more without.

Meister Eckhart   Mysticism   Germany   1300

above—below

And when that greater Self comes sea-like down
To fill this image of our transience,
All shall be captured by delight, transformed:
In waves of undreamed ecstasy shall roll
Our mind and life and sense and laugh in a light
Other than this hard limited human day,
The body's tissues thrill apotheosised,
Its cells sustain bright metamorphosis.

Sri Aurobindo   Yoga   India   1950

in existence

Zen is a way of liberation, concerned not with discovering what is good or bad or advantageous, but what is.

Alan Watts   Zen Buddhism   United Kingdom   1961

in diversity

If we penetrate deeper into the symbolic language of the myths . . . we shall see that the crude polytheism which appears superficially to exist in ancient Mexico is simply a symbolic pointing to natural phenomena. The two thousand gods of the great multitude . . . were for the initiated sages merely many manifestations of the One.

Irene Nicholson   Anthropology   United States   1959

child—God

No one points out the Supreme Deity to a child. We come unto our fathers.

K.A. Busia   Politics   Ghana   1973

in religion

Whatever form of Me any devotee with faith desires to worship, I make that faith of his firm and undeviating.

The Bhagavad Gita   Hinduism   India   600 BCE

in diversity

One must have King-recognizing eyes
To recognize the King in mean disguise.

    Jalal ad-Din Rumi   Sufism   Tajikistan, Turkey (Persia)   1230

in God

God is closer to me than I to myself.

    Saint Augustine   Christianity   Algeria (Rome)   430

of the godhead

All grace and glory and all divinity
Were here collected in a single form;
All worshipped eyes looked through his from one face;
He bore all godheads in his grandiose limbs.

    Sri Aurobindo   Yoga   India   1950

with God

See there within the flesh
Like a bright wick, englazed
The soul God's finger lit
To give her liberty,
And joy and power and love.

    Mechthild von Magdeburg   Mysticism   Germany   1250

with God

God's Holy Will is the center from which all we do must radiate; all else is mere
weariness and excitement.

    Jean-Pierre Camus   Christianity   France   1639

in truth

The best scenery is nought-to-see —
That is the Mind-Essence of Illumination.
The best gain is nought-to-get —
That is the priceless treasure of Mind-Essence.
The best food for satiation is nought-to-eat —
That is the food of beyond-form Samadhi.
The best drink is nought-to-quaff —
That is the nectar of the Bodhi-Mind.
Wisdom is but Self-awareness,
Beyond all words and talk!

. . .

He who realizes the truth of "nor-high nor-low,"
Has reached the highest Stage.
He who realizes the truth of no-action,
Is following the Supreme Path.
He who realizes the truth of no-birth, no-death,
Obtains the best that he can hope for.
He who realizes the truth of no-inference,
Has mastered the best logic.
He who realizes the truth of no-great, no-small,
Understands the teaching of the Supreme Vehicle.
He who realizes the truth of no-virtue and no-evil
Has acquired the Supreme Means.
He who realizes the truth of not-two,
Has attained the Supreme View.
He who realizes the truth of no-accepting and no-abandoning,
Knows the supreme way to practice.
He who realizes the truth of non-effort,
Approaches the highest Accomplishment.

Jetsun Milarepa   Tibetan Buddhism   Tibet   1135

in desire   with God

I cannot teach you how to pray in words.
God listens not to your words save when He Himself utters them through your lips.
And I cannot teach you the prayer of the seas and the forests and the mountains.
But you who are born of the mountains and the forests and the seas can find their prayer in your heart,
And if you but listen in the stillness of the night you shall hear them saying in silence,
"Our God, who art our winged self, it is thy will in us that willeth.
It is thy desire in us that desireth.
It is thy urge in us that would turn our nights, which are thine, into days which are thine also.
We cannot ask thee for aught, for thou knowest our needs before they are born in us:
Thou art our need; and in giving us more of thyself thou givest us all."

Kahlil Gibran   Mysticism   Lebanon   1923

in the Transcendent

Do not ask whether the principle is in this or in that; it is in all beings. It is on this account that we apply to it the epithets of supreme, universal, total. . . . It has ordained that all things should be limited, but is Itself unlimited, infinite. As to what pertains to manifestation, the Principle causes the succession of its phases, but is not this succession. It is the author of causes and effects, but is not the causes and effects. It is the author of condensations and dissipations (birth and death, changes of state), but is not itself condensations and dissipations. All proceeds from It and is under Its influence. It is in all things, but is not identical with beings, for It is neither differentiated nor limited.

Chuang Tzu   Taoism   China   286 BCE

in rest   in God

Wherefore, when you shall find yourself in this simple and pure filial confidence with our Lord, stay there, my dear Theotimus, without moving yourself to make sensible acts, either of the understanding or of the will; for this simple love of confidence, and this love-sleep of your spirit in the arms of the Saviour, contains by excellence all that you go seeking hither and thither to satisfy your taste: it is better to sleep upon this sacred breast than to watch elsewhere, wherever it be.

Saint Francis de Sales   Christianity   France   1616

In action   without realization

I was interrupted yesterday just when I was trying to formulate the experience I had. And now everything seems changed. That precise knowledge, that clear-sightedness has given place to a great love for Thee, O Lord, which has seized my whole being from the outer organism to the deepest consciousness, and all lies prostrate at Thy feet in an ardent aspiration for a definitive identification with Thee, an absorption in Thee. I implored Thee with all the energy I could summon. And once again, just when it seemed to me that my consciousness was going to disappear in Thine, just when all my being was nothing but a pure crystal reflection of Thy Presence, someone came and interrupted my concentration.

Such is, indeed, the symbol of the existence Thou givest me as my share, in which outer usefulness, the work for all, holds a much greater place even than the supreme realisation. All the circumstances of my life seem always to tell me on Thy behalf: "It is not through supreme concentration that thou wilt realise oneness, it is by spreading out in all." May Thy will be done, O Lord.

Now I understand clearly that union with Thee is not an aim to be pursued, so far as this present individuality is concerned; it is an accomplished fact since a long time. And that is why Thou seemest to tell me always: "Do not delight in the ecstatic contemplation of this union; accomplish the mission I have entrusted to thee upon earth."

And the individual work to be carried on simultaneously with the collective work is to become aware and take possession of all the activities and parts of the being, the definitive establishment of consciousness in the highest point, making possible both the prescribed action and the constant communion with Thee. The joys of perfect union cannot come until what has to be done is done.

First, union must be preached to all, afterwards work; but for those who have realised the union, every moment of their life must be an integral expression of Thy will through them.

The Mother   Yoga   France   1914

with God

In taverns better far commune with Thee
Than pray in mosques and fail Thy face to see!
O first and last of all thy creatures Thou,
'Tis Thine to burn and Thine to cherish me.

Omar Khayyam   Poetry   Iran (Persia)   1123

of opposites   spirit–senses

All the senses and their qualities reflect him but he is without any senses; he is
unattached, yet all-supporting; he is enjoyer of the gunas (modes of nature), though
not limited by them.

   The Bhagavad Gita   Hinduism   India   600 BCE

in time   through eternity

I claim from time my will's eternity,
God from his moments.

   Sri Aurobindo   Yoga   India   1950

in dualities

They only who love Me with steadfast mind
Can cross this glamour of Duality;
And they who rise above this Dualness
They only know Me as the One Sole Truth.
Crossing beyond this ever-battling Pair
Of Joy and Sorrow, mind now Proud now Low,
Elation and Depression, they attain
The state of Peace that knows not any change.

   The Bhagavad Gita   Hinduism   India   600 BCE

above–below

The unconsciousness of man is the consciousness of God.

   Henry David Thoreau   Transcendentalism   United States   1862

of the unconscious

If it were possible to personify the unconscious, we might think of it as a collective human being combining the characteristics of both sexes, transcending youth and age, birth and death and from having at its command a human experience of one or two million years, practically immortal. If such a being existed, it would be exalted above all temporal change; the present would mean neither more nor less to it than any year in the hundredth millennium before Christ; it would be a dreamer of age-old dreams and, owing to its immeasurable experience, an incomparable prognosticator. It would have lived countless times over again the life of the individual, the family, the tribe, and the nation, and it would possess a living sense of the rhythm of growth, flowering, and decay.

Carl Jung   Psychology   Switzerland   1953

inner–outer

The Immobile stands behind each daily act,
A background of the movement and the scene,
Upholding creation on its might and calm
And change on the Immutable's deathless poise.
The Timeless looks out from the travelling hours;
The Ineffable puts on a robe of speech
Where all its words are woven like magic threads
Moving with beauty, inspiring with their gleam,
And every Thought takes up its destined place
Recorded in the memory of the world.

Sri Aurobindo   Yoga   India   1950

form–formlessness

God is formless and God is with form, too, and He is that which transcends form and formlessness. He alone can say what else He is.

Sri Ramakrishna   Hinduism   India   1900

in the Divine

A life of gnostic beings carrying the evolution to a higher supramental status might fitly be characterised as a divine life; for it would be a life in the Divine, a life of the beginnings of a spiritual divine light and power and joy manifested in material Nature.
. .

This new status would indeed be a reversal of the present law of human consciousness and life, for it would reverse the whole principle of the life of the Ignorance. It is for the taste of the Ignorance, its surprise and adventure, one might say, that the soul has descended into the Inconscience and assumed the disguise of Matter, for the adventure and the joy of creation and discovery, an adventure of the spirit, an adventure of the mind and life and the hazardous surprises of their working in Matter, for the discovery and conquest of the new and the unknown; all this constitutes the enterprise of life and all this, it might seem, would cease with the cessation of the Ignorance. Man's life is made up of the light and the darkness, the gains and losses, the difficulties and dangers, the pleasures and pains of the Ignorance, a play of colours moving on a soil of the general neutrality of Matter which has as its basis the nescience and insensibility of the Inconscient. To the normal life-being an existence without the reactions of success and frustration, vital joy and grief, peril and passion, pleasure and pain, the vicissitudes and uncertainties of fate and struggle and battle and endeavour, a joy of novelty and surprise and creation projecting itself into the unknown, might seem to be void of variety and therefore void of vital savour. Any life surpassing these things tends to appear to it as something featureless and empty or cast in the figure of an immutable sameness; the human mind's picture of heaven is the incessant repetition of an eternal monotone. But this is a misconception; for an entry into the gnostic consciousness would be an entry into the Infinite. It would be a self-creation bringing out the Infinite infinitely into form of being, and the interest of the Infinite is much greater and multitudinous as well as more imperishably delightful than the interest of the finite. The evolution in the Knowledge would be a more beautiful and glorious manifestation with more vistas ever unfolding themselves and more intensive in all ways than any evolution could be in the Ignorance. The delight of the Spirit is ever new, the forms of beauty it takes innumerable, its godhead ever young and the taste of delight, rasa, of the Infinite eternal and inexhaustible. The gnostic manifestation of life would be more full and fruitful and its interest more vivid than the creative interest of the Ignorance; it would be a greater and happier constant miracle.

If there is an evolution in material Nature and if it is an evolution of being with consciousness and life as its two key terms and powers, this fullness of being, fullness of consciousness, fullness of life must be the goal of development towards which we are tending and which will manifest at an early or later stage of our destiny. The self, the spirit, the reality that is disclosing itself out of the first inconscience of life and matter, would evolve its complete truth of being and consciousness in that life and matter. It would return to itself — or, if its end as an individual is to return into its Absolute, it could make that return also, — not through a frustration of life but through a spiritual completeness of itself in life. Our evolution in the Ignorance with its chequered joy and pain of self-discovery and world discovery, its half fulfilments, its constant finding and missing, is only our first state. It must lead inevitably towards an evolution in the Knowledge, a self-finding and self-unfolding of the Spirit, a self-revelation of the Divinity in things in that true power of itself in Nature which is to us still a Supernature.

Sri Aurobindo   Yoga   India   1940

harmony in oneness

Harmony is the natural rule of the spirit, it is the inherent law and spontaneous consequence of unity in multiplicity, of unity in diversity, of a various manifestation of oneness.

Sri Aurobindo   Yoga   India   1940

in wholeness

A wheel was shone to me,
wonderful to behold . . .

Divinity is in its omniscience and
    omnipotence
    like a wheel,
    a circle,
    a whole,

    that can neither be understood,
    nor divided,
    nor begun nor ended.

Hildegard of Bingen   Mysticism   Germany   1163

of opposites

His being is a mystery beyond mind,
His ways bewilder mortal ignorance;
The finite in its little sections parked,
Amazed, credits not God's audacity
Who dares to be the unimagined All
And see and act as might one Infinite.
Against human reason this is his offence;
Being known to be for ever unknowable,
To be all and yet transcend the mystic whole,
Absolute, to lodge in a relative world of Time,
Eternal and all-knowing, to suffer birth,
Omnipotent, to sport with Chance and Fate,
Spirit, yet to be Matter and the Void,
Illimitable, beyond form or name,
To dwell within a body, one and supreme
To be animal and human and divine:
A still deep sea, he laughs in rolling waves;
Universal, he is all, — transcendent, none.

Sri Aurobindo   Yoga   India   1950

in contradiction

A.N. Whitehead speaks to us of the real which stands behind and beyond and within the passing flux of this world, 'something which is real and yet waiting to be realised, something which is a remote possibility and yet the greatest of present facts, something that gives meaning to all that passes and yet eludes apprehension; something where possession is the final good and yet is beyond all reach, something which is the ultimate ideal and the hopeless quest.'

Alfred North Whitehead   Mathematics   United Kingdom   1880

soul–self

An omnipotent indiscernible Influence,
He sits, unfelt by the form in which he lives
And veils his knowledge by the groping mind.
A wanderer in a world his thoughts have made,
He turns in a chiaroscuro of error and truth
To find a wisdom that on high is his.
As one forgetting he searches for himself;
As if he had lost an inner light he seeks:
As a sojourner lingering amid alien scenes
He journeys to a home he knows no more.
His own self's truth he seeks who is the Truth;
He is the Player who became the play,
He is the Thinker who became the thought;
He is the many who was the silent One.

Sri Aurobindo   Yoga   India   1950

of opposites   heaven–Earth

If anyone could follow all the way, to the ultimate term of all these teachings of
transcendence — with the Buddha passing beyond desire and fear and with the
crucified Christ to at-one-ment with the Father — surely it would be found that when
all pairs of opposites have been left behind, then duality and nonduality, egolessness
and egohood, heavenly truth and earthly truth have been left behind as well. This,
finally, is the meaning of the gentle scene of the coronation of Christ's earthly virgin-
mother Mary in heaven. She has risen carnally to that spiritual height where he, in
union with the Father, turns again with a gesture of total affirmation to the mother of
his earthly body and crowns her heaven's queen.

Joseph Campbell   Mythology   United States   1974

in martial arts   in strength

I set my mind on budo when I was about 15 and visited teachers of swordsmanship and jujutsu in various provinces. I mastered the secrets of the old traditions, each within a few months. But there was no one to instruct me in the essence of budo; the only thing that could satisfy my mind. So I knocked on the gates of various religions but I couldn't get any concrete answers.

Then in the spring of 1925, if I remember correctly, when I was taking a walk in the garden by myself, I felt that the universe suddenly quaked, and that a golden spirit sprang up from the ground, veiled my body, and changed my body into a golden one.

At the same time my mind and body became light. I was able to understand the whispering of the birds, and was clearly aware of the mind of God, the Creator of this universe.

At that moment I was enlightened: the source of budo is God's love — the spirit of loving protection for all beings. Endless tears of joy streamed down my cheeks.

Since that time I have grown to feel that the whole earth is my house and the sun, the moon and the stars are all my own things. I had become free from all desire, not only for position, fame and property, but also to be strong. I understood, "Budo is not felling the opponent by our force; nor is it a tool to lead the world into destruction with arms. True budo is to accept the spirit of the universe, keep the peace of the world, correctly produce, protect and cultivate all beings in Nature." I understood, "The training of budo is to take God's love, which correctly produces, protects and cultivates all things in Nature, and assimilate and utilize it in our own mind and body."

Kisshomaru Ueshiba   Aikido   Japan   1969

of planes of being   soul–psychic being

I have told you many times and I could not repeat it too often, that one is not built up of one single piece. We have within us many states of being and each state of being has its own life. All this is put together in one single body, so long as you have a body, and acts through that single body; so that gives you the feeling that it is one single person, a single being. But there are many beings and particularly there are concentrations on different levels: just as you have a physical being, you have a vital being, you have a mental being, you have a psychic being [soul], you have many others and all possible intermediaries. . . . But if you have united your consciousness with the psychic consciousness when you die you remain conscious of your psychic being.

The Mother   Yoga   France   1953

in the supramental being

A supramental or gnostic race of beings would not be a race made according to a single type, moulded in a single fixed pattern; for the law of the supermind is unity fulfilled in diversity, and therefore there would be an infinite diversity in the manifestation of the gnostic consciousness although that consciousness would still be one in its basis, in its constitution, in its all revealing and all-uniting order. . . .

The gnosis is the effective principle of the Spirit, a highest dynamis of the spiritual existence. The gnostic individual would be the consummation of the spiritual man; his whole way of being, thinking, living, acting would be governed by the power of a vast universal spirituality. All the trinities of the Spirit would be real to his self-awareness and realised in his inner life. All his existence would be fused into oneness with the transcendent and universal Self and Spirit; all his action would originate from and obey the supreme Self and Spirit's divine governance of Nature. All life would have to him the sense of the Conscious Being, the Purusha within, finding its self-expression in Nature; his life and all its thoughts, feelings, acts would be filled for him with that significance and built upon that foundation of its reality. He would feel the presence of the Divine in every centre of his consciousness, in every vibration of his life-force, in every cell of his body. In all the workings of his force of Nature he would be aware of the workings of the supreme World-Mother, the Supernature; he would see his natural being as the becoming and manifestation of the power of the World-Mother. In this consciousness he would live and act in an entire transcendent freedom, a complete joy of the spirit, an entire identity with the cosmic self and a spontaneous sympathy with all in the universe. All beings would be to him his own selves, all ways and powers of consciousness would be felt as the ways and powers of his own universality. . . . His own life and the world life would be to him like a perfect work of art; it would be as if the creation of a cosmic and spontaneous genius infallible in its working out of a multitudinous order. The gnostic individual would be in the world and of the world, but would also exceed it in his consciousness and live in his self of transcendence above it; he would be universal but free in the universe, individual but not limited by a separative individuality. The true Person is not an isolated entity, his individuality is universal; for he individualizes the universe: it is at the same time divinely emergent in a spiritual air of transcendental infinity, like a high cloud-surpassing summit; for he individualises the divine Transcendence.

Sri Aurobindo Yoga India 1940

with God

In a divine retreat from mortal thought,
In a prodigious gesture of soul-sight,
His being towered into pathless heights,
Naked of its vesture of humanity
As thus it rose, to meet him bare and pure
A strong Descent leaped down. A Might, a Flame,
A Beauty half-visible with deathless eyes,
A violent ecstasy, a Sweetness dire,
Enveloped him with its stupendous limbs
And penetrated nerve and heart and brain
That thrilled and fainted with the epiphany:
His nature shuddered in the Unknown's grasp.
In a moment shorter than Death, longer than Time,
By a power more ruthless than Love, happier than Heaven
Taken sovereignly into eternal arms,
Haled and coerced by a stark absolute bliss
In a whirlwind circuit of delight and force
Hurried into unimaginable depths,
Upborne into immeasurable heights,
It was torn out from its mortality
And underwent a new and bourneless change.
An Omniscient knowing without sight or thought,
An indecipherable Omnipotence,
A mystic Form that could contain the worlds,
Yet make one human breast its passionate shrine,
Drew him out of his seeking loneliness
Into the magnitudes of God's embrace.

Sri Aurobindo   Yoga   India   1950

spiritual vs. other types of oneness

So far as we really succeed in living for others, it is done by an inner spiritual force of love and sympathy; but the power and field of effectuality of this force in us are small, the psychic movement that prompts it is incomplete, its action often ignorant because there is contact of mind and heart but our being does not embrace the being of others as ourselves. An external unity with others must always be an outward joining and association of external lives with a minor inner result; the mind and heart attach their movements to this common life and the beings whom we meet there; but the common external life remains the foundation, — the inward constructed unity, or so much of it as can persist in spite of mutual ignorance and discordant egoisms, conflict of minds, conflict of hearts, conflict of vital temperaments, conflict of interests, is a partial and insecure superstructure. The spiritual consciousness, the spiritual life reverses this principle of building; it bases its action in the collective life upon an inner experience and inclusion of others in our own being, an inner sense and reality of oneness. The spiritual individual acts out of that sense of oneness which gives him immediate and direct perception of the demand of self on other self, the need of the life, the good, the work of love and sympathy that can truly be done. A realisation of spiritual unity, a dynamisation of the intimate consciousness of one-being, of one self in all beings, can alone found and govern by its truth the action of the divine life.

Sri Aurobindo   Yoga   India   1940

world—void   dream—waking   pain—pleasure   human—transcendent

He who sees the world and Voidness as the same,
Has reached the realm of the True View.

He who feels no difference between dream and waking,
Has reached the realm of True Practice.

He who feels no difference between Bliss and Voidness
Has reached the realm of True Action.

He who feels no difference between "now" and "then,"
Has reached the realm of Reality.

He who sees that Mind and Voidness are the same,
Has reached the realm of Dharmakaya.

He who feels no difference between pain and pleasure,
Has reached the realm of the True Teaching.

He who sees human wishes and Buddha's Wisdom as the same,
Has reached the realm of supreme Enlightenment.

He who sees that Self-mind and Buddha are alike,
Has reached the realm of True Accomplishment.

Jetsun Milarepa   Tibetan Buddhism   Tibet   1135

in the supramental

Mental nature and mental thought are based on a consciousness of the finite; supramental nature is in its very grain a consciousness and power of the Infinite. Supramental Nature sees everything from the standpoint of oneness and regards all things, even the greatest multiplicity and diversity, even what are to the mind the strongest contradictions, in the light of that oneness; its will, ideas, feelings, sense are made of the stuff of oneness, its actions proceed upon that basis. Mental Nature, on the contrary, thinks, sees, wills, feels, senses with division as a starting-point and has only a constructed understanding of unity; even when it experiences oneness, it has to act from the oneness on a basis of limitation and difference. But the supramental, the divine life is a life of essential, spontaneous and inherent unity. It is impossible for the mind to forecast in detail what the supramental change must be. . . . For the mind acts by intellectual rule or device or by reasoned choice of will or by mental impulse or in obedience to life impulse; but supramental nature does not act by mental idea or rule or in subjection to any inferior impulse: each of its steps is dictated by an innate spiritual vision, a comprehensive and exact penetration into the truth of all and the truth of each thing; it acts always according to inherent reality, not by the mental idea, not according to an imposed law of conduct or a constructive thought or perceptive contrivance. Its movement is calm, self-possessed, spontaneous, plastic; it arises naturally and inevitably out of a harmonic identity of the truth which is felt in the very substance of the conscious being, a spiritual substance which is universal and therefore intimately one with all that is included in its cognition of existence.

Sri Aurobindo   Yoga   India   1940

above—below   good—evil   with all

In the heart of my creation's mystery
I will enact the drama of thy soul,
Inscribe the long romance of Thee and Me.
I will pursue thee across the centuries;
Thou shalt be hunted through the world by love,
Naked of ignorance' protecting veil
And without covert from my radiant gods.
No shape shall screen thee from my divine desire,
Nowhere shalt thou escape my living eyes.
In the nudity of thy discovered self,
In a bare identity with all that is,
Disrobed of thy covering of humanity,
Divested of the dense veil of human thought,
Made one with every mind and body and heart,
Made one with all Nature and with Self and God,
Summing in thy single soul my mystic world
I will possess in thee my universe,
The universe find all I am in thee.
Thou shalt bear all things that all things may change,
Thou shalt fill all with my splendour and my bliss,
Thou shalt meet all with thy transmuting soul.
Assailed by my infinitudes above,
And quivering in immensities below,
Pursued by me through my mind's wall-less vast,
Oceanic with the surges of my life,
A swimmer lost between two leaping seas
By my outer pains and inner sweetnesses
Finding my joy in my opposite mysteries
Thou shalt respond to me from every nerve.
A vision shall compel thy coursing breath,
Thy heart shall drive thee on the wheel of works,
Thy mind shall urge thee through the flames of thought,
To meet me in the abyss and on the heights,
To feel me in the tempest and the calm,
And love me in the noble and the vile,
In beautiful things and terrible desire.
The pains of hell shall be to thee my kiss,
The flowers of heaven persuade thee with my touch.
My fiercest masks shall my attractions bring.
Music shall find thee in the voice of swords,

Beauty pursue thee through the core of flame.
Thou shalt know me in the rolling of the spheres
And cross me in the atoms of the whirl.
The wheeling forces of my universe
Shall cry to thee the summons of my name.
Delight shall drop down from my nectarous moon,
My fragrance seize thee in the jasmine's snare,
My eye shall look upon thee from the sun.
Mirror of Nature's secret spirit made,
Thou shalt reflect my hidden heart of joy,
Thou shalt drink down my sweetness unalloyed
In my pure lotus-cup of starry brim.
My dreadful hands laid on thy bosom shall force
Thy being bathed in fiercest longing's streams.
Thou shalt discover the one and quivering note,
And cry, the harp of all my melodies,
And roll, my foaming wave in seas of love.
Even my disasters' clutch shall be to thee
The ordeal of my rapture's contrary shape:
In pain's self shall smile on thee my secret face:
Thou shalt bear my ruthless beauty unabridged
Amid the world's intolerable wrongs,
Trampled by the violent misdeeds of Time
Cry out to the ecstasy of my rapture's touch.
All beings shall be to thy life my emissaries;
Drawn to me on the bosom of thy friend,
Compelled to meet me in thy enemy's eyes,
My creatures shall demand me from thy heart.
Thou shalt not shrink from any brother soul.
Thou shalt be attracted helplessly to all.
Men seeing thee shall feel my hands of joy,
In sorrow's pangs feel steps of the world's delight,
Their life experience its tumultuous shock
In the mutual craving of two opposites.
Hearts touched by thy love shall answer to my call,
Discover the ancient music of the spheres
In the revealing accents of thy voice
And nearer draw to me because thou art:
Enamoured of thy spirit's loveliness
They shall embrace my body in thy soul,
Hear in thy life the beauty of my laugh,

Know the thrilled bliss with which I made the worlds.
All that thou hast, shall be for others' bliss,
All that thou art, shall to my hands belong.
I will pour delight from thee as from a jar,
I will whirl thee as my chariot through the ways,
I will use thee as my sword and as my lyre,
I will play on thee my minstrelsies of thought.
And when thou art vibrant with all ecstasy,
And when thou liv'st one spirit with all things,
Then will I spare thee not my living fires,
But make thee a channel for my timeless force.
My hidden presence led thee unknowing on
From thy beginning in earth's voiceless bosom
Through life and pain and time and will and death,
Through outer shocks and inner silences
Along the mystic roads of Space and Time
To the experience which all Nature hides.
Who hunts and seizes me, my captive grows:
This shalt thou henceforth learn from thy heart-beats.
For ever love, O beautiful slave of God!

Sri Aurobindo   Yoga   India   1950

About the Editors

Ronald Jorgensen

Ron is an everyday mystic. He sees the mystical qualities in the common elements of life and always sees the world afresh. As a deep and eclectic explorer of our reality and with interests in nearly everything, he is charged with wonder and enthusiasm that is caught by his lifestyle and poetry. Always ready to share his original insights and to listen to those of others, Ron finds ways to nurture personal development through his writings on spirit and his teaching of tai chi and yoga. His depth and range of insights and dedication to this work have allowed Ron to take the seed of the book, plant it in a soil of knowledge and form, and grow it into this marvelous bouquet of expressions of oneness with colors, shapes and aromas that many find irresistible.

Born in Montana and raised in Washington, Ron did his undergraduate work at Washington State University. During his studies at Harvard University's Divinity School, he met the visiting Allen Ginsberg, which influenced him deeply for writing poetry.

Ron lived and worked in New York City for eight years as a consultant in management and educational technology with corporations, educational institutions and government agencies as clients. His most significant education began in the 1970's during his eight years in the Sri Aurobindo Ashram and Auroville in India where he studied and practiced Integral Yoga and worked on projects for an Ashram-related group, World Union. Ron makes his home in Enumclaw, Washington, at the foot of Mt. Rainier, and his most cherished other interests are music, hiking, dining, and good conversation laced with laughter.

William Leon

Bill is a dreamer and seeker of truths. Recognizing that the Ultimate Truth has varied dimensions and expressions, he seeks understanding through a broad exploration of knowledge and cultures in order to experience multiple points of view of the consummate One. He visualizes better lives for all in the world and journeys toward that through his own personal change and work. Immersion in the study of Integral Yoga led him to connect with the global community of Auroville, India (started by The Mother of Sri Aurobindo Ashram). As an Auroville International USA board member for over two decades, he has been a steady support.

Bill's education and wide-ranging studies of science and spirit have been useful in researching and organizing this collection. Moving frequently in his youth, he became fascinated by the diversity of cultural expression, and this influenced his life-long study of geography in the world and at four universities. After earning a Ph.D. from the University of Washington, he taught for 15 years at the University of Colorado at Colorado Springs and directed the Center for Community Development & Design, managing community research and development efforts throughout the state by his staff, students, and other faculty. Returning to Washington, Bill founded Geo Education & Research to provide program evaluation, community development, research, and educational services to non-profits, foundations, and government agencies, including the United Nations and the International Criminal Court. He lives in Lake Forest Park, Washington and volunteers on several local environmental and civic projects when he is not gardening, bicycling, or making his friends laugh.

Acknowledgements

Whatever name or two on the spine, a book is a work of community. In our case, quite a large one, that draws our loving gratitude for life's duration.

First, the Mother of Sri Aurobindo Ashram, India, started it all in a 1960 meeting. M. P. Pandit chose Ron to do it. He and A. B. Patel, both in that ashram, actively supported Ron in the early years. Sri Aurobindo brought them all together and inspired them and us.

Others who inspired us include Maggi Lidchi, Gary Delles, Wally Duchateau, Shyamraj Sharma, Carole Lazio, Bob Iden, Joetta Lawrence, Kathy Buss, Paul Tillich, Joseph Campbell, The Dalai Lama, Allen Ginsberg, Ruud Lohman, Gregory Corso, Jack Gilbert, Neal Cassady, Gary Larson, William C. C. Chen, Tom Brown, Palmer Hilty, June Maher, Jake Lehrer, and Ram Dass.

We are eternally grateful to the many helpers who put their loving devotion into this work. Several people played critical roles in the work's evolution. Doug Bates took the initial findings from notecards to a database that allowed us to more easily compile and edit the expressions. Raina Imig has been an insightful editor and graphics advisor. Maggie Greer, Agraha and Begabati Lennihan were essential editors. Robin Sherman provided key expertise in layout and book design. Other technical advisors include Edith Stadig, Angela Hryniuk, Philip Lightstone, Diane Thome, Michael Silverwise, Jim Sluga, Jim Balog, Agraha, and Murtaza Junejo of Print Fusion. The many quote sleuths who found and verified expressions include Rod Hemsell, Derek Rhys, Paula Bronte, Mary Bond, Carrie Stanley, Renata Kreidler, Valarie, Dave Ralph, Miranda Fox, Ananda and Abhishek Das, Crystal Vensand, Joe Johnston, Lucas Booher, Sinan Demirel, Rebekah Demirel, Sandy Buckman and many of the students who worked with Bill at the Center for Community Development & Design at the University of Colorado at Colorado Springs who also practiced "applied oneness" (who include Sarajoy Vanboren, Susan Dixon, Salena Vaughan, Aimee Cox, Danice Ditmar, Tammy Albin, Dorothy Macnak, Valerie Cass, Barbara Coast, Patricia Cole, Mary Dodge, Angela McGee, Pam Burton, Tim Pahel, John Stevens, Patricia Gavelda, Janis Phillips, Tom Light, Barry Cress, Steve Demarrias, Clark Friedrichs, Mary Jane Herrera, Nancy Noriega, Chuck Perry, Gregg Tugman, Ann Wiegert, Jim Griffith, Henrietta DeGroot, Patricia Middleton, Cecilia Gonzales, Rick Fitske, Scott Roscoe, John Stevens, Regina Earing, Diane Ahee, Thuylinh Nguyen, Pam Cherry, Robin Cunningham, Yolanda Robinson, Marie McIntire, Jodie Williams, Marian Swanger, Richard Foss, Lisa Sedlak, Sally Meadows, Bill Norkoli, Henry Rosoff, Megan Buffington, Marin La Riva, Deborah Woldruff, Sarah Aubrey, Vicky Mair, Sherry Marshall, Donna Micklich, Jonathan Batt, Lora Hahn, David Leitch, Donna Arkowski, Dan Stradtman, Soraya Baroumand, Kiet Nguyen, Marina Perkins, Suzan Kelley, Kathy Trask, Larizza Morales, Evelyn Alba, Brandie LaChance, Theresa Nallick, Rebecca Parkins, Sam Stuart, Carol Phelan, Priscilla Kaufmann, Barbara Gately, Sally Brown, Casey O'Neil, Skye Ridley, Sandy Trujillo, Carol Weissler, Darlene Montani, Dennis O'Rourke, Carol Huber, Lori Houser, and others). Since it took over 40 years, we may have forgotten some folks. If we did, please forgive us and do remind us that you worked on the book.

Others who supported us financially and in other crucial ways include Esther Margaret Thorpe Jorgensen, Jim and Patricia Jorgensen, Shu-Jung Wang, Martha, Sarah Jane Freymann, Rick Notestine, Dawn Bernasconi, Gail Miltimore, Diane Thome, Herb Coats, Roger and Lavinia Stanley, Rand Hicks, Douglas Manfredi, Gene and Annie Trobaugh, Elinor Ulman, Bill and Mif Decker, Ranko Petcovits, Dolores Armentrout, Kalpana Dave, Bobbi Nesmith, Garrin Ross, Dave and Millie Roberts, Gary Bowker, Sylvia Wallace, Gennie Barrett, Leonard, Dave Pook, Patty Megna, Corey, Caroline Kuknyo, and Diane Olson.

People who inspired and supported us in this work by their embodiment of oneness include Bob and Polly Leon, Jim and Evelyn Swann, Cyndi Swann, Avery Leon, Sera Han, Graysie, Danger, Max, Jivan and Anadi Swann, Jerry Swann, Marie Bjornson, Audrey Swann, Dylan Swann, Dale Swann, Anadi Carr, Bob, Melanie, Sam, John, and Casey Leon, Rut and Bobby Martin, Paul Blankenbecker, Sibby, David, John, Beth, and Amber Hagge, Leo and Bea (Boo Mama) Winston, Hal Belle Isle, the Lee family, Kim Nguyen, Richard Goodloe, Don Norman, Paul Ford, Dave Tetta, Kim Holscher, Shyamraj, Vikas, Manju, and Veena Sharma, Cosette Leciel, Joe McCrae, Francine Loeb, John Murphey, Joel and Michelle Levey, Agraha Levine, Rachel Price, Madani Knowles, Kathy Provazek, Ken Winnick, Cecily Kaplan, Will Ambrose, Richard and Nishi Carlson, Sylvia Wallace, Rebecca Purdy, Morgan and Tom Kellock, Sinan and Rebekah Demirel, Alan and Lori Safer, Fritz Fuhrmann, Diana Echeverria, Harry Atlas, Jeanne Downing, Paula Rowland, Jane Reisman, Marc Bolan, Anne Gienapp, Kasey Langley, Afsaneh Rahimian, Geoff Miller, Janette Moreno, Shelley Dillon, RobRoy Erickson, Leonor Robles, Sarah Stachowiak, Heidi Brown, Francis Zainoeddin, Jean Eisele, Karen Litfin, Louis Mangual, Caroline Kuknyo, Siggy Quante, Carol Sanford, J.W. Harrington, Vicki Scuri, Gilbert White, Nick Helburn, Dick Morrill, Bill Beyers, David Hodge, Craig Zumbrunnen, Clancy Philipsborn, Burrell Montz, Paul Covey, Deborah Elliott-Fisk, Craig Calhoun, Frances and Barbara Sheridan, Marion Sheridan, Wendy Berg, Babs Buttenfield, Steven Moss, Alice Ierley, Eve Gruntfest, Marc Weber, Karen Bruenig, Sarah Christiansen, Katie Warner, Judy Rice-Jones, Lynn Johnson, Sarah Qualls, Jody Fitzpatrick, Sandy Wurtele, Lynda Dickson, Jerry Carlton, Bob Durham, Cindy Sell, Mary Dodge, Larry Eubanks, Eric Morris, Peter Hein, Peggy Hupcey, T. Michael Smith, Scott Kieselbach, Bernie Jones, Bob Horn, George Weber, Jack Leaman, Connie Lorig, Elizabeth Wright Ingraham, Mike Riley, Bubba Snyder, Jim Bates, Jim, Null, Michael Barndollar, Jack Donahue, Calvin Gibson, Eric Swab, Ruben Martinez, William Barns, Tom Huber, Chuck Murphey, José Barrera, Bob Bergman, Fred Betz, Jr., Donna Chadd, Jules Guadin, Charles Vorwaller, Marvin Adams, Rebecca Bromley, Kip Peterson, Jack Bowman, Mark Tremmel, Rocky Sarter, George Marin, Cullen Ann Wheelock, David Carvey, Joanne Greek, Bill Lyons, Kee Warner, Michael Davenport, Paul Poppert, Deborah Sagen, other Board members of the Center for Community Development & Design, Dwayne Nuzum, E Gordon Gee, Kat Jorstad, Jim Beckenhaupt, Karen Gayle, Lindy Tudor, Bob Bixler, John Miller, Jay Beeton, Erika Archibald, Rishi and Kirti Hemsell, Kalaben Patel, Prakash Patel, Bhavana, B, Dakshina, Lisbeth, Savitra, Nadaka, Gopika, Wolfgang, Soleil, Rathinam, Rajaveni, Selvaraj, Shankar, Murugan, Jill, Swar, Surya Narayanan, Anandi, Kalya, Julian and Wendy Lines, Bryan and Fanou Walton, Constance Walker, Jeanne and Gordon Korstange, Jack and Mary Alexander, Mateo Needham, Renu Noegy, Lara Davis, Malcolm Boyer, Chetana Deorah, Binah Thillairajah, Chandresh Patel, Ed and Mindy Giordano, Nilauro Marcus, and John Robert Cornell.

Many libraries and other sources were invaluable to our research but especially facilities at the University of Washington, the University of Colorado at Colorado Springs, the Enumclaw Library, the King County Library System, Seattle Public Libraries, and Wikipedia. We also thank the many publishers who gave us permission to reproduce these expressions and, of course, the authors who wrote them.

Thanks also to the publishers and authors who gave their permission to us to use their work. We have diligently searched for the copyright holders of the many works still under copyright and we are grateful for their permission to use the small excepts or poems included in this work. If we have not found the holders and have included items authors or publishers do not wish to have included, we will remove them upon request. Please know that our inclusion of any of these works is not meant to usurp their mojo but to acknowledge, celebrate, and share their mastery of mystery so that others may find and enjoy the works of these authors. For this reason we have included a full bibliography.

Many, many others whose faces we recall, also vividly gave to this book in work, funding and meals, ears and eyes, laughs and hearts, and loves sustained by souls down to the nano-details which complete and give the radiance to it all.

Bibliography

The index has a more complete listing of authors. Please note that if you are searching for a particular author, some cultures list the family names first. We have kept this arrangement in the bibliography and in the index. Works with many or unknown authors are listed in the following section by title.

Adams, Henry: The Education of Henry Adams

Adyashanti: True Meditation: Discover the Freedom of Pure Awareness

Aldrich, Thomas Bailey: A Shadow of the Night

Alexander, Christopher: The Timeless Way of Building

Angelou, Maya: "On the Pulse of Morning"

Ansari of Herat: "Invocations" The Persian Mystics: Invocations of al-Ansari al-Harawi

Antiphon: On the Murder of Herodes

Archief, Bijbel: Theologica Germanica

Aristotle: The Basic Works of Aristotle

Arundale, G.S.: Freedom and Friendship: the Call of Theosophy and the Theosophical Society; Nirvana; You

Aseyev, Nikolai: "There Are Some Folk Who Money Covet"

Augustine, St.: City of God

Aurelius, Marcus: Meditations

Aurobindo, Sri: "Electron" in Collected Poems of Sri Aurobindo; Eric in Collected Plays and Short Stories of Sri Aurobindo; Savitri: A Legend and a Symbol; The Life Divine

Awoonor, Kofi: "Rediscovery"

Bahá'u'lláh: Gleanings from the Writings of Bahá'u'lláh; One Planet One People . . . Please; The Hidden Words of Bahá'u'lláh

Baldwin, Christina: Life's Companion: Journal Writing as a Spiritual Quest

Bartok, Bela: Letter to Octavian Beu

Bass, Franta: ". . . I Never Saw another Butterfly. . ." in Children's Drawings and Poems from Terezin Concentration Camp, 1942-1944

Beecher, Henry Ward: Prayers from Plymouth Pulpit

Benediktsson, Einar: "Wave-life" in Odes and Echoes

Benét, Stephen Vincent: Western Star

Bergholz, Olga: "Hope"

Berry, Wendell: "The Unforseen Wilderness" in Kentucky's Red River Gorge

Besant, Annie and Leadbeater, C.W.: "Talks on the Path of Occultism: A commentary on The Voice of the Silence"

Besant, Annie: An Introduction to Yoga; A Study in Consciousness; Dharma; Study in Consciousness; The Evolution of Life and Form; What the Mystic Means by The Eternal Now

Black Elk: Black Elk Speaks; The Sacred Pipe

Blake, William: Auguries of Innocence

Blavatsky, Helena Petrovna: Isis Unveiled; Raja-Yoga or Occultism; The Esoteric
    Character of The Gospels; The Secret Doctrine, Volume II; Transactions of the
    Blavatsky Lodge

Blok, Alexander: "A Red Glow in the Sky"; "Address delivered at the Celebration of the
    Eighty-Fourth Anniversary of the Death of Pushkin" in Wisdom Through the
    Ages

Boehme, Jacob: The Supersensual Life

Boone, J. Allen: Kinship with all Life

Bottomley, Gordon: "To Iron Founders and Others"

Brown, John: Reformers and Rebels

Browning, Elizabeth Barrett: "Aurora Leigh"

Buber, Martin: Zen and Hasidism; Interpreting the Hasidic Doctrine of Humility

Bucke, Richard: Cosmic Consciousness

Buddha, Gautama: Cullaviyuha Sutra; Dhammapada; Kokaliya Sutra; Mahayana Texts;
    Nolóka Sulta; Puróbheda Sutra

Bunyan, John: Pilgrim's Progress

Burke, Edmund: An Account of the European Settlers in America

Butler, Samuel: Butler's Note-Book

Campbell, Joseph: Beautyway: A Navaho Ceremonial; The Mythic Image

Camus, Jean-Pierre: The Spirit of St. Frances de Sales

Carey, Ken: Return of the Bird Tribes

Carlyle, Thomas: Life of Schiller; Sir Walter Scott

Carpenter, Edmund: Anerca; Eskimo Realities

Cassidy, Sheila: "The Peace of God," in Prayers for Peace

Césaire, Aimé: Return to My Native Land

Channing, William Ellery: My Symphony; Notebook: Children

Chardin, Pierre Teilhard de: The Phenomenon of Man

Chesterton, G.K.: All Things Considered

Chang Huai-kuan: Shu Tuan (Evaluation Of Calligraphy)

Chinmoy, Sri: "Inner flames of the United Nations"; "The United Nations and World-
    Union"; "The United Nations: Leader of the World Family" in The Garland of the
    Nation-Souls

Chŏn Ponggŏn: "Flower in a Classic Whisper" in World Order

Chuang Tzu: Chuang Tsu: Inner Chapters

Cicero, Marcus Tullius: De Senectute

Clinton, Hillary: Speech at Fourth World Conference on Women in Beijing

Colby, Frank Moore: Imaginary Obligations

Coleridge, Samuel Taylor: Biographia Literaria; Specimens of the Table Talk of S.T. Coleridge

Confucius: Sources of Chinese Tradition: Volume 1: From Earliest Times to 1600

Connolly, Cyril: The Unquiet Grave

Conrad, Joseph: Lord Jim

Coomaraswamy, Ananda: Good Work

Cotter, Joseph S.: Dunbar Speaker

Crimthainn, Áed Ua: Book of Leinster

Cyril of Alexandria: Commentary on the Gospel according to St. John

da Vinci, Leonardo: The Notebooks of Leonardo da Vinci

Dalai Lama, H. H. the 14th: Ocean of Wisdom: Guidelines for Living; The Global Community and the Need for Universal Responsibility;

Dass, Baba Hari: Fire Without Fuel: The Aphorisms of Baba Hari Dass

Dass, Ram: Be Here Now

David-Neel, Alexandra: Initiations and Initiates in Tibet

Davies, William Henry: "Men that Think"

DeBogart, Willard Von: Harmonic Neurons

de Saint-Exupéry, Antoine: Flight to Arras; The Wisdom of the Sands

de Sales, St. Francis: Treatise on the Love of God

Dewey, John: The Public and Its Problems

Dhul-Nun al-Misri: Sugi Saints East and West by Sadhu T. L. Vaswani

Diop, Birago: "Spirits"

Diop, Cheikh Anta: L'Afrique noire pré-coloniale in The Literature and Thought of Modern Africa: A Survey

Diop, David Mandessi: "To A Black Dancer" in Hammer Blows And Other Writings

Djoleto, Amu: "The Good Old Motto"

Donne, John: Sermons

Doren, Mark Van: December Setting

Dostoyevsky, Fyodor: The Brothers Karamazov; The Possessed

Drinkwater, John: "Abraham Lincoln"

Dumas, Alexander: The Three Musketeers

Durrell, Lawrence: Clea

Dyer, Wayne W.: You'll See It When You Believe It

Eddy, Mary Baker: Science and Health

Edgar, Lilian: Elements of Theosophy

Edwards, Brooke Medicine Eagle: Buffalo Woman Comes Singing: The Spirit Song of a Rainbow Medicine Woman; "In Essence"; Earth Song

Ehrenburg, Ilya: The Fantastic Adventures of Julio Jurenito

Einstein, Albert: "Letter to Robert. S. Marcus" in Mathematical Circles Adieu; "The Enlightened Mind" in Wisdom Through the Ages; "Science and Religion"; The World as I See It;

Elagin, Ivan: "Rough Draft"

Eliot, Sir Charles: Japanese Buddhism

Eliot, T.S.: The Elder Statesman

Emerson, Ralph Waldo: Address to Harvard Divinity School; "Each and All"; Essays; Journals; Lectures and Biographical Sketches; Letters and Aims: Progress of Culture; Letters and Social Aims; Nature; "Sea-Shore"; Society and Solitude: Works and Days; The Conduct of Life

Emre, Yunus: Yunus Emre Ve Tasavvuf

Erskine, John: The Complete Life

Farrell, James T.: Prejudices: A Selection

Fénelon, François: "Simplicity and Self-Consciousness" in The Complete Fénelon

FitzGerald, Robert D.: "Movement"

Florian, Miroslav: "Fatherhood" in New Writings in Czechoslovakia

Fox, George: "Epistle 115"; "Epistle 292 and letter from prison to friends in the ministry" in The Quaker Contribution

Froebel, Friedrich Wilhelm: Educated Man

Fromm, Erich: Man for Himself

Fuller, Buckminster: "the View from the Year 2000"; Buckminster Fuller Public Lecture at Columbia University: Synergetics: Explorations in the Geometry of Thinking

Fuller, Margaret: Summer on the Lakes; Woman in the Nineteenth Century

Fuller, Thomas: Gnomologia

Gandhi, Mahatma: An Autobiography or the Story of my Experiments with Truth; From Yeravda Mandir

Gibran, Kahlil: The Prophet

Gide, André: "Pretexts: Reflections on Literature and Morality"

Gió: The Burning Heart

Goddard, Gloria: To the Commonplace

Goethe, Johann Wolfgang von: Elective Affinities; Faust; The Experiment as Mediator between Object and Self

Gorky, Maxim: The Zykovs

Govinda, Lama Anagarika: The Foundations of Tibetan Mysticism

Grayson, David: Adventures in Contentment

Gregory of Nyssa, Bishop: The Creation of Man

Hafez: "Dropping Keys"

Hagedorn, Hermann: "The Bomb That Fell on America"

Haich, Elisabeth: Initiation

Hardy, Alister: The Biology of God

Hawking, Stephen: A Brief History of Time

Hazlitt, William: Characteristics

Heraclitus of Ephesus: 10th Fragment

Hesse, Hermann: Demian

Hildegard of Bingen: Meditations with Hildegard of Bingen

Hoffer, Eric: The Passionate State of Mind

Hofmann, Hans: Search for the Real

Holmes, Oliver Wendell: "To My Readers"; The Autocrat of the Breakfast Table

Hope, A.D.: "Palingenesia 'cognovi clipeum"; "Day-time and Night-time vision"

Horne, Richard Hengist: Orion

Howells, William Dean: Pordernone

Hoyle, Sir Fred: Frontiers of Astronomy

Hsun-tzu: Hsun-Tzu, Basic Writings

Huai-Nan-Tsze: The History of Great Light

Hubbard, Barbara Marx: For the Love of God

Hugo, Victor: Les Misérables

Hui-neng: Tan-Ching, Manual of Zen Buddhism

Humboldt, Wilhelm von: Gasammelte Schriften

Humphreys, Christmas: Exploring Buddhism

Hunt, James Henry Leigh: Men, Women and Books: Fiction and Matter of Fact; Book of Gems

Huxley, Julian: New Bottles for New Wine: Ideology and Scientific Knowledge, Huxley Memorial Lecture for 1950

James, Sr., Henry: The Philosophy of Henry James: A Digest

Jeffers, Robinson: "The Truce and the Peace"; "To the Rock That will Be a Cornerstone"

Jefferson, Thomas: "Letter from Thomas Jefferson to Isaac McPherson"

Jeremias, Alfred: The Worldview of The Sumerians

Jerome, Jerome K.: The Idle Thoughts of an Idle Fellow

Jesus Christ: The Bible

Jiménez, Juan Ramón: "Heroic Reason" in Selected Writings

Johnson, Jakobina: "Thou Golden Flower" in Odes and Echoes

Jones, Rufus: The Faith and Practice of the Quakers

Jorgensen, Ronald: "Christmas and the New Year, 1993"; "Tai Chi Song"; "The Holidays"

Joyce, James: A Portrait of the Artist as a Young Man

Judy: Dear God: Children's Letters to God

Jung, Carl: Civilization in Transition; Carl Jung Collected Works; Memories, Dreams, Reflections; Modern Man in Search of a Soul; The Archetypes and the Collective Unconscious; The Structure and Dynamics of The Psyche

Kadinalovska, Mirtala: "What a Pity"

Kalākaua, King David: "The Pearl"

Karenga, Maulana: Kwanzaa: origin, concepts, practice

Kautilya: Kautilìya-Arthasàstra

Kavanagh, Patrick: "Father Mat" in A Soul For Sale

Kayvan, Azar: Jam-i-Kay Khosraw

Keats, John: "Letter, 22 November 1817"

Keller, Helen: The Open Door

Kennedy, John F.: Address at United Negro College Fund Convocation, Indianapolis, IN; Speech in Berlin

Kerényi, C.: Askelpoios: Archetypal Image of the Physicians Evidence

Khan, Hazrat Inayat: The Complete Sayings of Hazrat Inayat Khan; The Unity of Religious Ideals

Kierkegaard, Søren: Journals; Stages on Life's Way

Kilmer, Joyce: "Servant Girl and Grocer's Boy"

Kim Ŏk: "Falling Flowers"

Klee, Paul: The Inward Vision

Komey, Ellis Ayitey: "Domination"

Kosek, Miroslav: ". . . I Never Saw another Butterfly . . .": Children's Drawings and Poems from Terezin Concentration Camp, 1942-1944

Krishnamurti, J.: At the Feet of the Master; You Are the World

Kuliev, Kaisyn: "A Woman's Bathing in the Stream"

Kunene, Mazisi: "Algerian Night — To the Martyrs — "

Kurashara, Shinjiro: "The Fox"

Lao Tzu: Tao Te Ching; Hua Hu Ching

Larcom, Lucy: "On the Beach" in The Poetical Works of Lucy Larcom

Lawrence, D. H.: Studio; The Poetry of the Present

Leadbeater, C.W.: A Textbook of Theosophy; The Christian Creed: Its Origin and Signification; The Hidden Side of Things

Lee, Christopher: "That Good Night"

Leeuw, J.J. van der: The Fire of Creation

Leon, William: "morning mountain's cloud"; "Playing Catch with My Soul or If Rumi Played Baseball"

Lieh-tzu: Works of Lieh-tzu

Longfellow, Henry Wadsworth: Endymion; Hyperion

Lowell, James Russell: A Fable For Critics; A Glance Behind the Curtain; Among my Books; An Incident In a Railroad Car; My Study Windows

Lugovskoy, Vladimir: "The Middle of the Century"

MacDonald, George: "A Lover's Thought of Love"

MacLaine, Shirley: Going Within

Magdeburg, Mechthild von: "Love Flows from God,"

Maharshi, Ramana: The Spiritual Teaching of Ramana Maharshi

Malraux, André: "Les Métamorphoses Des Deux"

Manitonquat: Love is Life Believing in Itself

Marquis, Don: Chapters for the Orthodox

Marti, José: Discurso en el Liceo Cubano; Our America; The Cuban Revolutionary Party

Martin-Chauffier, Louis: L'homme et la Bête

Marvell, Andrew: "The Definition of Love"

Masefield, John: "Dauber, Part 6"

McCord, David: Once and for All

Meera, Mother: Answers; Something Beautiful for God

Mencius: Works

Mencken, H. L.: Prejudices: Third Series

Mensah, A. Karpper: "Nation Feeling"

Meredith, George: The Ordeal of Richard Feverel; The Spirit of Earth in Autumn

Merrell-Wolf, Franklin: The Philosophy of Consciousness without an Object

Merton, Thomas: New Seeds of Contemplation; Thomas Merton on Zen; Thomas Merton: The Hidden Ground of Love (Letters)

Mickiewicz, Adam: "Over the Great Clear Pool"

Milarepa, Jetsun: The Hundred Thousand Songs Of Milarepa, Volume I

Millay, Edna St. Vincent: "God's World"; "Renascence"

Miller, Henry: The Air-Conditioned Nightmare; The Colossus of Maroussi

Miller, Joaquin: "Why, Know You Not?"

Miller, Joe: "If the Earth were only a few feet in diameter..." in Earth Ball brochure

Milton, John: Paradise Lost

Mohammed: The Koran

Montague, Charles Edward: Disenchantment

Montaigne, Michel de: "Apology for Raimond Sebond"; "Of the Resemblance of Children to their Fathers" in Essays

Montaigne, Michel de: "Apology for Raimond Sebond," in Essays

Moore, Thomas: "Believe Me, if All Those Endearing Young Charms"

Morley, Christopher: Inward Ho!

Morton, H. L.: Colombo's Canadian Quotations

Mother (Mira Alfassa): Charter of the Community of Auroville, India; Prayers and Meditations; Collected Works of The Mother; Education: Part One; Mother's Agenda; Questions and Answers; The Mind of the Cells; The Synthesis of Yoga [By Sri Aurobindo]: The Mother's Talks

Mudie, Ian: "Murray River at Haylands, 2 A.M."

Muir, John: My First Summer in the Sierra

Murchie, Guy: The Seven Mysteries of Life

Murphy, Michael: Golf in the Kingdom

Nágárjuna: "Nāgārjuna's Doctrine of the Eight NO's" in Treatise on the Middle Way

Needham, Joseph: Science and Civilization in China II

Needleman, Jacob: A Sense of the Cosmos

Ni Hua Ching: The Book of Changes and the Unchanging Truth

Nicholson, Irene: Firefly in the Night: A Study of Ancient Mexican Poetry and Symbolism

Nietzsche, Friedrich: Human, All Too Human; The Wanderer and His Shadow

Noriko, Ibaragi: "My Camera," in Dialogue

Norwid, Cyprian: "But Just to See"

Noyes, Alfred: "The Torch-Bearers"

Nyerere, Julius: Freedom and Socialism

Obama, Barack: Eulogy for Reverend Clementa Pinckney, June 26, 2015

Omar, ibn al-Khattab Caliph: Letter to Amr ibn al-As, Governor of Egypt

Orpheus: The Mystical Hymns of Orpheus

Ortega y Gasset, José: Meditations of Quixote

Over, Raymon Van: Sun Songs: Creation Myths from Around The World

Padmasambhava: The Tibetan Book of The Dead

Paine, Thomas: Rights of Man

Palinurus (Cyril Connolly): The Unquiet Grave

Pandit, M.P.: Pandit In America

Pascal, Blaise: Pensées; Thoughts

Pennington, Isaac: Works

Petrov, Avvakum: Russian Historical Library, Vol. 39

Phillips, Stephen: Paolo & Francesca

Plato: Parmenides; The Republic; Timaeus

Plutarch of Chaeronea: Whether the Athenians were More Warlike or Learned

Poignant, Roslyn: "Creation of the Cosmos"

Pope, Alexander: "Translations from Ovid: Sappho to Phaon"; "Essay on Man, Epistle I" in The Complete Poetical Works of Alexander Pope

Pososkov, Ivan: Paternal Testament

Proust, Marcel: Remembrance of Things Past: The Past Recaptured

Rajneesh, Bhagwan Shree: The Book of Secrets

Ram, N. Sri: Thoughts For Aspirants, Second Series

Rauch, Earl Mac: Buckaroo Bonzai and the Sixth Dimension

Reid, Dorothy E.: "Poem Carried As a Banner" in The Commonweal

Ricardo, Cassiano: "Nightfall"

Rice, Ruth Mason: "A Japanese Print"

Rilke, Rainer Maria: Wartime Letters

Rinpoche, Kalu: Personal Spirituality

Rinpoche, Songyal: The Tibetan Book of Living and Dying

Rochefoucauld, Francois de La: Maxims

Rogers, Samuel: "On a Tear"

Rothenberg, Jerome: Shaking the Pumpkin

Royce, Josiah: The World of the Individual

Rumi, Jalal ad-Din: Masnavi I Ma'navi

Rumiko, Kora: "The Tree"

Rush, Cherlynn A.: "Certitude" in World Order

Ruskin, John: Sesame and Lilies (Of Kings' Treasuries); Time and Tide

Russell, Bertrand: The Conquest of Happiness

Saadi: The Bustan; Gulistan

Sandburg, Carl: "Washington Monument by Night "in Slabs of the Sunburnt West

Sandoz, Mari: Crazy Horse

Santayana, George: The Life of Reason: Reason in Common Sense; The Sense of Beauty

Savage, Minot Judson: Where is God?

Schiller, Friedrich: The Death of Wallenstein

Schreiner, Olive: Letter to Havelock Ellis

Schrödinger, Erwin: "The Mystic Vision" in Quantum Questions: Mystical Writings of the World's Great Physicists

Schucman, Helen: A Course in Miracles

Schweickart, Russell: "No Frames, No Boundaries" in Earth's Answer

Schweitzer, Albert: The Philosophy of Civilization

Sevak, Paruyr: "My Belief"

Shakespeare, William: Hamlet; Othello

Shams-i-Tabrizi: Diwan-I-Shams-I-Tabrizi

Shaw, George Bernard: Pygmalion

Shelley, Percy Bysshe: A Defense of Poetry; Prometheus Unbound

Siéyés, Abbe: Preliminaire a la Constitution

Silesius, Angelus: The Cherubic Pilgrim

Silva, Rosemary: Lesbian Quotations

Smith, Walter Chalmers: "Ahura-Aoktha or the World's Wisdom"

Smuts, Jan C.: Holism and Evolution

Socrates: Crito

Somé, Malidoma Patrice: Ritual: Power, Healing and Community

Soustelle, Jacques: The Four Suns

Spinoza, Baruch de: Bartok, sa vie et son aeuvre

Stephens, James: "The Crest Jewel" in Collected Poems

Stickney, Trumbull: In the Past

Stoppard, Tom: Rosencrantz and Guildenstern are Dead

Storm, Hyemeyohsts: Seven Arrows

Sun Bear and Wabun: The Medicine Wheel

Suzuki, D. T.: On Indian Mahayana Buddhism

Tagore, Rabindranath: Fireflies; My Reminiscences; Stray Birds; The Gardener

Takahashi, Shinkichi: "Hand"; "Moon"

Talib, Ali ibn Abi: Sentences

Taliesin: "The Cad Goddeu" in Book of Taliesin

Tanikawa, Shuntaró: "Growth"

Tarkovsky, Arseny: "Lexicon"

Taylor, Andrew: "Norwich Sleeping"

Tennyson, Alfred Lord: "Ulysses

Terence: Heaughton Timoroumenos

Terts, Abram (Andrei Donatovich Sinyavsky): Russian Themes; The Icicle

Thaves, Bob: Frank & Earnest

The Earth Charter Commission: The Earth Charter

Thich Nhat Hanh: Being Peace

Thomas, Lewis: The Lives of a Cell

Thompson, Francis: The Mistress of Vision

Thoreau, Henry David: Journal; Walden

Til, Jon Van: Mapping the Third Sector

Tolle, Eckhart: The Power of Now

Trismegistus, Hermes: Thrice-Greatest Hermes

Tutu, Desmond: The Book of Forgiving: The Fourfold Path for Healing Ourselves and Our World; The Words of Desmond Tutu

Tyson, Neil deGrasse: Space Chronicles

Ueshiba, Kisshomaru: Aikido

United Nations Charter Commission: United Nations Charter

Urantia Foundation: The Urantia Book

Uvavnuk: Anerca

Vigny, Alfred de: Cinq-Mars

Villa, Jose Garcia: "The Way My Ideas Think Me"

Vinokurov, Yevgeni: "Music"

Voznesensky, Andrei: "Longjumeau"

Wang Pi: A Translation of Lao Tzu's Tao Te Ching and Wang Pi's Commentary

Washington, Booker T.: Fellowman

Wei Wu Wei (Terence Gray): Ask The Awakened; The Negative Way

Weil, Simone: The Need for Roots, Prelude to a Declaration of Duties toward Mankind

Wells, H.G.: The Outline of History

Weöres, Sándor: "The Lost Parasol"

White, Betty: The Road I Know By Steward Edward White

Whitehead, Alfred North: Science and the Modern World

Whitman, Walt: "Preface"; "A Song of the Rolling Earth"; "By Blue Ontario's Shore"; "Europe, The 72d and 73d Years of These States"; "Night on the Prairies"; "Poem of Remembrances for a Girl or a Boy of these States"; "So Long!"; "Song of Myself"; "To a Common Prostitute"

Wilbur, Richard: "Clearness" in Ceremony; "The Aspen and the Stream" in Advice to a Prophet

Wilder, Thornton: The Bridge of San Luis Rey

Williams, Tennessee: Sweet Bird of Youth

Wilson, Woodrow: "Address at Princeton University"

Winfrey, Oprah: Oprah Winfrey Speaks

Wittgenstein, Ludwig: Philosophical Investigations

Wolfe, Thomas: Death the Proud Brother

Woodward, William E.: George Washington: The Image and the Man

Wordsworth, William: "Lines Composed a Few Miles above Tintern Abbey"; "The Prelude"; "Lucy: Three Years She Grew in Sun and Shower"

Wright, Frank Lloyd: "Taliesin" in The Architectural Record, May 1914

Yeats, William Butler: "A Deep-Sworn Vow," in The Wild Swans at Coole; "A Meditation in Time of War," in Michael Robartes and the Dancer; "To the Rose Upon the Road of Time"

Yevtushenko, Yevgeni: "I am Earthman Gagarin"

Yi Yong-Sang: "I can love North Koreans To my Comrade, Sgt. Richard"

Young, Edward: "Love of Fame, Satire VI" in The Complete Works, Poetry and Prose of the Rev. Edward Young

Yousafzai, Malala: "Speech at the Youth Takeover of the United Nations"

Ywahoo, Dhyani: Voices of Our Ancestors

Zimmer, Heinrich: Philosophies of India

Zukav, Gary: The Dancing Wu Li Masters

Other Selected Sources

A Dictionary of Oriental Quotations (Arabic and Persian)

A Year of Grace

Afro-American Encyclopedia

Anthology: Quotations and Sayings of People of Color

Avataṃsaka Sūtra

Aztec Thoughts and Culture

Bartlett's Familiar Quotations

Beacon Book of Quotations by Women, The

Beauty of America in Great American Art, The

Bhagavad Gita, The

Bible, The

Birthright of Man

Book of Golden Precepts, The

Celtic Civilization

Chinese Epigrams Inside Out and Proverbs by Tehyi Hsieh

Chippewa Nation Code for Long Life and Wisdom, The

Colombo's Canadian Quotations

Commonweal, The

Complete Works of Sri Aurobindo, The

Creativity and Taoism

Dark Nights of the Soul: A Guide to Finding your Way through Life's Ordeals

Early Philippine Literature

East and West Series

Egyptian Book of the Dead

Egyptian Ideas of the Future Life

Encyclopedia of Religious Quotations, The

Essential Unity of All Religions

Famous Orators of the World and Their Best Orations

Four Masterworks of American Indian Literature

Great Quotations, The

Heart Sutra, The Prajnaparamita Sutras of Mahayana Buddhism, The

I Ching

International Thesaurus Of Quotations, The

Isha Upanishad

Koran, The

Laws of the Peruvians, 1594

Left News

Lend Me Your Ears: Great Speeches in History

Letters of the Scattered Brotherhood

Literature and Thought of Modern Africa: A Survey, The

Maha Upanishad

Mahabharata

Mandukyo Upanishad

Maori Myths and Tribal Legends

Mystics and Saints of Islam

Mythic Image, The

Perennial Philosophy, The

Quaker Contribution, The

Reformers and Rebels

Sacred Hindu Symbols

Saints and Sages

Saints who Moved the World

Sayings — Wise or Witty

Shwetashwatara Upanishad

Song of the Sky Loom

Talmud, The

Teachings of Sri Ramakrishna

Theosophist, The

Thesaurus of Anecdotes

Tibetan Book of the Dead

Torah, The

UNESCO Year of the Child

Vedas, The

World Union Journal

Yiddish Proverbs

Zen and Hasidism

Zenist

Index

There are four indices integrated here. They are organized and identifiable by font as follows: **author**; setting; nation; *facet of oneness.*

The honorific titles of authors are retained in the index after the name or surname of the author (e.g., Dalai Lama, His Holiness the 14th; Aurobindo, Sri; Thomas, Saint; Seattle, Chief; Theresa, Mother). Where no author is identifiable the work or organization is indexed (e.g., Torah, Bhagavad Gita, Isha Upanishad, United Nations Charter Commission).

The setting is the area of knowledge, inquiry, or action in which the author worked or lived. Even though many authors were eclectic contributors to multiple settings, we list the one they are most noted for, even though their contribution to this work may have been in another setting (e.g., Einstein's setting is listed as physics even though his contributions here are more philosophical).

Nations are groups of self-identified people and do not necessarily occupy the same areas as politically defined states. Nations (such as Native American Tribes) now located within other countries are listed under those countries (e.g., America (Zuni); Canada (Inuit)). Where authors are from places that are considered parts of multiple countries, the most recognized modern countries are listed first and others placed in parentheses (e.g., Pakistan (India)). Where nation or Tribe are not known, the larger geographic realm is listed (e.g., Africa, America). America is used as the nation for Native Americans because that is where most readers are likely to look for them, though all Tribes have different names for the territory. All other American authors are listed as coming from the United States.

The facet of oneness is the most detailed index and is useful for finding the specific expression one might be looking for. Many statements express multiple facets of oneness.